T0319819

Innovation and Employment

Process versus Product Innovation

Charles Edquist

Professor, Department of Technology and Social Change, Linköping University, Sweden

Leif Hommen

Assistant Professor, Department of Technology and Social Change, Linköping University, Sweden

Maureen McKelvey

Associate Professor, Department of Industrial Dynamics, Chalmers University of Technology, Gothenburg, Sweden

Edward Elgar

Cheltenham, UK • Northampton, MA, USA

Published by
Edward Elgar Publishing Limited
Glensanda House
Montpellier Parade
Cheltenham
Glos GL50 1UA
UK

Edward Elgar Publishing, Inc.
136 West Street
Suite 202
Northampton
Massachusetts 01060
USA

A catalogue record for this book
is available from the British Library

Library of Congress Cataloguing in Publication Data

Edquist, Charles, 1947–
    Innovation and employment : process versus product innovation /
Charles Edquist, Leif Hommen, Maureen McKelvey.
        p. cm.
    Includes bibliographical references and index.
    1. Technological innovations—Economic aspects. 2. Employment (Economic theory). 3. Economic development. I. Hommen, Leif. II. McKelvey, Maureen D. III. Title.

HC79.T4 E3 2001
338'.064—dc21

00–065408

ISBN 1 84064 414 1 (cased)
      1 84064 427 3 (paperback)

Printed and bound in Great Britain by Biddles Ltd, *www.biddles.co.uk*

Contents

Figures

Tables

Preface

The relations between innovations, growth and employment are extremely complex, but also very important from a socioeconomic and political point of view - and thereby from a research and policy point of view. The complex whole can be divided into the relations between (1) innovations and growth, (2) innovations and employment and (3) growth and employment. These relations are represented in Figure P.1.

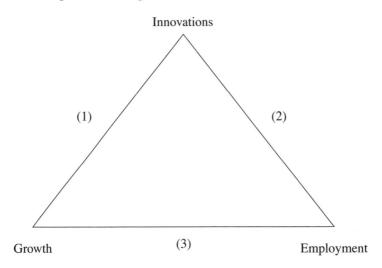

Figure P.1   Interrelations of innovation, growth and employment

Innovations and employment ('2' in Figure P.1) will be the main focus in this book. However, we will also address the relations between growth and employment ('3' in Figure P.1). Let us here set the stage for this discussion.[1]

When politicians discuss remedies for the unemployment problem, they often claim that more rapid growth is what would solve or mitigate it. Such a statement is unclear in the sense that it does not specify what kind of growth is meant. Is it, for example, economic growth (GDP growth) or productivity growth? Everyone talking about 'growth' and employment should be specific on this issue, since the employment consequences of these two kinds of growth are *very* different!

It is increasingly important for both policy makers and social scientists to make such distinctions, and to clarify their implications for employment, given the rise in recent years of public concern about the idea of 'jobless growth' due to technological unemployment. Popular works articulating such concern - for example, Jeremy Rifkin's book on *The End of Work* (Rifkin, 1995) - have gained a very broad audience. In the policy literature there has been a growing realization that 'we are once again passing through a period in which a gap is opening up between the speed of technical progress ... and our capacity to ... provide new job opportunities' (Commission of the European Communities, 1994: 4).

As the OECD *Jobs Study* (OECD, 1994a, 1994b, 1994c) argues, it is necessary to develop a more detailed and differentiated understanding of the relation between 'growth' and employment, since some kinds of 'growth' destroy jobs while other kinds create jobs. The OECD study has therefore emphasized that the development of adequate solutions to the problem of high unemployment will depend, in large part, on a 'dynamic perspective' on technology/employment relationships - one that 'emphasises the role of innovation and technological advance in the very processes of growth and structural change' (OECD, 1994b: 165). From such a perspective, it can be seen that some kinds of growth reduce employment and other kinds increase employment. Hence, the 'employment intensity of growth' differs between various kinds of growth, and the source and content of growth have significant employment implications (Commission of the European Communities, 1994: 57–60).

A crucial question therefore arises: which kinds of growth lead to more jobs and which do not? This is a central question addressed in this book.

We analyse types of growth mainly through a taxonomy of different kinds of innovations. The main categories relate to the dichotomies of product versus process innovation and manufacturing versus service production. However, each category is in turn further differentiated. This is done by distinguishing types of process and product innovations, and by relating the inputs of knowledge (levels of R&D or human capital) involved in different kinds of production to their innovative output.

To the extent possible, our analysis specifies the employment consequences of different types of innovations. This is done at various levels of analysis - from the micro level of the firm, through sectoral and national levels of economic organization, to the international or global level. However, because of the bias in the availability of data, the sectoral level will be addressed most thoroughly.

The book has three parts. Part I addresses the theoretical approach and conceptual framework. Part II discusses the relationship between innovations and employment, using existing empirical material in order to analyse how different kinds of growth affect job creation and destruction. Part III summarizes findings and presents conclusions and policy implications.

This book is based on research funded and carried out in the project entitled 'Innovation Systems and European Integration' (ISE), funded by Targeted Socio-Economic Research, DG XII, European Commission.[2] The sub-project in which this research was conducted dealt with 'Innovations, Growth and Employment' and the main objective was to increase our understanding of the sources of growth and employment as perceived by the systems of innovation approach in contrast to traditional approaches. The relations between innovations and growth ('1' in Figure P.1) as perceived by different theoretical approaches were analysed by Björn Johnson and Birgitte Gregersen in other work carried out within the same ISE sub-project (Gregersen and Johnson, 1998a, 1998b).

In its original form this book was presented and discussed on several occasions as a research report within the ISE research project. The authors wish to thank those ISE members who commented on earlier drafts of the manuscript: Birgitte Gregersen, Johan Hauknes, Björn Johnson, Mireille Matt, Svend Otto Remoe, Keith Smith and Morris Teubal. We are indebted to them and to the whole ISE group for their collegial assistance. We are grateful to the Swedish Council for Research on Working Life (RALF) and the Swedish National Board for Industrial and Technical Development (NUTEK) for funding that helped us to complete this project. Björn Elsässer and Jan Fagerberg also deserve our gratitude for having read and commented on later versions of the manuscript. In addition, the authors wish to acknowledge the support and advice provided by colleagues in the Systems of Innovation Research Programme at the Department of Technology and Social Change of the University of Linköping, Sweden. Naturally, the authors accept all responsibility for any faults in this book.

NOTES

1. We will also return to the issue of growth and employment in later sections, including Part III, where Chapter 6 presents our main conclusions.
2. ISE consisted of nine research groups in nine European countries. It had the overall purpose of elaborating the systems of innovation approach with respect to:

   (1) Evaluation of this new understanding of the development of science, technology and innovation and the implications thereof for economic growth and employment.
   (2) Developing new policy options and implications on this basis.

   Two summary reports were produced within ISE. The reader interested in policy issues is advised to consult *The ISE Policy Statement* (Edquist et al., 1998), which is written for politicians and policy makers concerned with innovation policies and policies closely related to this field, for example, policies dealing with education, R&D, economic growth and employment. It deals with policy implications in an integrated manner.

The second report is *The ISE Final Report* (Edquist, 1998), which describes and summarizes the basic scientific findings and policy implications for each of the sub-projects in ISE. The sub-projects were clustered in two phases:

1. Policy implications of the state of the art
   - Policy implications of systems approaches to innovation
   - Innovations, growth and employment
   - European integration and national systems of innovation
2. Issue-oriented empirical sub-projects
   - Science-based technologies and interdisciplinarity
   - Public technology procurement as an innovation policy instrument
   - Financing innovation
   - Corporate governance and innovation performance
   - Technological entry: diversification vs new innovators

Thirty-one research reports were produced on these issues in the sub-projects of phases 1 and 2. It is necessary to consult these research reports for the detailed basis of the arguments presented in the two summary reports. The research reports, together with the two summary reports, are all included on a CD-ROM titled *ISE: Innovation Systems and European Integration* (Edquist and Texier, 1998). The CD-ROM is available, free of charge, from the Systems of Innovation Research Programme, Department of Technology and Social Change, University of Linköping, Sweden. All the material contained in the CD-ROM is also available on the Internet at the following address: http://www.tema.liu.se/tema-t/sirp/index.htm.

PART I

Theoretical Approach and Conceptual Framework

In order to outline and explain the perspective from which we will consider the relations between innovations and employment, our first two chapters briefly describe our theoretical approach, methodology and conceptual framework. Later chapters provide further elaboration of theories and concepts, as necessary to discuss the empirical evidence.

Our theoretical point of departure is the so-called systems of innovation (SI) approach. As an emerging current of thought in the economics of innovation, this approach offers a non-linear perspective that is highly relevant to the study of economic growth – particularly growth based on innovation. SI approaches are especially appropriate to an understanding of the interactions and interdependencies – for example between the 'supply side' and the 'demand side' – in processes of innovation. They can also be used to relate innovations to processes of economic development and growth. In our first chapter, we briefly summarize some general characteristics of SI approaches and relate them to broader theoretical developments in the economics of innovation. This chapter also outlines our overall assumptions and methodology.

In our second chapter, we proceed on this basis to develop a conceptual framework that distinguishes among different kinds of innovation using a systems-oriented approach. We argue that a differentiated concept of innovation – one that includes more than just technical process innovations – is needed to grasp the complicated relationships between innovations and employment.

1. A systems of innovation perspective on employment

Although the relations between growth and employment are complex and difficult to grasp, they are also very important. Not all kinds of economic growth lead to more employment and not all kinds of productivity growth, as it is normally measured, lead to less employment.[1] We also know from the 'growth accounting' literature (for example, Abramovitz, 1989, 1993; Denison, 1962; Maddison, 1991; Solow, 1957) that the 'residual', often equated with 'technical change', is a major source of productivity growth, although the causal relationships have seldom been clearly specified.[2]

In discussions about causes and effects of economic growth and productivity growth, creation and destruction of employment is an important part of the puzzle. It is, moreover, an especially complicated part, since the relationships between innovation and employment are seldom direct and immediate. Instead, the effects over time of technical change or innovation on employment are usually mediated by a number of offsetting factors (Vivarelli, 1995). These include effects on demand in other industries and sectors, 'real income' (or purchasing power) effects on the overall level of demand, and 'adjustment' effects in labour markets (for example, wage movements) that partly compensate for the substitution of labour (ibid.: 27–38). Moreover, all these factors are affected by macroeconomic conditions and the institutional and organizational characteristics of the economy (Vivarelli and Pianta, 2000: 1–11).

As indicated by Gregersen and Johnson (1998a; 1998b), there is a great deal of theorizing and a huge literature on growth and its sources. Since practically everyone agrees that innovation is a crucial source of growth, this implies that much has been written on 'technical change' and growth and much theoretical work deals with the issue. This is, however, not true to the same extent for the relations between innovation and employment, and we know less about this relation.[3]

We argue that the systems of innovation (SI) approach offers a useful way of analysing the relations between innovation and employment, for the following reasons.

One important consideration is that the SI approach offers researchers and policy makers a more discriminating account of issues pertaining to innovation and employment than the approaches aligned with conventional economic theory. Mainstream economic theory has traditionally had a primary focus on 'short-run problems of optimal resource allocation within a static framework, from which technological change ha[s] usually been excluded' (Rosenberg, 1986). By concentrating attention on the issue of responsiveness to price signals, mainstream economic theory has neglected the analysis of innovation as a process guided to a large extent by 'responses to other signals and responses transmitted through other forms of social interaction than market exchange' (Nielsen, 1991). More importantly, technical change was traditionally seen as a process occurring outside the economic, or market, sphere.

In contrast, the SI approach incorporates both explicit principles of change and a view of innovation as a collective learning and selection process, inherited from evolutionary economics (Nelson, 1987). Evolutionary economics explicitly treats technical change and innovation as processes of search and learning by economic actors. These processes depend on how individual actors, such as firms, respond to incentives and disincentives in the selection environment (Nelson, 1990; Nelson and Winter, 1982). Moreover, following institutional economics (Hodgson, 1991), the SI approach bases explanations of evolutionary patterns of change on the decisions and actions of organizational actors in relation to institutional rules.[4] Accordingly, it examines how general characteristics of innovation as a collective process are manifested in different societal contexts. Thus, the SI approach can be used to compare how efficiently different institutional frameworks and combinations of agents point innovative activities in directions that are favourable for economic growth (Lundvall, 1992; Nelson, 1993).

The SI approach is focused on the determinants of product and process innovation. The literature in this tradition has so far not dealt with the consequences of innovations, for example for growth and employment, to the same extent. However, we believe that it has a great potential for doing so because of its insistence on treating innovation and technological change as endogenous factors in economic systems. For this reason, the SI approach offers a more promising perspective on the dynamics of employment generation than standard economic theory. In the latter, innovation and technological change have largely remained exogenous. 'As a result, the causal connections between technological change and economic growth are poorly understood' (Carlsson, 1995: 1). More recently, new economic growth theory has moved towards incorporating technical change and skills into economic theorizing (Romer, 1986, 1990), but the SI approach and underlying heterodox economic theories have gone further (Verspagen, 1992).

The emergence of SI approaches and their characteristics have been dealt with by Edquist (1997a: section 3).[5] Nine characteristics of the approaches were identified there:

1. *They place innovation and learning processes at the centre of focus.* This is based on the understanding that innovation is a matter of producing new knowledge or combining existing elements of knowledge in new ways. It is thus, in a broad sense, a 'learning process'.

2. *They adopt a holistic and interdisciplinary perspective.* They are 'holistic' in the sense that they try to encompass a wide array – or all – of the determinants of innovation that are important. They are 'interdisciplinary' in the sense that they allow for the inclusion not only of economic factors but also of organizational, social and political factors.

3. *They employ historical perspectives.* Since processes of innovation develop over time and involve the influence of many factors and feedback processes, they are best studied in terms of the 'co-evolution' of knowledge, innovation, organizations and institutions.

4. *They stress the differences between systems, rather than the optimality of systems.* The differences between systems of innovation are a main focus, rather than something to be abstracted away from. This means conducting comparisons between existing systems, rather than between real ones and an ideal or 'optimal' one (since an optimal system of innovation cannot be specified).

5. *They emphasize interdependence and non-linearity.* This is based on the understanding that firms almost never innovate in isolation but interact more or less closely with other organizations, through complex relations that are often characterized by reciprocity and feedback mechanisms in several loops. This interaction occurs in the context of institutions – for example, laws, rules, regulations, norms and cultural habits.[6] Innovations are not only determined by the elements of the systems, but also by the relations between them.[7]

6. *They encompass both product and process innovations, as well as sub-categories of these types of innovation.*[8] This is based on the understanding that developing a differentiated concept of innovation – that is, one which is not solely restricted to the conventional emphasis on process innovations of a technical nature – is necessary to comprehend the complex relations between growth, employment and innovation.

7. *They emphasize the central role of institutions.* They do so in order to understand the social patterning of innovative behaviour – for example, its typically 'path-dependent' character – and the role played by institutions and by organizations. While organizations of different kinds are conceptualized as the main actors, or 'players', in processes of innovation, institutions are understood as defining 'the rules of the game'. Institutions

and organizations are also considered to be reciprocally related to one another. On one hand, organizations such as firms are to a large extent institutionally defined and regulated (through law, for example). On the other hand, organizations often act as agents of institutional change.

8. *They are still associated with conceptual diffuseness.* Thus, further development will involve making progress from the present state of 'conceptual pluralism' to a clearer specification of 'core concepts' and their precise content – a gradual selection process in which pluralism and ambiguity will be reduced by degrees.

9. *They are conceptual frameworks, rather than formal theories.* Recognizing that SI approaches are not yet at that stage of development where they are capable of 'formal' (abstract) theorizing leads to an emphasis on empirically based 'appreciative' theorizing. Such theorizing is intended to capture processes of innovation, their determinants, and some of their consequences (for example, productivity growth and employment) in a meaningful way.

As indicated by this discussion, innovations and learning are placed at the very centre of focus in the SI approach. The proposition that the approach has – implicitly, if not explicitly – a rather differentiated innovation concept forms the point of departure for making the explicit distinctions used in this book and discussed in Chapter 2. On this basis, an analytical framework for the study of the relations between innovations and employment is proposed.[9] By dividing the broad category of 'innovation' into its components, it is possible to study each in more detail, how they are related to each other, and their impact on employment and growth.

In order to make sense of a complicated mass of empirical evidence and of theoretically based assumptions and analysis, we have found it necessary to address initially the immediate, or direct, effects of innovations on employment. We discuss these before addressing what are known as compensating, counteracting, or offsetting factors, that is, those that are relevant to a dynamic analysis over time. Our goal is a dynamic analysis involving the different levels of economic systems. However, the existing state of the art requires, in our opinion, that we start by sorting out the direct and more immediate effects of innovation on employment. We can then begin to address systemic complexity by disentangling how innovations affect productivity growth, and thereby the demand for labour, in different sectors. Having done that, we can then turn to questions about growth in markets, competitiveness and economic growth, addressing them in relation to the dynamic and secondary employment effects of innovation. In this context we will deal with interactions in systems of innovation.

Let us address some general theoretical objections to conducting such a 'partial' analysis of the employment impacts of innovation. Many economists tend to argue that it would be highly advantageous to deal with the employment impact of innovation in a general equilibrium framework. That would mean looking at an economic system as a whole and dealing with the simultaneous determination of all prices and quantities of all goods and services, and adding to that the consequences of innovation for employment. To our knowledge, no one has ever attempted to conduct such an analysis, and it seems that it is not possible to carry out a general equilibrium analysis of innovation and employment for the time being, partly for reasons of (un)availability of empirical material. Another reason is that mainstream economic models have problems in dealing with product innovation (Lundvall, 1985; Pasinetti, 1981; Vivarelli, 1995). A further reason is that innovation processes have evolutionary characteristics that tend to prevent the achievement of states of equilibrium (Dosi, 1982, 1988; Edquist, 2000, forthcoming).

Anyone arguing that a general equilibrium analysis of the relations between innovation and employment is the only acceptable one, therefore, also has the burden of demonstrating its viability. Moreover, a theoretical problem arises because general equilibrium analysis often assumes full employment as well as perfect competition. Within such a framework, employment and unemployment become non-issues.

Labour economics has avoided, rather than solved, this theoretical problem. Due to assumptions made about the natural 'clearing' of perfect labour markets, equilibrium analysis in labour economics often tends to regard unemployment as an ephemeral phenomenon, associated with transitory market imperfections.[10] Alternatively, equilibrium analysis may introduce structural problems and lag effects that obstruct market clearing. In theories of the 'non-accelerating inflation rate of unemployment' (NAIRU), for example, a certain level of unemployment is posited as the equilibrium point at which inflation stabilizes (Layard, Nickell and Jackman, 1991). In this case, however, the analysis does not normally take innovation into account, since NAIRU theory assumes that productivity does not rise and may even fall as firms increase their output. The failure to include the possibility of productivity increases due to innovation is one of the major flaws of this theory.[11]

Ideally, our current approach to analysis would identify not only the most important direct consequences of innovation for employment, but also second- and third-order ones. Although not fully achieved here, striving in that direction will gradually take us closer to what the term 'general' in general equilibrium analysis essentially implies, that is, an approach which takes into account that everything is tied together with everything. That is how we, at least, interpret the standard definition of a general equilibrium analysis, which refers to an approach that 'looks at an economic system as a whole' (Pearce, 1986: 167). Having said that, we note that our epistemological foundations have nothing to do with the term 'equilibrium' in general equilibrium analysis, since innovation is the enemy of equilibrium (see above).

A general equilibrium approach is normally used to analyse how economies adjust to exogenous 'shocks' and eventually re-establish a state of balance, or equilibrium, achieved when the markets are 'cleared'. In our approach, however, innovation is regarded as endogenous, rather than exogenous. We also focus on mechanisms internal to the economic system that can operate to prevent outcomes associated with 'market clearing'. (One such outcome would be full employment, achieved through 'natural' processes of market adjustment.) These mechanisms can generate alternative kinds of economic results (such as either high or low unemployment).

Analysing not only the direct but also the indirect employment effects of innovation in a manner consistent with an SI approach means abandoning assumptions of equilibrium and perfect competition. Instead, it requires accounting for sources of disequilibrium and market imperfections – a task at which we make only a beginning here.

The approach described above is reflected in the structure of this book. Chapter 2, which completes Part I, introduces the basic distinctions between different kinds of innovation more formally. Part II of the book (Chapters 3, 4 and 5) then considers the relationships between the various types of innovation, on the one hand, and employment, on the other. Part III (Chapters 6 and 7) summarizes the arguments and addresses policy implications and issues for further research.

The theoretical discussion will be 'appreciative' (Nelson, 1994) rather than 'formal' – that is, we shall try to stay relatively close to empirical substance and argue in verbal terms. None the less, the theoretical grounds for our reasoning are spelled out, and hence the 'appreciative' theoretical discussion will lead to the generation of hypotheses.

We believe that our main contribution to the literature is to conduct a systematic review of the empirical evidence in relation to our conceptual and theoretical framework. We do this by formulating and discussing a series of hypotheses. There are, in total, 19 hypotheses. Most of them are grounded in existing empirical work. Some others are based on theoretical reasoning. Of course, our hypotheses can only be properly tested, or answered, through additional empirical work that explicitly addresses them. In cases where hypotheses cannot be explicitly formulated because the evidence and ideas are especially tentative, we have instead spelled out future research questions.

In this book, we have no ambitions to test the hypotheses systematically or answer the questions conclusively. We do, however, want our hypotheses, research questions and tentative conclusions to stimulate further research into the matters we address.

NOTES

1. Economic growth means increased GDP and productivity growth means larger production per employed person or per hour worked.
2. We later specify what 'technical change' may mean.
3. This is not to deny that there is a large literature on the issue. The literature on innovation (technical change) and employment seems to have emerged in 'waves'. For earlier reviews of the literature, see Edquist (1992; 1993a).
4. Although the term 'institution' is often used to denote both, we here explicitly distinguish between 'institutions' in the sense of laws, rules and norms and 'organizations' as consciously created actors with explicit objectives. See Edquist and Johnson (1997: 46–7).
5. The use of *approaches* in plural form indicates that there are several variants of the SI perspective. They include national, sectoral and regional systems of innovation approaches, as discussed in section 2 of Edquist (1997a). The sectoral ones are presented in Breschi and Malerba (1997) and Carlsson (1995); the national ones in Lundvall (1992), Nelson (1993) and Nelson and Mowery (1999); and the regional ones in Braczyk et al. (1998). All these contributions – and others – are discussed in the introduction to Edquist and McKelvey (2000), which is a two-volume collection of 43 central articles on SI approaches.
6. The concepts of institutions and organizations are specified and their roles in innovation are discussed in Edquist and Johnson (1997). They make a distinction between institutions and organizations that follows North's (1990) analogy of discriminating between 'the rules of the game' and the 'players' in the game. On this basis, they present a definition of institutions as 'sets of common habits, routines, established practices, rules or laws that regulate the relations and interactions between individuals and groups', and a definition of organizations as 'formal structures with an explicit purpose and [that] are consciously created; ... players or actors' (Edquist and Johnson, 1997: 46–7).
7. Systems-oriented theories dealing with interactions and inderdependencies contributing to innovation are discussed as antecedents of the SI approach in Edquist and Hommen (1999). Interactions between firms and other organizations in processes of innovation have been analysed empirically in Edquist, Eriksson and Sjögren (2000).
8. These sub-categories are introduced in Chapter 2, below.
9. This framework is partly based upon earlier work (Edquist, 1997b).
10. Thus, for example, Chennells and Van Reenen (1998), who have used a 'partial equilibrium' model to analyse the impacts of technological change on the structure of employment and wages, make the following comment: 'Note that there is no unemployment in this model since the labour market clears' (ibid.: 6).
11. 'If increased capacity utilisation and, over the longer term, an increased and more technologically advanced capacity allow a growth of the feasible wage, then there may be no unique "equilibrium" point (NAIRU) with only that one level of unemployment associated with non-accelerating inflation' (Michie and Pitelis, 1998: 43–4). Both unemployment and inflation could even decline simultaneously.

2.   Specification of basic concepts

Definitions may be neither right nor wrong, but they may be useful or not, depending upon their purpose. Conceptual clarity is, however, a virtue because it enables us to evaluate and compare research. For this reason, we will first specify some central innovation concepts in a way that makes them useful for the study of employment effects, which are discussed in Part II (Chapters 3, 4 and 5).

The key distinctions used here are between product and process innovations. With respect to product innovations we distinguish between material goods and intangible services and, regarding process innovations, between technological and organizational innovations. The first distinction, between product and process, is well established in the literature, having originated with Joseph Schumpeter. He defined product innovation as 'the introduction of a new good ... or a new quality of a good' and process innovation as 'the introduction of a new method of production ... [or] a new way of handling a commodity commercially' (Schumpeter, 1911: 66). Dividing products into the categories of goods and services is a long-standing convention in the economics literature. The distinction between technological and organizational process innovations is also well established (see, for example, Utterback and Abernathy, 1975).[1]

Thus the original vision of Schumpeter and the legacy of heterodox economic theory and research help us advance a differentiated conception of innovation. Certainly, a differentiated conceptualization of innovation would be of great practical utility within evolutionary and institutional economics, including the SI approach. Such a conceptualization is important because it helps us analyse the relative dynamics of different sectors, including their impact on employment and economic growth.

In mainstream economic theory, innovation is, more or less explicitly, often assumed to be limited to process innovations.[2] At the same time, however, it can be argued that product innovations are probably more important than process innovations in many respects.[3] A historical comparison shows that over the past hundred years there have been tremendous cultural, social and technological transformations resulting from the development and diffusion of new products. Just assume away the automobile, the telephone, the computer and the television!

Product innovation, leading to the substitution of old goods and services or to the satisfaction of new needs, is the main mechanism behind structural change in economies. It propels development to a larger extent than increasing efficiency through process innovations. Several prominent economists and economic historians have associated periods of economic growth with major growth industries and with institutional change (Abramovitz, 1989; Kuznets, 1972). This is probably the reason why authors developing the SI approach, especially Carlsson (1995), Lundvall (1992) and Nelson (1993), all emphasize product innovations in their concepts of innovation.[4]

In principle, the SI approach has no problems in capturing and dealing with product innovation. In practice, however, there are a number of problems to be confronted in operationalizing the distinction between product and process innovation. These difficulties have been addressed most thoroughly by Archibugi, Evangelista and Simonetti (1994), who provide a comprehensive review of the various definitions that have been used. These authors find, by comparing definitions at different levels of aggregation, that 'For 96.9 percent of the innovations, the classifications are not consistent: they may appear as either products or processes, according to the approach adopted' (ibid.: 15).

However, these authors also 'acknowledge that ... the distinction between product and process innovations is a useful tool for analysis' and propose, as a remedy to the problem of inconsistent classification, that 'it would be good practice for those who employ these terms to explain very clearly which meaning they attach to them' (ibid.: 21). Complying with this advice, a specification of our basic concepts follows, as does a discussion of the methodological problems in using these definitions when reviewing existing empirical research.[5] The present work reviews empirical studies based mainly on firm-level definitions of product and process innovation (European Commission, 1993; OECD, 1996c).

The inclusion of organizational, as well as technological, change within a comprehensive taxonomy of innovations may also be thought problematic. However, if the objective is to understand the growth and employment effects of innovation, there are strong reasons for also including organizational innovation in the analysis. Developments in industry have led managers and researchers to give increasing emphasis to organizational change as a source of productivity growth, competitiveness and employment. By now, all are familiar with 'just-in-time' and 'lean production'. Arguments stressing the importance of organizational change are persuasive. Although Japanese auto assembly plants in the USA use process technologies similar to their US counterparts, the Japanese 'transplants' are more productive than domestic plants (Womack, Jones and Roos, 1990: ch. 4).[6] Organizational forms may be 'national' – that is, rooted in and emerging from specific characteristics of societies – or 'firm-based' and 'international' at the same time, as shown by transplant factories.

Leaving aside the question of origins, it can be argued that organizational changes are important process innovations. They are also vital for the development and use of technological innovations. Nevertheless, the study of organizational innovations is neglected compared to the study of technological innovations. An agenda for future research is therefore to develop much more comprehensive knowledge about the emergence and diffusion of organizational innovations and their socioeconomic consequences. Due to its relative neglect, the marginal return of work along this path can be expected to be high. (See Appendix B.)

In order to relate our analytical framework to the empirical evidence and theoretical explanations, the product–process distinction is below complemented with other taxonomies. First, in order to analyse the relative impacts of innovations on employment, we need to know more about the types of products involved. The classification used here is the common one of 'investment', 'consumer' and 'intermediate' products. (See section 2.3.) Second, in order to understand the dynamics of sectors, we want to be able to classify sectors based on the relative investment in new knowledge. We therefore use the classification of 'high-technology', 'medium-technology' and 'low-technology' manufacturing sectors. (See section 2.4.) The definitions introduced below are related to manufacturing, but Chapter 4 complements these for services by addressing the relative knowledge intensity of different service sectors. These taxonomies are also important aids to disentangling, and understanding, the relative importance of different types of innovations and their impacts on employment in different sectors.

2.1 PRODUCT INNOVATIONS

Product innovations are new – or better – products (or product varieties) being produced and sold; it is a question of *what* is produced. The products may be brand new to the world, but they may also be new to a firm or country, that is, diffused to these units. In his original definition, Schumpeter referred to goods or qualities of goods 'with which consumers are not familiar' (Schumpeter, 1911: 66). The category of product innovations, however, can include both *new goods* and *new services*. New goods are material product innovations in manufacturing and the primary sectors. In contrast to goods, services are intangible; they are often consumed simultaneously to their production and they satisfy non-physical needs for the user (Hauknes, 1994). Only products produced for the market (commodities) are addressed here, which means that goods and services produced for direct use by the producer (within the household) are excluded.[7] The reason is that the focus of this book is on employment in the sense of wage labour.

Some examples of product innovations in goods production would include a genetically modified strawberry, a new alloy produced from metals in the nineteenth century, the automobile around the turn of the century, an industrial robot in the 1960s, the microwave oven, high-definition TV in the 1990s, a new processor for PCs, a new pharmaceutical, or a mobile telephone.

Examples of product innovations in services include the (first) offer of a curly hairstyle, heart transplants in the 1960s, a new insurance payment plan for drivers who lose their licences, a new financial service such as 'home banking', mobile telephone calls, video-on-demand over the telecom network, access to the Internet, consulting in the field of building process automation systems in engineering companies, consulting in the field of organization and management, provision of advice to firms about innovation management, education with regard to the European Union legal system, legal advice with regard to intellectual property rights, or the design and maintenance of computer systems in firms.

The definition of product innovation given above might seem fairly clear. However, in empirical work it is sometimes tricky to identify a new product. To begin with there is the problem of determining whether a product is new at all. A main difficulty with respect to the identification of product innovations is that of distinguishing between minor changes and those that represent major changes. In the case of a new microprocessor it is easy. But what about a new flavour of a sausage?

The distinction between 'minor' and 'major' changes in products is thus not always easily drawn. However, it remains possible to distinguish between 'minor' (trivial) and 'major' (non-trivial) product changes, and to reserve the term 'product innovation' for the latter. For example, the EC *Harmonized Innovation Surveys* questionnaire of 1991/92 gives the following definition of 'minor' changes, which are not recognized as product innovations in the Community Innovation Survey:

> We leave out changes which are purely aesthetic (such as changes in colour or decoration), or which simply involve product differentiation (that is, minor design or presentation changes which differentiate the product while leaving it technically unchanged in construction or performance). (European Commission, 1993: 2)

The reason for excluding such changes is the widely differing economic and technical significance of different product innovations, which in turn motivates the creation of taxonomies (Archibugi, 1989; Freeman, Soete and Townsend, 1982; Simonetti, 1991).[8]

Here we will also cite the definitions of 'significant' and 'incremental' innovation that have been used in data collection instruments for much of the empirical research that this book refers to (European Commission, 1993; OECD, 1996c). The innovation surveys regularly conducted by bodies such as the EC and the OECD have continued to rely upon a conventional dichotomy between significant and incremental innovation. The terms used are consistent with the *Oslo Manual* distinction between 'a technologically new product' and 'a technologically improved product' (OECD, 1996c). In EC innovation surveys, these categories have been translated, respectively, as '*significant innovation* ... involving radically new technologies, or ... combining existing technologies in new uses' and '*incremental innovation* ... enhanced ... through use of new components or materials ... [or] improved by partial changes to one or more of the sub-systems' (European Commission, 1993). Trivial or 'minor' product changes are, as noted above, excluded by these terms.

The distinction between 'significant' and 'incremental' product innovations is important for us because it implies a difference in the market situations of innovative products. 'Significant' product innovations are often associated with new markets; 'incremental' product innovations are generally associated with existing markets (OECD, 1996c). As argued in Chapter 4, different types of product innovations have different potentials to create jobs.

2.2   PROCESS INNOVATIONS

Process innovations are new ways of producing goods and services; it is a matter of *how* existing products are produced. Schumpeter's (1911: 66) original definition referred to a 'method of production' or 'way of handling a commodity' that is 'not yet tested by experience in the branch of manufacture concerned'. We divide process innovations into technological or organizational ones. *Technological* process innovations are units of real capital (material goods) which have been improved through technical change. *Organizational* process innovations are new ways to organize work; a new organizational form is introduced. (See also Appendix B.)

Neither of these types of process innovation can have large socioeconomic effects until they are widely diffused. Variation in long-term growth rates among industrial countries has been consistently related to differences in their level of technological advancement (Maddison, 1991). Similarly, the spread of 'techno-economic paradigms' – in which there is an appropriate alignment of new forms of productive organization with pervasive new 'core technologies' – has been identified as a major factor in the explanation of Kondratieff cycles or long waves of economic development (Freeman, Clark and Soete, 1982; Freeman and Perez, 1988).

The relations between technological and organizational process innovations and the categories of goods and services are partly problematic. (See also Appendix A.) The main difficulties have to do with one's perspective in relation to questions of location in the economy. Economists have been aware for some time that whether an innovation concerns a process or a product depends very much on whose perspective one is adopting (Kuznets, 1972). Archibugi, Evangelista and Simonetti (1994) give the example of where the (objective) criterion of location of 'first use' is employed. They state that ascertaining 'that the innovation has been used for the first time within the innovating firm ... would imply that it is a process', while 'innovations that are used for the first time outside the innovating firm may be labeled as products' (ibid.: 10). However, this is not necessarily the case, except from the perspective of the originating firm. A purchaser might subsequently also use the product as a process innovation. Let us address these definitional issues and also discuss some relationships between product and process innovations.

Technological process innovations are new *goods* that are used in the process of production.[9] These new goods are what most people think of as investment goods, although they can also include intermediate goods. Examples include paper and pulp processing machines, industrial robots and IT equipment.

An investment good may be a product innovation initially and a process innovation at a later stage. An industrial robot is a product innovation when produced by ABB in Västerås and a process innovation when used by Volvo in Göteborg.[10] As argued above, the location or perspective is important in determining whether a material artefact is a product or process at different times. The investment good may initially have been a product for one firm, then bought and used as a process innovation by another firm. Or it may have originated as a process innovation within one firm that later produced it on a larger scale and sold it as a product to other firms.

Within the production sphere, there are also other kinds of relations between material product and process innovations which can be important.[11] In some cases the production of new products requires new process technologies. An example is the production of a new kind of integrated circuit with a smaller line breadth. It absolutely requires new lithographic and other process technologies. Other product innovations do not require new process technologies. An example could be a new kind of pump, which can be produced in the same mechanical factory as old kinds. A third kind of relation along this dimension is when the same product – or a very similar one – is produced with radically different process technologies. An example is human growth hormone, previously extracted from human brains and now produced through genetically engineered cells.[12]

Organizational process innovations are new ways to organize business activities such as production or R&D and have no technological elements as such. They have to do with the coordination of human resources. Examples of recent organizational process innovations are just-in-time production, TQM (total quality management) and lean production. Like many technological process innovations, they are normally initially developed through processes of trial-and-error and learning-by-doing within the innovating firms. They are not usually based on formal R&D activities.[13] In contrast to many technological innovations, they are, as a rule, diffused to new firms by copying the vanguard firms.[14] Moreover, this diffusion is facilitated by the fact that there are normally no property rights associated with organizational innovations.[15] (For further discussion, see Appendix B.)

Organizational process innovations are intangibles – that is, they are non-material. Therefore they are never goods but they might be sold as services in some cases. For example, the process of copying is sometimes facilitated by organization consultants, who are then 'social carriers' of organizational knowledge. In other words, the knowledge basis behind organizational innovations may sometimes be sold as consultancy *services*, thereby becoming commodified. Thus some organizational process innovations could have been previously bought as intangible products (that is, services) from a seller – or, vice versa, an intangible product can be bought and later used as an organizational process innovation. However, it is likely that only a tiny share of all organizational innovations become service products. Most organizational innovations are not services and are not products sold on markets at all.[16] In other words, the categories of services and organizational innovations are fairly independent of each other, although they have similar characteristics in several respects.[17]

As discussed above, organizational innovations are not always included in discussions of product versus process innovations. However, there are at least three good reasons for doing so here:

1. Organizational changes are important sources of productivity growth and competitiveness and they might also strongly influence employment.[18]
2. Organizational and technological changes are closely related and intertwined in the real world and organizational change is often a requirement for successful technological process innovation.[19]
3. All technologies are created by human beings and this is achieved within the framework of specific organizational forms. They are 'socially shaped' by the organizational forms.[20]

At present, organizational innovation is an important but under-theorized topic in the literature on systems of innovation. Organizational innovations are not included in the innovation concepts used by Carlsson and Stankiewicz (1995) and Nelson and Rosenberg (1993) in theorizing about systems of innovation. In Lundvall (1992) innovations other than technological ones are mentioned, but they are not systematically analysed. An exception is chapter 5 in Lundvall

(1992), which deals with work organization and the innovation design dilemma (Gjerding, 1992).

The emergence of new organizational forms, their diffusion, as well as the interaction between these forms and technological innovations can – in principle – be analysed within an SI approach.[21] It may simply be achieved by including organizational innovation in the innovation concept – in a pragmatic spirit.[22] However, organizational innovations take place under different circumstances and are governed by different determinants as compared to technological innovation (Edquist, 1997a: section 3.6), even though they are also closely related to technological innovation in their development. Because of these similarities and differences, this section has tried to propose clear distinctions and will continue to do so through the coming chapters, which analyse the empirical material.

2.3 INVESTMENT, CONSUMER AND INTERMEDIATE PRODUCTS

When specifying concepts earlier in this chapter, we noted that, from a dynamic perspective, some innovations can first be product innovations and later process innovations, or vice versa. This complication must be taken into account in analysing the employment effects of innovation. As we argue in Chapter 5, some artefacts can play both the roles of job 'creators' and job 'destroyers' at different times, or in different situations. The possibility of a 'double' (negative as well as positive) employment effect depends on whether or not an artefact can be both a product innovation and a process innovation. This makes it important to classify innovations according to 'final demand'.

As a basis for further discussion of these points in Chapter 4, we present here a classification of products and product innovations into three categories: *consumer products*, *investment products* and *intermediate products*.[23] These are well-established categories and useful for the analysis of dynamic relationships, as indicated in an earlier discussion by Kuznets (1972: 433–5). It can be seen from the examples given below that both goods and services can be classified into these three categories.

Consumer products are goods and services that are consumed (by households) for their own sake to satisfy current wants. Examples are prefabricated food, haircuts and heart transplants.

Investment products are durable products that are intended to be used as factor inputs for further production. These products imply an initial sacrifice of consumption/welfare followed by (expected) subsequent benefits, since resources are devoted to producing non-consumable products instead of products intended for immediate consumption. Industrial robots and some kinds of consultancy advice to firms – for example with regard to building a process automation system – are examples of investment products.[24] Investment goods such as industrial robots are often called capital goods.

Intermediate products are used by firms to produce other products, rather than for final consumption, but they are rapidly used up, so they are not investment goods. Raw material (for example steel), components, mobile telephone calls and legal advice for current business problems can serve as examples.[25]

2.4   HIGH-, MEDIUM- AND LOW-TECHNOLOGY SECTORS

Another important basis for the classification of innovations is the categorization of manufacturing and service sectors according to the level of investment that firms make in the search for innovations (in, for example, R&D). Distinctions are commonly made among high-technology, medium-technology and low-technology manufacturing sectors, and similar distinctions can be developed for service sectors. Such categories are important in analysing the employment effects of innovation, as argued in Chapter 4.

The categorization of manufacturing sectors according to their level of technology is based, as a rule, on R&D investment. This standard practice, as well as some of the difficulties it involves, has been described and explained as follows:

> For example, the OECD maintains a classification of high-technology, medium-technology and low-technology manufacturing sectors based on their relative R&D expenditures or *R&D intensity* (ratio of R&D expenditures to gross output). Computers, communications, semiconductors, pharmaceuticals and aerospace are among the high-technology and high-growth OECD sectors and are estimated to account for about 20 per cent of manufacturing production. Countries' output, employment and trade profiles can be drawn based on the relative roles of their high-, medium- and low-technology sectors. However, current indicators of R&D intensity are confined to manufacturing sectors: they have not been developed for the fast-growing services portion of OECD economies. Nor do these indicators take account of R&D purchased from other industrial sectors, either embodied in new equipment and inputs or disembodied in the form of patents and licences. More complete indicators of total R&D intensity, including both direct R&D efforts and acquired R&D, need to be developed. (OECD, 1996d: 247–8)

Chapter 4 uses the original OECD definition of R&D expenditures in manufacturing sectors. It further argues that high-, medium- and low-technology categories in service sectors can be measured by the proportion of highly educated people employed. Service sectors with a high proportion of employees possessing advanced educational qualifications are similar to R&D-intensive manufacturing sectors in some ways. Since they often conduct little or no R&D on a formal basis, it might be inaccurate to label such service sectors as 'high-tech'. However, they can be called 'knowledge-intensive'. As shown in Chapter 5, innovation-based interactions between 'high-tech' sectors in manufacturing, on the one hand, and 'knowledge-intensive' sectors in services, on the other, have important consequences for employment.

2.5   SUMMARY

Because the category of innovation is extremely complex and heterogeneous, it is necessary and useful to make analytical distinctions. The primary one proposed here is between product and process innovations. Within this, process innovations are further distinguished into technological and organizational, and product innovations into material goods and intangible services. These distinctions are represented in Figure 2.1.

We have also proposed some additional, complementary distinctions. Thereby, products are divided into investment, consumer and intermediate products. Further, manufacturing and service sectors are divided into high-, medium- and low-technology or, in the case of services, knowledge-intensity sectors, based respectively on R&D intensity or educational level of the labour force. Part II (Chapters 3, 4 and 5) of this book shows how these distinctions are useful for an analysis of relations between innovations and employment.

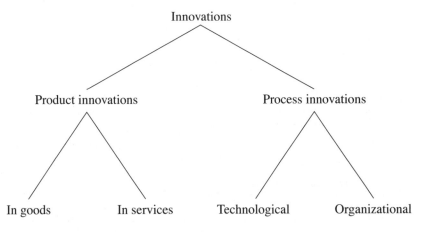

Figure 2.1   Different kinds of innovations

NOTES

1. Utterback and Abernathy (1975), in their work on the product life cycle, demonstrated the link between the product/process distinction and the distinction between technological and organizational innovations by generating a model of development in which different firm structures, or transformations of a firm's organizational structure, are related to the relationship (or balance) between product and process innovation.
2. However, some neoclassical models deal with the emergence of new products.
3. See the introductory section of Chapter 4.
4. More generally, these authors also stress the importance of sectoral differences, particularly in terms of institutions and knowledge. We address these differences by means of the categories discussed in sections 2.3 and 2.4.
5. Other important methodological problems concern levels of aggregation and the character of final demand (Archibugi, Evangelista and Simonetti, 1994). The present work will be careful to identify the different levels of aggregation used in the studies referred to. At a later point in the book, the problem of 'final demand' will be dealt with by considering distinctions among product innovations as 'investment', 'intermediate' and 'consumer' products (see sections 2.3, and Chapter 5, sections 5.2 and 5.3). For further discussion, see Appendix A.
6. This pattern of performance in the US auto industry, first identified in comparative research conducted during the late 1980s, has been found to persist in subsequent, follow-up research. According to this later research, Japanese assembly plants in North America were in 1993 second only to those in Japan itself in terms of productivity and other performance criteria (Lansbury and Bamber, 1997: 212, table 12.5). This research, which repeats earlier national comparisons, also indicates that (apart from the 'benchmark' plants of Japanese firms situated in Japan) the plants of US firms exhibited the least positive change between 1989 and 1993 (ibid.).
7. This exclusion also applies to 'internal markets' within firms – such as, for example, the case where a firm has a computer department which 'sells' its services to other departments of the firm. It also applies to the case when a process innovation (for example, an industrial robot) is designed, produced and used within the same firm – in our sense, it never becomes a commodified product.
8. As this matter has been discussed extensively elsewhere, Appendix C only briefly reviews some main arguments and concepts.
9. For reasons of simplification, here only material elements are included in the concept of technological process innovation. This obviously means that services cannot be technological process innovations. When the conceptual basis has become more solid, immaterial elements (like skills and knowledge) might be introduced into the concept. However, there may be strong arguments why they fit best in the category of organizational process innovations.
10. Only investment goods may appear in two 'incarnations' in this way. It is not possible for consumer goods to do so.
11. Generally, therefore, empirical studies have shown strong interrelation of product and process innovation at the firm level (Archibugi, Casaratto and Sirilli, 1987; Kraft, 1990; Lunn, 1986). However, this relationship is neither simple nor deterministic (Rosenberg, 1976), and requires clear specification.
12. The growth hormone example is discussed in detail in McKelvey (1996).
13. Hence original organizational process innovations normally emerge within the using firm; they are seldom sold and bought on the market, as technological process innovations often are.
14. Hence they are normally not exchanged on markets at this diffusion stage.
15. This they have in common with most service products.
16. Nevertheless, these innovations may have important effects on both production costs and the delivery of products, and so may have a significant impact on products and product markets. Additional arguments for the study of (both 'market' and 'non-market') organizational innovations are presented below.

17. The strength of this link should be established empirically. It would also be useful to know whether or not the link grows stronger, and under what circumstances.
18. Thus, 're-engineering' techniques, which are organizational changes, have been shown to result in significant productivity increases and reductions in employment. See, for instance, the example given in Hammer and Champy (1993: 36-9).
19. This is, for example, shown in Nyholm (1995).
20. The discussion of these reasons is developed in Edquist (1997a).
21. Since there are organizational forms in most areas of human activity, it is useful to talk about such forms in different 'spheres' or at various levels of aggregation. For example, the organizational form in an R&D department influences the design of product technologies – some of which are later transformed into process technologies. The organizational form where the process technology is used – that is, in the process of production – influences the implementation of the technology. See Edquist (1992; 1997b).
22. This is, for example, done by Dosi: 'In an essential sense, innovation concerns the search for, and the discovery, experimentation, development, imitation, and adoption of new products, new production processes and new organisational set-ups' (Dosi, 1988). The relations between the three innovation categories mentioned by Dosi are discussed in some detail in Edquist (1997b) for manufacturing goods as well as for services.
23. This classification follows the distinction between final and derived forms of demand made in J. Schmookler's (1996) major analysis of the central role of demand in determining the focus and volume of innovation and technical change.
24. The rationale for classifying this kind of consultancy advice as an investment service is that it is used as an input for future production just like the automation system. However, many other kinds of consultancy advice are not used over time in the same way.
25. Some products may be both consumer and intermediate products, for example milk used for drinking and for producing chocolate – or mobile telephone calls. It depends on what the product is used for.

PART II

Innovations and Employment

Understanding how and why different types of innovation affect the creation, or destruction, of jobs is one crucial and important part of the puzzle of the overall relationship between (1) innovation and growth, (2) innovation and employment, and (3) growth and employment. (See Figure P.1 in the Preface.) The definitions given and motivated in Chapter 2 provide us with conceptual tools for specifying the very different types of employment impact that different innovations can have.

The purpose of the following three chapters is to explore, debate and discuss the impacts of different kinds of innovations on employment. In doing so, we want to identify what types of innovations and sectors are likely to create jobs for the future – and which are likely to lose them. From this standpoint, Chapter 3 addresses process innovations, Chapter 4 product innovations and Chapter 5 dynamic effects.

Having stated such grand objectives, let us just say that the current book will take us some distance down this road but by no means lead us to the end. However, it provides new ways of thinking about the problems and potential solutions and thereby contributes to the development of a future research agenda in the field.

Although our work is focused on the relations between innovation and employment, following this road means that productivity, productivity growth, market growth and economic growth must at times be brought into the analysis. One particularly important reason for this is that productivity growth and market growth are dynamic links between innovation and employment.

Productivity is the relation between value added (in which it is important to note that intermediates are deducted) and either labour (labour productivity), capital (capital productivity) or a weighted average of the two (so-called total factor productivity (TFP)), using (in the most common definition) the share of wages in value added as weights. Labour productivity is defined as the ratio between production (measured as value added or production value) and labour input (measured as number of employed or number of hours worked).

Accordingly, changes in labour productivity can sometimes lead to changes in employment, especially when process innovations are the reason for the change. Labour productivity is the most common productivity measure. In this measure, other inputs (like capital) are disregarded. Therefore, labour productivity is a partial measure of productivity and a narrow concept. The same is true for capital productivity.

When the term 'productivity' is used in this book, labour productivity is normally meant. Change in labour productivity is often seen as an approximation of the development of material welfare and is a relevant measure in discussions related to employment issues. Most productivity data available also relate to labour productivity, and therefore it is natural to make international comparisons based on these figures.

To capture the relations between the use of resources and production as a whole, all factors of production should, however, be taken into account. This is done by the concept of TFP. Change in TFP is often said to be caused by 'technical change'. This assumed relationship comes from the neoclassical growth model of Solow in the 1950s (1957). Let us quote him at some length:

> If Q represents output and K and L represent capital and labour inputs in 'physical' units, then the aggregate production function can be written as $Q = F(K,L;t)$. The variable t for time appears in F to allow for technical change. It will be seen that I am using the phrase 'technical change' as a shorthand expression for *any kind of shift* in the production function. Thus slowdowns, speedups, improvements in the education of the labour force, and all sorts of things will appear as 'technical change'. (Solow, 1957: 345)

It is reasonable to assume that a 'shift' in the production function should be interpreted to include, in addition to what Solow explicitly mentions above, all technological and organizational process innovations. Since he argues at the macro level and discusses in terms of an *aggregate* production function, there is nothing that, in principle, excludes product innovations from being incorporated into his notion of 'technical change'. And, in a one-sector model, it does not really matter, of course. It is interesting to note, however, that nowhere in his article does Solow include product innovations in 'technical change'. Nor does he explicitly mention product innovations at all. He even comes close to excluding them explicitly when he writes: 'Obviously much, perhaps nearly all, innovation must be embodied in new plant and equipment to be realised at all' (ibid.: 354).

At a lower level of aggregation, it is important to distinguish between process and product innovation. Here a process innovation leads to a *shift* in the production function, while a product innovation leads to a completely *new* production function. Later mainstream growth economists have, however, seldom attempted to take product innovation into account, but have continued to focus on process innovation in the spirit of Solow. In this book, we argue that it is crucial to make a distinction between process and product innovation and to take both of them into account in analyses of growth and employment consequences of innovation.

3. Process innovations and employment

This is the first of three chapters that explore and discuss the relations between innovations and employment. The chapter focuses on process innovations. Process innovations refer to how things are produced, and can be technological or organizational. They are necessary for firms and countries to increase productivity and to maintain competitiveness relative to others. In this connection, competitiveness is usually considered to be largely a matter of cost reduction – and, often, of reducing labour costs.

In a static perspective, process innovations thus often have the potential to reduce employment, but there are also second- and third-order effects which may increase employment – so-called 'compensation effects'. The following sections address the immediate impacts of process innovation in different sectors. Moreover, they provide a basis for the discussion in Chapter 5 of (possible) compensation effects, other dynamic elements and relevant theoretical questions.

3.1 TECHNOLOGICAL PROCESS INNOVATIONS

Technological process innovations (such as new machinery used in factories) are normally labour saving and often capital using per unit of output. Usually, therefore, new process technologies increase labour productivity and potentially reduce employment in the firm, country, sector or region where they are introduced. Hence the 'immediate' effect on employment is negative. However, second- and third-order consequences may partly offset the immediate effect – or even (more than) balance it, at least in principle.

Hypothesis 1   The labour-saving effects of technological process innovations vary widely between sectors – in manufacturing as well as in service production.

This hypothesis is broadly consistent with much of the evidence from empirical work reviewed in the OECD *Jobs Study* (OECD, 1994b; 1995b). The review addresses both manufacturing and services at the sectoral level across OECD countries. For manufacturing, 'When the record for productivity growth by subsector is compared with that for employment, a mixed picture emerges' (Johnson, 1995: 56). This means that there are different groups of sectors with different relationships between productivity growth and employment.

The mixed picture is illustrated by the three subsectors of basic metals, chemicals, and machinery and equipment. In nearly every country where basic metals had the strongest productivity growth, employment in that sector declined as a share of total employment in manufacturing. However, the reverse was true of chemicals, which was not only highest or nearly highest in terms of productivity growth in most countries, but whose share of employment also rose in almost all countries. A similar pattern was found in machinery and equipment – a rising share of manufacturing employment in nearly every country, including those where this sector had the highest productivity record. There are country-specific variations on these trends, but 'all countries reveal a wide range of productivity experience across subsectors, whether the trend for all manufacturing is high (Japan) or low (Canada)' (ibid.: 55). This evidence indicates interesting differences across sectors, which we shall address later in this book. It also indicates that countries may take different paths of development and sectoral specialization, which may be related to specific national factors.

The OECD *Jobs Study* also indicates that the service industries have begun to present a 'mixed picture' in terms of the employment effects of productivity gains (ibid.: 52). The service sector as a whole is far from homogeneous. It is difficult to arrive at uniform measures of output and thus problematic to compare countries and sectors. None the less, 'industries such as finance, insurance and real estate, and communication consistently generate more output per worker than service industries such as wholesale and retail trade' (ibid.). For the OECD as a whole, the sector including finance, insurance and real-estate services has been one of the leaders in the generation of new service employment. However, the strongest contribution to such employment growth has come from a sector with a lower level of productivity growth than wholesale and retail trade – namely, community, social and personal services (OECD, 1996b: 71).[1]

This sectoral variation in the relationship between productivity growth and employment is consistent with the findings of earlier, country-specific research about different sectors. For example, Levy, Bowes and Jondrow (1984) examined five traditional US goods-producing industries and found that patterns of demand growth in some, such as mining and aluminium, compensated partly or completely for initial job losses, while this did not occur in other industries, such as steel and automotive manufacturing. Similarly, the UK Tempo programme conducted five different branch and sector studies, based mainly on manufacturing industries but also including some service industries. It arrived at projections of increased employment levels in IT-based branches (electronics, telecommunications, instruments, engineering, and the graphics and printing industries), and reduced employment levels in other manufacturing branches (Freeman and Soete, 1987).

Moreover, recent German research, covering both manufacturing and services, found a positive correlation between productivity and production changes across sectors, but reported that the employment effects varied. In industries where productivity growth outstripped production growth, employment declined (Blazecjak, 1991). This was mainly the case in manufacturing industries (including chemicals, plastics, cars, aerospace, scientific instruments and textiles). The reverse tendency, of innovation creating increased employment under conditions of expanding production, was found in some other manufacturing industries (such as manufacturing machinery and office machinery) and also in some service industries (such as communications and insurance). Hence, in a longer-term perspective, employment growth expanded when the market expanded alongside productivity growth. Such market growth is often closely associated with the development of new products, to be discussed in Chapter 4.

Hypothesis 2 The variation in labour saving caused by technological process innovations is larger between service sectors than between manufacturing sectors.

Again, research conducted by the OECD (1996a; 1996b) supports this hypothesis. For manufacturing, there tends to be a consistent pattern in the relationship between technological change and employment. A regression analysis of employment by manufacturing sectors across countries indicated that 'on average, over many sectors there is a tendency for higher productivity growth in individual sectors to be negatively associated with employment in the given sector' (Johnson, 1995: 55). There are, however, important sectoral variations in manufacturing, as discussed under Hypothesis 1.

In services, there is a much less consistent pattern. A study of employment growth across the OECD countries found that for four core service sectors, 'Almost all of the increase in the share of total employment in the services can be attributed to the two of the four core sectors that least resemble each other' (OECD, 1996b: 73). One 'core sector' is FIRB (financial, insurance, real-estate and business services), which is a heavy user of process technology with a large proportion of skilled workers. The other is CSPS (community, social and personal services) in which not all, but many subsectors (especially the privately provided services) tend to have a majority of less-skilled workers (ibid.).[2]

Thus, employment growth in services has come mainly in one sector that is more uniformly dominated by high-skill employment (FIRB) and in one sector with a more uneven skill profile, including a larger proportion of low-skill employment (CSPS). We note, however, that the empirical evidence concerning CSPS addresses both private- and public-sector services.[3]

At this point it is helpful to provide a brief clarification and explanation of the nomenclature employed in the OECD literature cited above. This terminology will be used extensively throughout the remainder of the book – in particular, when we refer to the categories FIRB and CSPS.

The OECD divides services as follows:

> There are four core services sectors: wholesale and retail trade, restaurants and hotels; transport, storage and communications; finance, insurance, real estate and business services (FIRB); and community, social and personal services (CSPS). (ibid.: 71–3)[4]

Of the two 'employment leaders' in services – CSPS and FIRB – CSPS is particularly important. CSPS, due to its large size and fast rate of employment growth, is clearly the OECD world's primary 'employment growth' sector. CSPS accounted for 30 per cent of all OECD employment in 1991 and its rate of employment growth was ranked among the top five sectors (including both manufacturing and service sectors) in seven of eight OECD countries (OECD, 1996b; Sakurai, 1995). This ranking is depicted in Table 3.1, which shows that Denmark is the exception.

The growth of employment in both FIRB and CSPS has been attributed primarily to increased demand, and productivity growth in general has had a negative impact on employment growth (Sakurai, Ionnidis and Papaconstantinou, 1996). However, the specific contribution of technological change to productivity growth in the service industries has remained difficult to establish. Due to 'measurement difficulties', existing research has only been able to establish an 'erratic' connection between new process technology and employment in services (Brynjolfsson, 1991).

Due to the lack of good indicators and comparable statistics, it is very difficult to determine whether there are country-specific patterns of sectoral variations in the relationship between productivity growth due to technological process innovation and employment growth in services. We do know, however, that there are important historical differences among countries in terms of the sectoral pattern of employment creation in services.

As an example of such differences, during the 1960–90 period among OECD countries, 'all four Nordic countries have experienced very sharp increases in the share of public-sector employment' in services. At the same time, more moderate increases were recorded in other European countries and Canada. The corresponding share of public-sector service employment 'remained particularly low in Japan and Australia' (Johnson, 1995: 52).

These results can be compared with those of another, previously cited, study

Table 3.1 Ten highest employment growth industries in eight OECD countries

	Canada 1971–86	Denmark 1972–88	France 1972–85	Germany 1978–86	Japan 1970–85	Netherlands 1972–86	UK 1968–84	USA 1972–85
1	CSPS	Real estate	FIRB	Non-ferrous	Computers	Real estate	FIRB	Real estate
2	Computers	Finance	Computers	Aerospace	CSPS	Aerospace	CSPS	Computers
3	FIRB	Pharmaceutical	CSPS	Computers	FIRB	CSPS	Government	Finance
4	Hotels	Government	EGW	CSPS	Electronics	Communication	Trade	Hotels
5	Plastics	Instruments	Communication	Motor vehicles	Plastics	Government	Pharmaceutical	CSPS
6	Aerospace	Electronics	Government	Hotels	Government	Finance	Transport	Mining
7	W&R trade	Other transport	Electronics	Government	Motor vehicles	Motor vehicles	Plastics	Electronics
8	Government	Communication	Aerospace	FIRB	Aerospace	Hotels	Construction	W&R trade
9	Motor vehicles	EGW	Hotels	Plastics	Trade	EGW	Food	Aerospace
10	Mining	Non-electrical machinery	Transport	EGW	EGW	Transport	Electronics	Instruments

Source: Adapted from Sakurai (1995), table 5.

of patterns of employment creation during the same period (specifically, during the 1970s and 1980s) in eight OECD countries (Sakurai, 1995). Significantly, the latter study found that only Denmark – the one Nordic country examined – did not include CSPS in its list of the five sectors with the fastest rate of employment growth (ibid.: 150). Comparing these results – depicted in Table 3.1 – supports the speculation that CSPS has figured more importantly as an 'employment leader' in countries with a lower rate of increase in public-sector employment. Countries with higher rates of job creation in public services may simply have organized and paid for, in the form of government services, employment that would otherwise be included in CSPS. In those countries where such employment was instead organized on a basis that would lead to inclusion in CSPS, this would be recorded by the OECD as 'private sector employment' – even though it might occur within government-owned enterprises.

Although it is difficult to establish country-specific variations, we do know that the productivity of specific service industries, to the extent that it can be measured, has varied widely across countries (OECD, 1994b). Finally, we know that the overall rate of employment creation in services also differs among countries. The rate is much faster, for example, in Japan and the USA than it is in Europe (McKinsey Global Institute, 1994).

Hypothesis 3   Employment tends to increase in those manufacturing sectors that are growth sectors, and these sectors are closely associated with high-technology sectors.

Research examining a period from the early 1970s to the late 1980s for manufacturing sectors in eight countries has shown that productivity growth and process technology have affected employment negatively. The result holds both in total manufacturing and in individual industry segments (Sakurai, 1995).

A significant exception to this pattern has been in the case of high-wage and high-technology segments. There, higher domestic and export demand outweighed the labour-saving effects of new process technology (ibid.).

We can also refer to research that employed a more systematically comparative approach to investigate the effects of structural and technological change on manufacturing employment in the six largest OECD countries. It found that 'growth sectors' (with increases in both employment and value added) are associated with 'high-technology' (higher R&D intensity) industries whose products are in strong demand. In other manufacturing industries, this 'virtuous cycle' of technological development, growth in product markets and increasing employment does not occur (Pianta, Evangelista and Perani, 1996). A similar pattern has been revealed in country-specific research on manufacturing sectors (Meyer-Krahmer, 1996; Vivarelli, Evangelista and Pianta, 1995). In conclusion, then, empirical evidence strongly supports Hypothesis 3.

Hypothesis 4 In some service sectors technological process innovations lead to very large productivity increases and thereby potentially to large labour savings.

We possess only crude measures of service-sector productivity. One is the contribution per worker (by sector) to the average annual growth of GDP. Using this measure, the OECD has made a cross-country comparison of longer-term sector and industry performance in both services and manufacturing. This comparison indicates that while productivity growth in services has generally lagged behind that of manufacturing over the past two decades, productivity growth in some service sectors is above the level of manufacturing in several countries.[5] One such service sector is transportation, storage and communication; another is utilities (OECD, 1994b).[6] Both sectors are heavy investors in new process technology, and since neither has made any large contribution to employment growth in services, it may be inferred that process innovation has had strong labour-saving effects in these industries.[7]

For most of the same (and other) countries, however, a second study shows that FIRB is nearly equal to, equals or is above transportation, storage and communication and utilities in its level of capital investment in new process technology (Papaconstantinou, Sakurai and Wyckoff, 1995: table 5).[8] Yet the productivity growth of FIRB, while high relative to many other segments of services, has tended to be well below the level of manufacturing in all countries (OECD, 1994b). FIRB's contribution to the growth of employment has been high throughout the OECD (OECD, 1996b). Thus there tends to be a marked pattern of both above- and below-average productivity growth in service sectors investing strongly in new process technologies. Moreover, the relationship of this pattern to the pattern of service-sector employment growth is not well understood. However, the combination of product innovation and increased market demand is probably relevant here, as discussed elsewhere in this book.

The FIRB sector is especially puzzling in this connection. Given the above-mentioned 'measurement difficulties', together with what is known about capital investment in new process technology in this sector, it is difficult to point to evidence for FIRB which directly supports the proposition that its capital investments should translate into high productivity growth based on labour saving.

Country-specific studies rather than comparative ones, however, allow for the correction of measurement problems and offer more insight. The most comprehensive evidence addresses the US situation. For the finance, insurance and real-estate subsector (that is, the FIRB sector, excluding business services) in the USA, for example, Baily and Gordon (1988) found that measurement errors underestimated the productivity by about 1.1 per cent per year before 1973, and by 2.3 per cent thereafter. The US finance, insurance and real-estate subsector's net share of non-residential capital stock was found in this study to be almost equal to that of the entire manufacturing sector. Its share of investment devoted to computers and communication equipment was found to be nearly double that of manufacturing (ibid.).

Thus productivity growth due to new process technology in FIRB industries may have been fairly high – but so too has been the rate of employment growth in FIRB industries. For example, employment in the finance, insurance and real-estate industries and in other capital-intensive service industries (including air transport, telecommunications, retail and wholesale trade, and health care) in the USA expanded by 23 per cent during the 1980s (National Research Council, 1994).

The same pattern of significant employment growth in capital-intensive service industries is also found across the OECD. This employment growth pattern, however, has to be viewed against the background of a general decline in the growth rate of service employment across the OECD countries since the 1960s (OECD, 1996b: graph 3.2, table 3.6). Moreover, a recent analysis of service-sector employment growth suggests that investment in new process technologies, which is a major source of productivity growth, has generally had a negative impact on job creation (Sakurai, 1995). Thus 'new demand', rather than 'new technologies' *per se* (that is, innovations in process technology) appears to be the primary source of the employment growth, in both FIRB and services in general (OECD, 1996b: 75).

One conclusion that can be drawn is not only about the diversity of service sectors but also that testing the above hypotheses requires disaggregation into a large number of goods and service sectors. Such disaggregation is certainly more interesting than an empirical analysis in 'average' terms of large aggregates such as 'manufacturing' and 'service production'. More importantly, it is necessary if we are fully to understand employment effects of innovation.[9]

3.2   ORGANIZATIONAL PROCESS INNOVATIONS

Organizational process innovations also influence productivity and employment. Some of them substantially increase labour productivity in the process of production – with corresponding reductions of employment (per unit of output). Womack, Jones and Roos (1990: figure 4.5) claimed that the time needed to assemble a car during the period when they conducted their research (the late 1980s) could vary between more than 100 hours and around 20 hours. The lower figure was due to a large extent to 'lean production', a new organizational form emanating from Japan (ibid.: ch. 4).[10] These kinds of organizational process innovations are similar to technological ones from a productivity and employment point of view, and therefore the compensation mechanisms involved are similar.[11]

At a level of aggregation involving more than one firm, other kinds of organizational innovations, such as kanban or just-in-time production, reduce the amount of capital engaged in work-in-progress (in inventories or in transport) (Aoki, 1990). This does not necessarily influence the volume of production, nor the amount of labour used (per unit of output). These kinds of organizational innovations are interesting from an employment perspective since they can increase (capital) productivity – and thereby competitiveness – without reducing employment. They are different from most technological process innovations in this respect (Edquist, 1992).

Hypothesis 5 There are different kinds of organizational process innovations. One category is similar to technological process innovations with regard to the factor-saving bias – that is, they are labour saving. Another class is capital saving without direct effects on employment levels.

This distinction, between labour-saving and capital-saving organizational innovations, is seldom made in discussions of organizational innovations in industry. Instead, the more common approach is to regard organizational innovation as an intervening variable in processes of technological change – that is, as a means of 'realizing' the productivity potential of investments in technological process innovations (particularly information technology) by amplifying their labour-saving effects (Baldwin and Johnson, 1995; Lynch and Black, 1995; OECD, 1996b: 138–40; Osterman, 1990: 44–5).

This approach is taken, for example, by authors who discuss organizational innovations in manufacturing as an undifferentiated category of productivity-enhancing forms of work organization (for example, Alänge, Jacobsson and Lindberg, 1996). One group of such authors speaks broadly about 'a new paradigm of how to manage a business' – one contributing substantially to the reduction of labour input per unit of output in manufacturing (ibid.). They cite several firm-level examples of dramatic reductions in employment. However, their discussion assumes that employment reductions due to combined technological and organizational process innovations in individual manufacturing firms simply mirror the broad trend towards 'industrial growth accompanied by a continuous reduction in industrial employment' (ibid.: 1).

More discriminating approaches tend to yield different results. Given the rather crude 'state of the art' with respect to the conceptualization and measurement of organizational innovations (see Appendix B), an analysis of the employment impacts of organizational innovations at higher levels of aggregation than the individual firm is difficult. International comparisons tend to reveal little about the effects on productivity and employment that are specific to organizational, as compared to technological, process innovation.

More detailed results have been obtained at the national level (Australian Manufacturing Council, 1994; Nutek, 1996), and even more so in sector- or industry-specific studies (Greenan, 1995). However, even studies conducted at these lower levels of aggregation suggest that 'there are few direct links' among organization, productivity and employment (OECD, 1996b: 140). In other words, the relations between specific organizational innovations and changes in productivity or employment are usually complicated by intervening factors. In order for there to be positive effects on productivity (and, thereby, some impact on employment), 'it is the bundle of strategies associated with workplace reorganisation, including enterprise training and a highly skilled work-force, which improves performance' (ibid.).

Some recent German research on 'new production concepts' has sought to overcome these difficulties by combining the analysis of survey data with that of qualitative empirical investigations conducted at the level of individual firms (Dreher et al., 1995). Subsequent survey research, based on the results of this combined analysis, investigated certain types of organizational innovations. Specifically, it examined innovations such as just-in-time (JIT) production which are aimed at reducing the amount of capital tied up in inventories and other 'buffers'. These 'new production concepts' were analysed with respect to their capacity to increase labour productivity in terms of schedule effectiveness.[12] It was found that 'although these concepts do help to reduce material stocks, they do not provide direct solutions for time schedule problems or the reduction of lead times' (Dreher, 1996: 12). One interpretation of these results is that organizational innovations of a capital-saving type, in and of themselves, have neutral and possibly even positive effects on employment. One reason seems to be that while there is a reduction in material stocks, and thus physical capital, labour is still required to solve problems of scheduling and coordination in production. These problems may even increase under conditions where 'buffers' are absent.

These findings must, of course, be interpreted in relation to those of comparable studies conducted at a national level. National studies, including both surveys and case-study investigations, have usually concentrated on the question of whether organizational change can significantly improve labour productivity (Betcherman et al., 1994; Ichniowski, Shaw and Prennushi, 1994). The focus has usually been on labour-saving organizational changes, and a key issue has been to determine the specific contributions of organizational process innovations to improved labour productivity. Results include that the net employment effects of organizational innovations of this type tend to be negative (Campbell, 1993), and that their positive effect on productivity is indirect in the sense that it is mediated by other, intervening variables (Lynch and Black, 1995).[13] They are thus similar to technological process innovations in this respect.

A further level of research into whether or not organizational process innovations can improve productivity and thereby have an impact on employment concerns the micro level of individual firms.[14] At this level, it has been found that labour-saving organizational changes tend to result in higher levels of employment induced by improved productivity only when they are introduced in combination with technological process innovations (Greenan, 1995). However, Hörte and Lindberg (1992) argue that, in the Swedish case, investment in new organizational forms has a higher marginal productivity than investment in new production technology (ibid.).

It is thus possible to identify, on the basis of existing research literature, evidence of both capital-saving and labour-saving types of organizational innovation. However, few studies seek to differentiate between them. One exception is the work by Nyholm (1995). This study indicates that certain ('managerial') types of organizational change which were introduced in combination with new technology had more positive effects on productivity than other types of organizational change (in 'work organization'). Nyholm's study places capital-saving organizational innovations such as JIT in the category of 'changes in work organization'. Conversely, it assigns labour-saving organizational innovations such as 'horizontal' management structures to the category of 'managerial innovations' (ibid.: 20). This distinction implies that the second type of organizational change – that is, innovation in 'work organization' – is much less likely to have an immediate effect of 'labour saving'. Instead, it is more likely to be 'capital saving'.

The labour-saving type of organizational change – that is, 'managerial innovations' – was found to have a far more positive effect on productivity. Improved productivity was achieved by making more effective use of advanced technologies – but this in turn required the development of a more highly qualified labour force (ibid.: 27). However, despite the fact that it had a less positive effect on productivity, the capital-saving type of organizational change – that is, innovations in 'work organization' – was also found to be associated with 'increased responsibility/competence among the employees' (ibid.: 20). Thus the study suggests that some organizational innovations can be both 'capital saving' and 'labour enhancing'. However, 'labour enhancing' here refers only to a qualitative change in the skill level of labour inputs.[15] It does not refer to a quantitative increase in employment.

One problem that should be noted about this study is that the evidence remains ambiguous, in at least one important respect. That is, it does not allow us to consider the employment impacts of organizational process innovation in isolation from those of technological process innovation. In addition, the two types of organizational change identified by Nyholm as 'changes in work organization' and 'changes in management structure' need to be more clearly distinguished.[16]

Hypothesis 6   Organizational process innovations require different kinds of investment than technological ones. Due to the kinds of investment that they require, organizational process innovations more directly affect the type of employment created.

This hypothesis addresses some of the most salient differences between technological and organizational process innovations. Few, if any, organizational process innovations require large R&D resources for their emergence or development, and for implementation most will require almost no fixed capital investment (McGuckin, 1994).[17] However, other kinds of investment will be necessary. They include fees for consultants, training and education of the labour force, and other efforts consciously to implement organizational changes.

   Given the difficulties of measurement, it may not be possible to arrive at accurate figures for such investment. Even where the specific contribution of organizational innovation to output and productivity can be identified, organizational change cannot be reduced to a readily quantifiable input measure of 'investment' (ibid.). By definition, however, organization has to do with the coordination of human resources – and, hence, with strategies and forms of investment in 'human capital' (Miller, 1996). And, as Machlup (1980) reminds us, it is qualitatively different from physical capital as a form of 'knowledge capital' because it is vested in people: 'embodied in individual persons, specially schooled and trained "knowledge carriers" and qualified workers with acquired skills' (ibid.: 430–431).

   There are a number of empirical studies that stress the strong connection between organizational innovation and investment in human capital (Baldwin and Johnson, 1995; De Meyer, 1994; Greenan, 1995; Osterman, 1990; Tan and Batra, 1995). The bulk of these studies also indicate important implications for the quality or type of employment created. Nyholm (1995), for example, shows that the apparent bias of advanced manufacturing technologies towards the use of more highly skilled labour cannot be directly attributed to technological change *per se*. Instead, it is more closely related to 'the interrelations and organisational structures in which the new technologies are used', specifically 'new organisational forms ... making use of multi-faceted competence and multi-skilled labour' (ibid.: 26–8).

These developments at firm and industry levels have important implications for national economies. While firms have strong incentives for investing in technological process innovations, they confront numerous disincentives for investing in the development of skilled labour. The most fundamental of these is the problem of appropriating the full benefit of investments in skills transferable to other firms.[18] This can be analysed as a reason for the separation of responsibilities for 'generic' and 'firm-specific' investments in human capital between public education and private (firm-based) training, respectively (Becker, 1975).

This division of responsibility, however, has become increasingly problematic to identify and maintain. A recent survey of cross-national evidence indicates that the combined effect of technological and organizational innovation in the workplace has not only increased the demand for workers possessing higher levels of 'generic' skills. It has also increased the rate at which 'knowledge and skill developed outside the work situation are likely to become obsolete before they are put to use' (Stern, 1996: 189). This is thus a situation which 'makes it relatively more efficient to locate the creation and acquisition of productive knowledge close to the actual productive process' (ibid.). Historical and comparative evidence indicates that this is most likely to occur in countries that have created arrangements providing special economic incentives to counteract the 'natural' disinclination of firms to invest in training (Koike and Inoki, 1990; Soskice, 1994).

3.3 SUMMARY AND FUTURE RESEARCH QUESTIONS

The foregoing discussion of process innovations has used the analytical distinction of technological and organizational process innovations to analyse their impacts on productivity and employment.

Section 3.1 discussed technological process innovations. We argued that the immediate employment effect of technological process innovations is negative. The review of evidence also showed considerable sectoral variation. Further, it showed that product innovation and the dynamic effects of increasing demand in certain growth sectors affects the final results of process innovations on employment.[19]

Section 3.2 then discussed organizational process innovations. Further distinctions were made here between labour-saving and capital-saving organizational innovations. The last-mentioned type of process innovation appears to have (potentially) neutral employment impacts. For the other, the immediate impact on employment is consistently negative.

In general, we have very limited systematic knowledge about productivity gains, factor-saving biases and employment implications of organizational process innovations and their diffusion. At the same time we know that organizational process innovations are economically and socially very important. Moreover, this is true for both manufacturing and services, for example in the banking sector (OECD, 1996b: ch. 6). Thus there is a great need for systematic empirical research on organizational process innovation. In particular, work is needed on the impact of various kinds of organizational process innovations on employment and productivity, as well as how this compares with the impact of technological ones.

An example of an area where further research on the impacts of organizational process innovations is required is indicated by recent debates on 'unbundling' or 'outsourcing'. Stronger support for the proposition that certain types of organizational innovations may have neutral or even positive effects on employment might be provided by research testing the 'unbundling' hypothesis. That is the proposition that certain structural changes within manufacturing firms not only result in employment reductions at the firm level but also externalize functions formerly internal to the firm. Thereby, some studies have suggested, equivalent employment is generated through the creation of new firms, often in other sectors, such as in the case of rapidly growing segments such as 'producer services' or 'business services' (Barker, 1990; Tschetter, 1987).

Recent evidence suggests that the 'unbundling' hypothesis has some credibility. The US manufacturing sector lost over 600 000 jobs from March 1991 to the middle of 1993, but two-thirds of these losses were compensated for by increases in producer service-sector employment of 'temporary workers'. These temporary workers were 'hired by manufacturing firms ... trying to maintain flexibility and cut costs' (OECD, 1996d: 41). In this case, 'unbundling' did not fully compensate for employment loss but did mitigate it.

All in all, this type of organizational change may thus result in job reallocation, both within sectors and intersectorally.[20] It may sometimes have neutral effects on total employment, globally speaking (Alexander, 1996). Even if that is the case, this type of organizational change does not necessarily have neutral effects at the level of national economies. It may involve the reallocation of employment from one country to another.

Existing research indicates that 'unbundling' is not a major source of employment growth. A static breakdown of employment gains made by the services sector in eight countries from the early 1970s to the mid-1980s has shown that increased outsourcing of services was the primary factor behind employment increases only in one sector in one country. This was the financial services sector in the UK (Sakurai, 1995).[21] However, a second study argues that increased outsourcing of services 'was the secondary factor behind job growth in this particular sector [the financial services], or some portion of it, in every other country except the United States' (OECD, 1996d: 41).

Significantly, research on European producer services (defined to include finance, banking, insurance, real-estate and business services) has indicated that most of these services are not being purchased by manufacturing industries, as the 'unbundling hypothesis' suggests, but by other service sectors (ENRS, 1995). This is quite interesting in relation to the relative dynamics of services and manufacturing.

Perhaps the most extreme form of 'unbundling' described in current research literature is the rise of 'small-firm networks' in conjunction with the decentralization of large, vertically integrated corporations (Sabel, 1989). This development is widely held to have had positive effects on both the quantity and quality of employment (Loveman and Sengenberger, 1990). Moreover, it cannot be linked directly to technological change, since 'new technologies ... undoubtedly allow for the decentralisation of production ... but make it just as possible to have flexible centralised production with attendant economies of scale' (Perrow, 1993: 118).

Significantly, small- and medium-sized enterprises (SMEs) appear to have had a very strong positive influence on the expansion of employment in sectors such as producer services. In Europe, the highest demand for producer services has come from medium-sized firms (51 to 500 employees) where 56 per cent of such services has been outsourced, while smaller and very large firms have purchased only 37 per cent of their producer services from external sources (ENRS, 1995). Thus, whether or not it is due to the 'unbundling' of large firms, the growth of SMEs appears to have had some positive impacts on employment. In particular, SMEs have added significantly to the demand for producer services.

Given the relatively poor state of current knowledge regarding organizational process innovations, it might be preferable to address these issues initially through case studies. The empirical evidence discussed in relation to the foregoing hypotheses indicates the usefulness of the conceptual distinctions proposed here between technological and organizational process innovations. It also shows that the proposed distinction between labour-saving and capital-saving types of organizational innovations is useful.

Let us mention a number of questions and tentative answers which could be addressed in empirical studies of organizational process innovations. We concentrate on these because the agenda for research is least developed here. We also refer the reader to the discussion of organizational innovations in Appendix B.

Questions

1. What are the effects of organizational process innovations on employment and productivity, and how do these differ from the effects of technological

process innovations? Do the answers to these questions differ between time periods, countries and sectors?

2. In particular, what is the importance and role of organizational process innovations in specific service sectors?
3. Are organizational process innovations important for the development of new service products?
4. Are organizational process innovations more important for productivity and employment than technological ones in service production?
5. What is the quantitative importance of service products as organizational process innovations, that is, of consultancies, design services, training and education services, and R&D sold on the market?

With reference to Question 1, there is some evidence to suggest that organizational process innovations may, in some cases at least, make a greater contribution to productivity than technological ones (Hörte and Lindberg, 1992). It has also been shown that organizational innovations do not necessarily have a negative effect on employment (Nyholm, 1995).

With respect to Questions 2 and 3, the answers should vary depending on the sector, given the bifurcated pattern of employment growth in services led by two very different core sectors (OECD, 1996b). For policy-oriented research on the employment impacts of innovations, these sectors – FIRB (financial, insurance, real-estate and business services) and CSPS (community, social and personal services) – are obviously especially important sites for research.

Regarding Question 4, the observation has been made that certain technological process innovations – specifically, information technologies – are closely linked to the emergence of organizational innovations in services (OECD, 1986). This linkage has been referred to as a basis for explaining an apparent reversal of the industry life cycle in hitherto 'mature' sectors within services (Barass, 1986).[22] Research comparing the evidence for and against this proposition in FIRB and CSPS might reveal much about the relative importance of technological and organizational change for employment growth in each sector. Some important and useful beginnings have been made in case-study research (Casadio, 1995; Hirschhorn, 1988), which could be a starting-point for future research.

Question 5 is properly a topic for empirical research, the theoretical basis of which should include the 'unbundling hypothesis' (OECD, 1996b) and reference to key concepts concerning innovation networks (Freeman, 1991; Matthews, 1996). 'Unbundling' and its connection with 'small-firm networks' were briefly discussed earlier in this section.

Finally, there are reasons for moving from process to product innovations in the analysis here. Lundvall (1985) has theoretically illustrated the employment consequences of (technological) process innovations within the framework of a one-commodity 'corn-economy' model. He assumes that technical progress – in the sense of increased productivity resulting from process innovations – takes place permanently. This increases productivity and real income per capita – in terms of corn. At a certain point in time the physical limits for corn consumption would be reached, and the income elasticity of corn would start to fall. In such a model, saturation of demand would constitute an absolute limit for growth. Further productivity growth must lead to a fall in employment. He concludes the argument as follows:

> 'In the real world this barrier to growth is overcome exactly by the development of new use-values and new consumer needs. If we abstract from product innovation, we abstract from the most important of factors counteracting stagnation and unemployment' (Lundvall, 1985: 28).

This indicates interesting and important issues about product innovations, which are explored in the next chapter.

NOTES

1. It is possible to argue that productivity growth is more limited in the case of community, social and personal services than in wholesale and retail trade because in the former there are fewer possibilities for achieving greater efficiencies in production based on standardization that would permit both economies of scale and the substitution of equipment for labour. As one recent account of 'the service economy' observes,

   > Many service activities are so unique and different from case to case that only limited rationalisation is possible. This is especially the case in the person-related services (bodycare, health, childcare, care for elderly, education). But also information services ... and maintenance and repair of physical objects are often individualised. (Illeris, 1996: 56)

   However, Herzlinger (1997) convincingly argues that those American hospitals that specialize are engaged in the production of standardized products. She shows that they can thereby dramatically improve performance.
2. The other two core sectors are: (1) retail and wholesale trade, restaurants and hotels; and (2) transport, storage and communications.
3. FIRB services are mainly provided by the private sector. CSPS services, however, involve a 'mix' of public and private provision that varies across countries. Consequently there are ambiguities concerning whether the statistical data on CSPS (and other services, such as transport and communications, where there may also be a similar 'mix' of provision) refer to public or private services, or both.

   OECD statistics on services, which are cited extensively in this book, are a case in point. OECD statistics on CSPS and the other main service sectors often refer explicitly to 'private sector services' (OECD, 1994b: 157). Moreover, OECD publications often describe CSPS statistics with the explicit qualification 'excluding government provided services' (ibid.). On this basis, it might seem natural to conclude that OECD sources exclude public-sector provision from the composition of CSPS.

   In reality, however, the OECD statistics on CSPS normally only exclude 'public administration' from this sector (ibid.). In some instances, moreover, 'public administration' is also included as a separate sub-category of CSPS (ibid.). Thus the only rule of exclusion that is strictly and consistently adhered to by the OECD with respect to CSPS concerns the exclusion of 'government provided services' (ibid.).

In OECD sources, then, it is usual that only 'government services' are equated with the public sector. All other services are, in effect, normally treated as belonging to the private sector. As one commentator points out, the OECD employs 'a very narrow definition of public employment, excluding publicly owned enterprises' (Furåker, 1990: 11).

4. According to the explanation provided by Sakurai (1995), these four sectors represent broad divisions of the private services sector only (ibid.: 137–40). They do not include public-sector services, which are covered by the separate category 'Government Services' (ibid.: table 1). However, as indicated in the preceding note, this definition of public-sector services, usually employed by the OECD, is very restrictive. It effectively excludes a broad range of publicly owned (that is, government-owned) enterprises (Furåker, 1990: 11).

5. The countries referred to in this comparison are France, Germany, Japan, the UK and the USA (OECD, 1994b: table 4.2.1).

6. The 'content' of the transport, storage and communication sector is made evident by its name. Utilities refers to the provision of 'infrastructural' products, or economic 'resource inputs' such as electricity, gas and water. These are material goods, but their delivery involves a large service component, leading to their inclusion, in some classifications, within the service sector. For further discussion, see Smith (1997), especially section 3.

7. For example, although the transportation, storage and communication sector includes telecommunications, one of the most rapidly growing sectors in services, Table 3.1 shows that 'Communication' has been ranked among the five highest employment growth industries during the 1970s and 1980s in only two out of eight selected OECD countries (France and the Netherlands). This evidence suggests that new process technologies in this sector have generally had a strong labour-saving effect, diminishing the 'employment intensity' of otherwise rapid economic growth.

8. The countries referred to in the second study cited here include Australia, Canada, Denmark, Italy and the Netherlands, in addition to France, Germany, Japan, the UK and the USA.

9. Although important, disaggregation is very difficult to achieve today with regard to service production, because of the nature of existing data. Indicators and data need to be developed. However, some new sources of data, such as the European Community Innovation Survey (CIS) have already made possible some pioneering work on the employment and productivity impacts of technological process innovations in services. A leading example of the type of disaggregated analysis that it is possible to conduct with such data is provided by the recent work of Rinaldo Evangelista (2000). By disaggregating the FIRB sector, in particular, Evangelista develops a much more detailed empirical account of 'innovation and employment in services' than has hitherto been available in the research literature.

10. Womack et al. carried out their research on 'lean production' in the late 1980s. However, as discussed in note 6 in Chapter 2, follow-up research conducted in the 1990s has produced some very similar findings. Even in the original research on 'lean production', the figure of 'more than 100 hours' for assembly of an automobile referred to an unusual case – that of luxury car production. The market for 'hand-made' luxury cars has, of course, persisted into the 1990s. It is reasonable to assume on this basis that so have the extremely long periods of time required for the production of such cars, even though the cycle times may have been somewhat reduced. The production cycle times have certainly been reduced for other (non-luxury) types of cars, most of which can now be produced in well under 20 hours. Even so, the basic pattern of Japanese superiority in automobile assembly has persisted. See note 6 in Chapter 2.

11. Compensation mechanisms are discussed in Chapter 5, section 5.1.

12. In this study, 'schedule effectiveness' refers to a reduction of labour time per unit of output, achieved through 'reduction of lead times and (increased) ability to meet delivery deadlines' (Dreher, 1996: 12).

13. A summary of the findings of this and other, related, studies indicates that what is meant by an 'indirect' effect of specific organizational innovations on productivity is a relationship

between these two variables in which 'the line of causality is ... circuitous and relies on the combined use of a bundle of work practices and organisational structures' (OECD, 1996b: 140).

14. Such research normally takes into account the operation of 'compensation mechanisms' leading to second-order employment effects. How these mechanisms affect the relationship between productivity and employment can be briefly explained as follows. Productivity-improving organizational process innovations, especially those which are 'labour saving', will normally have an immediate impact of reducing employment per unit of output. It follows logically that they can only lead to increased employment through the operation of compensation mechanisms such as those that would operate to increase the 'market' of the firm – that is, its level of output. We discuss such mechanisms in Chapter 5, section 5.1.

15. Higher qualification requirements do, however, imply higher levels of investment in human capital.

16. The author makes the following remark about the interpretation of findings concerning the lower impact on productivity of 'changes in work organization', as compared to 'changes in management structure':

> this does not necessarily reflect that work organisation is less important than management structures. The answers with regard to changes in work organisation must be interpreted with considerable caution because of the inherent difficulty of differentiating between radical changes in work routines and minor adjustments in the work processes in a questionnaire. (Nyholm, 1995: 20)

17. Nevertheless, they may certainly be accompanied by technological process innovations.

18. This is because workers who are initially employed and trained by one firm can subsequently take jobs with another firm – which does not then have to provide them with training but is able, instead, to capture the benefits of the first firm's investment in training.

19. Product innovation is discussed in Chaper 4 and dynamic effects in Chapter 5.

20. Hence, 'unbundling' is a kind of organizational change which involves several firms – just like, for example, JIT.

21. The countries examined in this study were: Canada, Denmark, France, Germany, Japan, the Netherlands, the UK and the USA.

22. Industries and firms have been shown to have different organizational characteristics at different points in this cycle, and to progress from an initial concentration on product innovation to a later concentration on process innovation (Utterback and Abernathy, 1975). A reversal of this cycle implies movement in the opposite direction, that is, towards both a renewed emphasis on product innovation and the (re-)emergence of organizational characteristics normally considered to be typical of the initial stages of development but not the later ones. Thus there is a linkage between product innovation and organizational process innovation in 'mature' service industries adopting new process technologies. See also the later discussion of the 'reverse product cycle' thesis under Hypothesis 16.

4. Product innovations and employment

A product innovation occurs when something new is produced (and sold), either for the first time ever or for the first time in a firm, or in a country or region.[1] This means that new economic activities are established, or existing activities change direction. Thereby product innovations involve changes in the structure of production. This may also include new investments in buildings and machinery, and/or using existing resources for new purposes. The immediate impact on employment may be positive if new areas are developed, or the immediate impact on employment may be neutral if labour is transferred from one area to another.

Despite their apparent importance for economic and industrial dynamics, product innovations are a neglected issue in mainstream economic theory, as is also true for the analysis of their impact on employment. In large part, this is due to the fact that product innovations are usually dealt with as 'one compensation mechanism among others' in respect of process innovations, rather than being addressed separately, as a special kind of determinant of employment. For example, this 'compensation' approach is followed by Vivarelli (1995), who provides a comprehensive review of theories of compensation and compensation mechanisms. It should be noted, however, that Vivarelli's own argument is that product innovation, as opposed to other compensation mechanisms, is an especially powerful factor in the reduction of technological unemployment caused by process innovation (ibid.: 169).

Vivarelli's reasoning is highly consistent with that of Pasinetti (1981), who developed a theoretical model demonstrating the existence of labour-saving technological trajectories in established industries as an 'unavoidable process' (Pasinetti, 1981: 227). Moreover, he argued that the marginalist solution of decreasing wages would have a negative, not positive, compensating effect: 'a diminution of personal incomes, which would reduce, not stimulate, demand' (ibid.: 231). In this view,

> The correct answer to the problem is clearly that of introducing the machines, of producing with them the same physical quantities as before with fewer workers, and of employing the workers that have become redundant in the production of other commodities, old and new. Or, alternatively, to increase for all the proportion of leisure time to total time. (Ibid.: 77)

A similar approach emphasizing the importance of product innovation for employment is suggested in the hypothetical example from Lundvall (1985) cited at the end of Chapter 3, section 3.3. This line of reasoning has been developed most fully by Katsoulacos (1984), who drew attention to the special character of product innovation as a 'differentiating mechanism' with both 'displacement' and 'welfare' effects for labour. By 'displacement effect', Katsoulacos meant job losses, and by 'welfare effect', he meant job creation and increased income resulting from product innovation. According to Katsoulacos, the 'displacement effect' is primarily associated with process innovation, due to its labour-saving impacts. 'Displacement' may or may not occur in product innovation. Even when it does occur in connection with product innovation, though, the 'displacement effect' will be subordinate to a dominant 'welfare effect'. The 'welfare effect' refers to the role of product innovation in the generation of employment and income (including increases in real income, due to price reductions). On this basis, Katsoulacos argued that 'in determining the effect of product innovation on the level of employment, the primary factor involved is the "welfare effect" implying generation of employment' (ibid.: 83).

Katsoulacos argued that the welfare effect could occur, even where product innovation was of an incremental nature, to the extent that it involved the entry of new firms and greater competition.[2] A somewhat different, though complementary, line of reasoning has been put forward by Freeman and Soete (1987), who concentrate on shifts in demand, rather than increases in welfare. They argue that if new products succeed at all, it is because economic demand for them increases. If labour, following such changes in demand, shifts from declining to growing sectors or firms, technological unemployment should not occur.

We will divide the consideration of product innovation and employment into a discussion of material goods (section 4.1) and intangible services (section 4.2).

4.1 NEW MATERIAL GOODS

A considerable part of industrial R&D goes to the development of new and/or better products (rather than processes), although this figure varies among countries.[3] Of course, the figure also varies among sectors, just as 'R&D intensity' generally varies among sectors.[4] Intuitively we might expect there to be more new goods – that is, more product innovation – in R&D-intensive sectors of manufacturing than in other sectors.[5] Examples of R&D-intensive sectors are electronics and pharmaceuticals.

Hypothesis 7 New goods originate more often from R&D-intensive manufacturing sectors than from other sectors.

A recent European study of international patterns of generation and diffusion of new technology-based goods (Papaconstantinou, Sakurai and Wyckoff, 1995) reports the following results: 'Innovations are developed mainly in a cluster of high technology manufacturing industries; a different cluster of services are the main acquirers of technologically sophisticated machinery and equipment' (ibid.: 3).[6]

For further evidence, we can refer to the first Community Innovation Survey (CIS), which collected comprehensive European data on the generation of new products by industry.[7] In this survey, product innovation was measured as the proportion of 1992 output (in sales and exports) constituted by new products. New products were defined as products incrementally or significantly changed or newly introduced during 1990–92 (European Commission, 1993: 2). A recent analysis of the CIS data (Calvert et al., 1996) reports the following results for manufacturing industries:

> The industries with the highest proportion of output in new products are generally the ones we would expect:
>
> Office Machinery
> Motor Vehicles
> Other Transport
> Electronic Equipment
> Radio, TV, Communications Equipment
> Instruments
>
> Indeed, these are precisely the industries that have higher than average R&D intensities and are generally regarded as being at the forefront of innovation. (Ibid.: 8)

The authors make note of one exception:

> The only anomaly is that chemicals appears as below average in terms of innovation, but is above average in terms of R&D intensity. One explanation for this could be the fact that in this industry (especially in industrial chemicals) process innovation is much more important than product innovation. (Ibid.)

With respect to the above exception, it should be emphasized that the point made about 'chemicals' does not apply to the pharmaceutical industry, which is at the forefront of product innovation and which is also a part of the chemical industry. With respect to the main body of evidence, it could also be added that 'motor vehicles' are normally not considered to be a highly R&D-intensive sector. In this industry, however, quality-based competition dictates a fairly high level of incremental product development. As a final point of explanation, 'other transport' is R&D intensive since it includes aerospace.

Similar results were obtained from another, more recent analysis of the CIS data, which sought to correct for reliability problems (see note 7) by concentrating on data from five participating countries (Denmark, Germany, Italy, the Netherlands and Norway) with 'more solid results' (Pianta, 2000: 83). In this analysis, manufacturing industries were classified, on the basis of how their R&D expenditures were allocated, into two main groups: 'process innovation-based industries' and 'product innovation-based industries' (ibid.: 90–93). Industries belonging to the latter group were described as follows:

> The list of industries in product innovation-based industries includes: leather and footwear; furniture and other industries; chemical products; electrical apparatus; radio, TV and communication equipment; machinery and equipment; office and computing machinery; motor vehicles; other transport; professional goods. (Ibid.: 91)

This list very closely parallels the previously cited list of industries with the highest proportion of output in new products. The main difference is the inclusion of 'leather and footwear' and 'furniture and other industries'. (What the second source terms 'professional goods' is called 'instruments' by the first.) Otherwise – with the exceptions and anomalies already noted – most of the industries included in both lists are classified as 'high-tech' industries due to their relatively high levels of R&D expenditure.

To summarize the discussion here, different sources of evidence comparing sectors across countries support the hypothesis that R&D-intensive manufacturing sectors tend to generate more product innovations in material goods than other manufacturing sectors.

Hypothesis 8 Across countries, the pattern of diffusion for product innovations in material goods is different from that for process innovations. So are the determinants.

This point is important because countries that seem to be technological leaders in one may not be so for the other. Or a country like Japan may be a leader in both during a certain period.

Let us take flexible automation technologies in the engineering industries of five OECD countries during the 1980s as an example of the diffusion of technological process innovations. The four flexible automation technologies are computer-controlled machine tools, industrial robots, computer-aided design (CAD) and flexible manufacturing systems (FMS). Together these technologies represented a major technological breakthrough in the engineering industry[8] – the most important one since the steam engine and electricity, as analysed in detail in Edquist and Jacobsson (1988). Some conclusions relevant here are the following.

The degree of diffusion was, in the mid-1980s, much greater in Japan and Sweden than in the UK, the USA and West Germany. Sweden was, in other words, the only 'old' industrial country that kept pace with Japan with regard to the diffusion of automation technologies in the engineering industry. In addition, differences in the degrees of diffusion were very large among the five countries. Robot density was, for example, 14.5 times greater in Japan than in the UK, and FMS density was 9 times greater in Sweden than in West Germany.

However, at the country level, the pattern of diffusion of product innovations has been radically different, as illustrated by production in the R&D-intensive sectors, identified above as important generators of product innovations. Here Sweden is far behind Japan and also falls behind the USA, the UK and many other OECD countries. In contrast, Japan is a leading country with regard to the diffusion of both process and product technologies in the senses given above (Edquist, 1989; Edquist and McKelvey, 1992: table 1; 1996).

Moreover, the determinants of diffusion differ in processes and products. Determinants of the diffusion of process innovations include structure of industry, relative factor prices, regional wage differentials, rate of unemployment and union attitudes (Edquist, 1989: 4–5). For the diffusion of product innovations, important factors include differing propensities of firms to stay locked into their 'core business' in different countries, and differences in state policies (such as subsidies to old sectors, incentives to diversification and currency depreciations) (Edquist and McKelvey, 1992: 52–63). Hence the radically different diffusion patterns between process and product innovations in various countries result from different determining factors that vary across countries. To the extent that product and process innovations have different employment effects, a concentration on the diffusion of one or the other type of innovation influences the potential for job destruction and creation in different countries.

Hypothesis 9   There is a strong association between the production of R&D-intensive goods and new goods on the one hand and high labour productivity, high productivity growth and rapid market growth on the other.

There is support for this hypothesis in the recent research literature (OECD, 1996b: ch. 3). The connection between high-tech (or R&D-intensive) goods, productivity growth and market growth has, for example, been demonstrated in Edquist and McKelvey (1992; 1996), Edquist (1993b) and Tyson (1992:

35). Learning curves are also steeper for R&D-intensive goods production, which is also often associated with positive externalities. This means that a country with a – relatively speaking – large production of R&D-intensive goods can be expected to experience a higher productivity growth (and a higher economic growth) than other countries.

Much evidence about the relation between high-technology sectors and market growth is based on international comparisons of sectoral performance. Thus a comparative analysis of six OECD countries has found that growth sectors appear to be associated with higher R&D intensity, and that those with the highest rates of investment and innovation experienced greater output and employment growth (Pianta, Evangelista and Perani, 1996). That the R&D-intensive sectors and growth sectors in terms of output and employment are to a large extent the same has also been shown in Edquist and Texier (1996).[9] Intuitively, we also expect the market for new goods to grow faster than for old goods, and we have previously indicated (under Hypothesis 7) that new goods most often originate from R&D-intensive sectors.

The importance of innovation for export performance in OECD countries is well known, and has been demonstrated statistically through time-series analysis of country- and industry-level data (Fagerberg, 1988a; Soete, 1981). More recently, it has been demonstrated, through analysis of CIS data, that export shares for industries and firms are also positively influenced by innovation inputs:

> The results show that for the sample as a whole there is a positive relationship between export shares and innovation intensity (after controlling for country and industry effects), i.e., a higher proportion of innovation inputs leads to higher export share at the company level. This is particularly the case for firms in the following sectors: Textiles, Rubber & Plastics, Chemicals, Non-Metallic Minerals, Machinery and Other Transport. (Calvert et al., 1996)[10]

At the national level, there is a systematic association between GDP per capita, investment, patenting and R&D intensity. Thus, 'Across the 20 OECD countries, the greater the GDP per capita, the higher are the levels of investment and R&D per employee and international patenting activity (both per capita and per unit of export)' (Pianta and Meliciana, 1994: 10). However, a higher overall level of R&D intensity (R&D expenditure as a percentage of GDP) does not always translate into a higher growth rate.[11] R&D intensity alone is not a sufficient condition for rapid GDP growth. Instead, what matters is whether or not the R&D is concentrated in growth sectors. In other words, R&D activities have to be translated into production activities.

National growth rates have been found, in this connection, to be positively related to countries' aggregate degree of technology (or sectoral) specialization (ibid.). More specifically, high national growth rates have been found to be closely linked to certain sectoral specializations, especially high-technology ones (Pianta, Evangelista and Perani, 1996).

Within the OECD, for the period from 1980-82 to 1990-92, the sectoral specialization of Japan has been largely in the 'growth sectors', while the four major European economies have had a disproportionate concentration in 'sectors in restructuring'.[12] The USA has had a pattern of specialization that is midway between the Japanese and European patterns (ibid.). Only in Japan, where 'the fields of specialisation of technology ... are the same [as those] showing the fastest growth in production and employment for the whole of advanced countries', has there been a positive association between growth in technology, production and employment (Pianta, 1996: 12). In other words, the sectoral specialization of Japan's economy has been concentrated primarily in 'growth sectors' and, historically, this unique circumstance has led to a 'virtuous cycle' of economic development.

However, the recent Asian crisis has shown that even the Japanese model of specialization can run into serious difficulties, due to a number of structural and institutional factors. During the 1990s, it has instead been the US economy which has been forging ahead to create jobs and economic growth, to a large extent in high-tech sectors with extensive innovations, primarily of a product character. In the case of Europe, however, there has been no similar improvement during the same period. According to a very recent analysis, Europe in the 1990s remained 'specialised in process-innovation oriented industries, where the employment impact of technology is particularly negative' (Pianta, 2000: 88).

This may be an appropriate place to refer to what has begun to be called the 'new economy' during the last three years or so. This expression is now widely used and may mean many things. It sometimes denotes the new and rapidly growing firms with a rapidly rising value on various stock exchanges. For some, this rise in value is only a positive thing; for others, it is a stock exchange bubble, which is bound to disappear in a future crisis. The 'new economy' might also simply mean the increasing number of IT firms. Sometimes the expression means the production of new products in new sectors. For some people, the 'new economy' means the rapid growth of electronic trade, or the growth of the 'digital economy' or the 'e-commerce economy'. It may also refer to the fact that the US economy has performed extremely well in a macroeconomic sense during most of the 1990s – with high GDP and productivity growth, high employment creation and low inflation. The relations between central economic indicators such as economic growth, employment and inflation seem to have changed. The fact that the expression is used in so many different senses means that it is analytically useless, unless made more precise.

Here we will specify the 'new economy' to mean the sharp increase in labour productivity growth in the US economy that occurred in the mid-1990s. According to Stephen Oliner and Daniel Sichel, economists at the Federal Reserve in Washington DC, the annual growth of labour productivity in the non-farm business sector jumped from 1.61 per cent between 1991 and 1995 to 2.67 per cent between 1996 and 1999 (Wolf, 2000). This increase was 1.06 per cent in absolute terms and 66 per cent in relative terms – that is, a remarkable increase.

With regard to the forces behind the 'new economy', practically everyone stresses that technical change and other kinds of innovations are central.[13] As indicated, many also point out certain kinds of new technologies, that is, information technologies. Another common characteristic of all interpretations of the 'new economy' is that it is restricted to certain sectors of production. Within goods production those mentioned most often are computers, semiconductors and communications equipment; in service production, software, financial services, media and consulting are often mentioned. This sectoral approach means that a macro perspective is less useful than a meso (or micro) one both for the mode of analysis and for policy design. Sector-oriented changes must be analysed with a sectoral approach. And policies should be sector oriented if the above is sensible.[14]

We agree that a sectoral approach is useful in analysing the 'new economy', although we believe that it should not be confined to certain specific technologies (such as IT). There have historically been other 'waves' of innovation (for example, electricity and automobiles) and in the future there might be others (for example, bio-tech). The manufacturing sectors most often mentioned, and pointed out above, are all high-tech or R&D-intensive ones and the service sectors are knowledge-intensive ones. We have previously pointed out (under Hypothesis 3 and at the beginning of this discussion – that is, under Hypothesis 9) that these sectors have always been characterized by high productivity and high productivity growth. These characteristics also imply high wages and high profits. It could be added that these sectors also tend to perform better than traditional sectors on the stock markets in the long term. We have also previously indicated (in the discussion under Hypothesis 7) that product innovation is more common in these sectors than in more traditional ones.

From such a perspective it can be argued that the 'new economy' might not be that 'new' at all. First, as mentioned above, there have been earlier 'waves' of knowledge-based innovation and new ones may come. Second, we have shown (at the beginning of the discussion under Hypothesis 9) that the proportion of manufacturing that is 'high-tech' has been larger in the USA than in Europe for a long time. And the growth of high-tech production has been even more pronounced in the USA in the latter half of the 1990s than it has been in Europe and Japan during the same period. One possible interpretation of the 'new economy' phenomenon is therefore that the knowledge-intensive sectors have recently become larger in the USA – that is, they have grown more rapidly – and that this has resulted in substantial effects on macro productivity growth and other macro variables.

This interpretation is consistent with the fact that productivity has been growing more rapidly in the USA in the late 1990s than before. Since, as we will later show (for goods, in the discussion under Hypotheses 10–13, and for services under Hypothesis 19, especially) the production of new goods (and also of new services) leads to more jobs as well as higher measured productivity, this interpretation is also consistent with the fact that both employment and productivity have grown more rapidly in the late 1990s in the USA than earlier. In this way the pace of structural change of the economy has increased, mainly through a higher intensity of product innovation. According to this interpretation, the so-called 'new economy' may have existed for decades – or maybe 'always'. However, the kinds of product innovations that provide the basis for it have changed – and might change also in the future.

The 'new' phenomenon that has started to appear in the US economy in the latter half of the 1990s is thus primarily that the knowledge-intensive sectors, dominated by product innovation, have become larger. This is the main factor that lies behind the recent impressive performance of the US economy. It is also likely that this will diffuse to other economies like the European one(s). For example, there are strong signs that the innovation and growth dynamics of the Swedish economy started to change in the late 1990s.

The earlier part of the discussion under this hypothesis (9) referred to evidence supporting the identification of R&D-intensive sectors as growth sectors. Subsequently, the discussion referred again to evidence first cited under Hypothesis 7 in support of a positive association between R&D-intensive goods and new goods. Finally, the discussion reviewed evidence concerning the positive dynamic effects of technology specialization in growth sectors on productivity, growth and employment (the historical case of Japan and the USA in the 1990s). It concluded with some observations on the 'new economy'. Taken together, these various sources of evidence suggest that there is a positive association between the production of R&D-intensive goods and new goods on the one hand and high labour productivity, high productivity growth and rapid market growth on the other.

Hypothesis 10 Employment grows faster in R&D-intensive industrial sectors than in other sectors.

There is much empirical evidence that supports this proposition (OECD, 1994a: ch. 4; OECD, 1996b: ch. 3). Such evidence can be found at the firm, sectoral and national levels.

At the firm level, there appears to be an association between the production of R&D-intensive goods and employment. A study of the Netherlands reports that while R&D intensity in general has a slightly negative impact on employment growth (and an opposite effect, it may be inferred, on productivity) in firms, those with high rates of product-related R&D have above average employment growth rates (Brouwer, Kleinknecht and Reijnen, 1993).

Similarly, a French study of manufacturing firms discovered that, at the sectoral level, product innovation created more employment than did process innovation (Greenan and Guellec, 1996). This study also reported, however, that process innovations resulting in higher labour productivity were a more important mechanism for increasing employment at the firm level. The explanation offered is that 'a firm reducing its costs gains employment at the expense of its competitors, whereas a firm [producing] a new product experiences a lower [though still positive] gain [in employment] but [one that is] due [in this case] to an increase in demand addressed to the sector' (ibid: 1).[15] Thus we need to distinguish generation or destruction of employment at the different levels of firm and sector.

International comparisons of the economic performance of different sectors are fairly clear on the association between R&D intensity and growth. In manufacturing, in particular, it has been established that the R&D-intensive sectors have the greatest ability 'to generate more inventions and to lead to growing production and employment' (Pianta, 1996: 12). This has been shown in an analysis of employment changes in the manufacturing sectors of the six largest OECD countries, where it was found that innovation, increasing production and increasing employment are concentrated in a few highly R&D-intensive industries (Pianta, Evangelista and Perani, 1996). From a more detailed analysis of the dynamics of employment growth by sector in one country, the same study concluded that '[a] labour increasing pattern has been found only in sectors characterised by higher design and engineering expenditure and higher shares of product innovations' (ibid.: 13).

Some German research (Meyer-Krahmer, 1992) reviewed in Meyer-Krahmer (1996) offers particularly illuminating results. This research found that R&D-intensive sectors of West German industry enjoyed 'outstanding growth' during the 1980s, increasing their share in industrial employment from 39.5 per cent to 44 per cent by 1990. Since 1984, moreover, the net additional jobs created in industry were all in R&D-intensive sectors. Despite the slight reversal of this dynamic suffered in the early 1990s, these sectors continued to have an increasing significance, expanding while others contracted. 'The non-R&D-intensive sectors stagnated in comparison at the shrunken level reached during the recession' (Meyer-Krahmer, 1996: 217).

For the aggregate of advanced OECD economies, those manufacturing sectors showing the highest rates of R&D intensity – that is, the 'high-technology' industries – have experienced higher levels of growth in productivity and employment than others. This is shown, for example, in Figure 4.1, which illustrates the relationships among R&D intensity, productivity growth and employment growth in manufacturing for the G-7 countries. The figure shows that productivity growth and employment were negative for low-technology industries, positive for medium-technology industries and very large (highly positive) for high-technology industries.

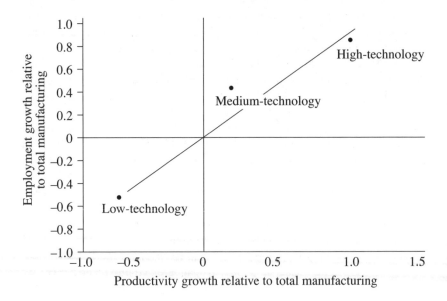

Source: Adapted from OECD (1996b: graph 3.7).

Figure 4.1   Productivity and employment growth in manufacturing, for high-, medium- and low-technology industries, 1970–93

However, the benefits of increased productivity, output and employment have been distributed unevenly across national economies (Vivarelli, Evangelista and Pianta, 1995). Significantly, it is those countries that have specialized in R&D-intensive industries with higher levels of product innovation (notably, Japan and the USA) that have had the strongest performance with respect to employment, even in the context of recession (OECD, 1996b: ch. 3).

Hypothesis 11 The increased productivity (and productivity growth) associated with new goods does not mean reduced employment (per unit of output), but instead reflects changes in the nominator (value added) in the labour productivity ratio.

In mainstream economic theory, productivity measures are intended to measure 'technical change' – following Solow (1957). In the context of the production function in general equilibrium theory, however, 'technical change' normally only means process innovations. Hence, if we assume that there are no changes in process technologies, nor any organizational process innovations, there will be no productivity growth.[16] But, as we have seen, empirical evidence indicates something else, namely that new goods are associated with high productivity and high productivity growth.

A possible explanation might be the following. Productivity as normally measured is, in reality, influenced by a number of factors other than changes in process technologies.[17] Other factors which might explain why sectors which tend to have new goods are associated with high productivity include:

- the market form (imperfect competition),
- factors of production are not flexible (for example, the capital stock cannot vary in the short run),
- economies of scale,
- the level of aggregation, and
- the fact that inputs and outputs are heterogeneous (quality can change) (Assarsson, 1991: 199–200).

Reasons for focusing on goods innovation here are that sectors with a high degree of goods innovation have been shown empirically to be characterized by high labour productivity and high labour productivity growth. Although process innovations, of course, also occur in these sectors, it is reasonable to assume that some of the other factors listed above constitute an important impact on productivity measures.

On the basis of the foregoing discussion, it can be argued that the higher productivity and higher productivity growth associated with new products does *not* mean reduced employment in the sense of less labour per unit of output. Instead, the source of this labour productivity growth is mainly the *numerator* in the labour productivity ratio between production value (value added) and employment.

In the numerator we have price-based measures of output (for example, value added). Of the five other factors influencing productivity listed above, two can lead to significantly increased prices. They are imperfect competition and quality changes in output. Hansson (1991) has shown that productivity measures are significantly influenced if the fact that markets are not characterized by perfect competition is taken into account.[18]

Assarsson (1991) argues that quality changes can significantly influence productivity measures, but that their influence is also very hard to measure. Quality changes in output mean that the content or character of goods and services changes. With these changes, prices also change. The problem is that information about prices does not indicate how much of a price change can be accounted for by a quality change (ibid.: 248).

Quality improvements of goods and services can be equalized with product innovations. The extreme case of a quality change is that nothing similar at all existed on the market before; a completely new product has appeared. This makes it, in practice, impossible to account for quality changes in productivity calculations (Assarsson, 1991: 203–4).

As goods innovations are brand-new goods or improved ones, they represent quality changes. Moreover, imperfect competition is evident in that they are often also associated with property rights through patents or with secrecy and they are in scarce supply – all factors that might lead to monopoly pricing. Both quality changes and monopoly pricing show up as productivity increases. Such 'productivity increases' (as they are measured) have nothing to do with a reduced amount of labour needed for producing a certain physical volume of output. Neither are they caused by 'technical change' in the sense of changes in process technology.[19]

The source of such productivity growth, then, is an increased price of the good – and not a reduced amount of labour needed for producing a certain physical volume of output. This source of productivity growth is not taken into account by mainstream economics, which assumes 'technical change' or process innovation to be the primary source of productivity growth.

The fact that the *source* of the productivity growth is different for process and product innovations partly explains why the immediate employment effects can be so different between these two categories of innovation.

Hypothesis 12   The productivity increase related to goods innovation does not refer to increased physical output, but to an increased price of that output. However, such productivity increases matter for the welfare of the members of the unit producing the innovation.

The increased productivity associated with new products is not increased productivity in a physical sense but only 'as measured'. It is an economic measure in price terms. More goods, in physical terms, are not produced with a given amount of labour. Neither is the same physical amount produced with less labour. In this sense, the total 'welfare' of the world in physical terms has not increased. However, the 'welfare' of those individuals, firms, regions and countries that produce the new goods has increased. They have appropriated a larger share of world output. In other words, the measured productivity increases caused, for example, by monopolism, matter for the distribution of welfare.[20]

Hypothesis 13   The production of new goods might lead to more jobs, as well as higher measured productivity.

In contrast to process innovations, productivity growth and more jobs may go hand in hand with the production of new goods. In other words, some kinds of productivity growth are compatible with job creation,[21] while other kinds mean that jobs disappear. These differences are crucial for the macroeconomic consequences of innovation.

In addition to the supporting evidence already reviewed (see, in particular, Hypotheses 8 to 12), the conclusions of a recent comparative analysis of the six largest OECD economies conducted by Vivarelli, Evangelista and Pianta (1995) support this hypothesis. This analysis compared the structure and performance of four major European economies (France, Germany, Italy and the UK), Japan and the USA. The results obtained indicate that the sectoral specialization of economies affects the productivity–employment relationship. Thus, 'in Europe ... the "virtuous cycle" between technology, growth and employment is much weaker and is often replaced by negative links', due to the fact that 'investment and innovation have focused on the restructuring of traditional sectors ... and are associated [with] large labour-saving effects' (ibid.: 7).

In other words, a growth pattern and sectoral specialization concentrating on process, as opposed to product innovation, has led to productivity growth, but not job creation, in Europe. In contrast, the Japanese economy has (until the 1990s) had a 'virtuous cycle' of innovation, productivity and employment. The US economy has historically occupied a position between those of the European and Japanese situations, but during the 1990s showed much more of a 'virtuous cycle'.

Let us in this context review the recent historical performance of the Swedish and overall European economies with regard to the production of industrial goods in the high-tech and other 'growth' sectors. We have selected those seven industrial sectors where production value has grown most rapidly in the OECD as a whole during the 1975–91 period. These growth sectors are: Printing and Publishing (ISIC 342), Drugs and Medicine (ISIC 3522), Plastic Products (ISIC 356), Office and Computing Machinery (ISIC 3825), Radio, TV and Communications Equipment (ISIC 3832), Electrical Apparatus (ISIC 3839), and Aircraft (ISIC 3845). Most of these are also those sectors that are normally classified as the R&D-intensive industries[22] (Edquist and Texier, 1996: 109).

Employment in these sectors grew by 50 per cent in the OECD as a whole during 1975–91, while the number of jobs in the rest of industry remained about the same (Edquist and Texier, 1996). This shows that there was a tremendous employment growth in some industrial sectors in all OECD countries taken together. These sectors are the so-called 'growth sectors'.

In Sweden, however, there were about 210 000 jobs in the 'growth sectors' in 1975, and 190 000 in 1991, while the number of jobs in the rest of industry decreased by 20 per cent. If employment in Swedish industry had grown at the same rate as in the OECD as a whole in the growth sectors during this period, then there would have been 315 000 jobs in the growth sectors in 1991 (Edquist and Texier, 1996). This is 125 000 more jobs than the actual number.[23] This should be related to the fact that there were about 870 000 jobs in industry in Sweden in 1991.[24]

Historically, then, during the 1970s and 1980s there has been a lack of structural change in Swedish industry in the direction of high-growth sectors characterized by a high level of R&D intensity. These are, as shown previously, those sectors dominated by product innovation rather than process innovation. This historical lag has obviously had large consequences for industrial employment in Sweden (Edquist and Texier, 1996). Moreover, it may be argued to have been a crucial factor behind the rate of unemployment of about 10 per cent during the late 1990s.[25]

A study of the proportion of R&D-intensive products produced by Swedish industry concluded that Sweden has negatively specialized in the production of high-technology (R&D-intensive) goods relative to other OECD countries (Edquist and McKelvey, 1996). This also points to the strong correspondence between this class of products and that of 'growth products'.[26]

In the European Union as a whole the situation is strikingly similar.[27] In 1976 the proportion of industrial value added emanating from the growth sectors in the EU was about 18 per cent. For the USA and Japan it was 19 per cent and the figure for Sweden was 21 per cent. In other words, the differences were quite small. In 1991 the corresponding figures were 22 per cent for the EU and Sweden and 29 per cent for the USA and Japan. Hence the gap between the EU and the USA/Japan increased from 1 per cent to 7 per cent, which means that the EU changed its structure of industry towards growth (and R&D-intensive) sectors much less than the USA and Japan (Edquist and Texier, 1996).

Change in the proportion of industrial employment located in the growth sectors between 1976 and 1991 is shown for different national and international categories in Table 4.1. In 1976 this figure was 13 per cent for the EU, and by 1991 the EU figure had risen to 21 per cent. US industrial

Table 4.1 Proportion of industrial employment in growth sectors, 1976-91

	1976	1991
EU	13	21
USA	23	30
Japan	21	29
OECD	17	26

Source: Calculations by C. and H. Edquist from the OECD's STAN database.

employment in the growth sectors increased from 23 per cent to 30 per cent during this same period. For Japan, there was an increase from 21 per cent in 1976 to 29 per cent in 1991. The average figure for industrial employment in the growth sectors across the OECD as a whole was 17 per cent in 1976; it had risen 26 per cent by 1991.

For the R&D-intensive sectors the corresponding 1991 figures for the proportion of industrial employment growth were 16 per cent for the EU, 21 per cent for the USA, 22 per cent for Japan and 19 per cent for the OECD as a whole. These figures are displayed in Table 4.2. Because of the dynamic character of high-tech production in the USA during the 1990s, the differences between the USA and Europe can be expected to be at least as large today as they were in 1991. The pattern briefly described here might be a major factor behind the fact that in early 2000 the rate of unemployment was about 10 per cent for the EU, but only 3–4 per cent for the USA. It was about 4–5 per cent for Japan.

We have previously shown that product innovations create employment and that there is a close relation between product innovation and R&D intensity. Therefore, the correlation between industrial structure and employment is not a coincidence. There is likely to be a causal relation between them, and the workings of the relationship have been discussed above.

Table 4.2 Proportion of industrial employment growth in R&D-intensive sectors, 1991

	1991
EU	16
USA	21
Japan	22
OECD	19

Source: Calculations by C. and H. Edquist from the OECD's STAN database.

4.2 NEW INTANGIBLE SERVICES

Product innovations also include new services, as discussed in Chapter 2, section 2.1. Service product innovations mean that new economic activities are generated and, as in the case of new goods, service innovations can therefore generate employment.

The preceding discussion of new goods (under Hypotheses 7 to 9) has argued that there is more product innovation in R&D-intensive sectors. Further, it has argued that there is a correlation between production of R&D-intensive goods on the one hand and high productivity and high productivity growth on the other. In addition, it has argued that the market grows faster for new goods than for other goods.

This section proposes similar arguments for service sectors. However, a word of caution is in order. It should be noted that this undertaking will be somewhat limited and constrained by the fact that services production has not been studied as thoroughly as goods production, given 'the intractable statistical problems associated with its measurement and thus the limited data available' (OECD, 1996b: 71). None the less, we will propose some hypotheses.

Hypothesis 14 Service sectors with a large proportion of highly educated people can be classified as 'high technology' or 'knowledge intensive'.

In the case of services, how to define a category of 'high technology' – that is, R&D-intensive – sectors is less clear. This is so because formal R&D is less important for the development of new services; moreover, it is not clear what formal R&D actually is in this context.[28] Thus R&D intensity measured in monetary terms is less applicable. One option is to measure the level of technology in terms of human resources instead of R&D expenditures. This implies that a high proportion of highly educated people would indicate a high 'knowledge intensity'.[29] A high level of knowledge intensity in services would thus correspond with 'high technology' or 'high R&D intensity' in manufacturing.

A positive association between 'knowledge intensity' (as defined above) and 'R&D intensity' has already been shown to exist in the 'high-technology' sectors in manufacturing. It is generally understood, moreover, that this key relationship implies another one – between specially qualified 'human resources' and the capacity for innovation. The notion that similar correlations might also occur outside of a handful of 'high-tech' manufacturing industries has also gained wider acceptance in recent years. All of these ideas, in fact, have been essential to the rationale for the OECD's development of a framework for compiling data on stocks and flows of human resources in science and technology (HRST). In order to analyse and forecast the innovation capacity and performance of nations, regions and sectors, the OECD has attempted to formulate a coherent set of statistical guidelines for conceptualizing and measuring HRST, codifying these in the so-called *Canberra Manual* (OECD, 1995d). As used in that source, HRST 'would ideally refer to the human resources actually or potentially devoted to the systematic generation, advancement, diffusion and application of scientific and technological knowledge' (ibid.: 9).

A 'human resources' approach to identifying advanced service sectors forms an important part of the definitional and methodological basis for a recent classification of sectors according to their level of 'knowledge intensity' (Lee and Has, 1995). This classification was developed, in part, to overcome the limitations of existing measures of R&D intensity with respect to capturing the role of knowledge in the economy, particularly in the service sectors where these measures are less applicable.[30]

In this 'human resources' approach, three indicators of R&D activity are combined with three indicators of human capital content to create an index of knowledge intensity.[31] Sectors are classified as 'high-knowledge' if two of their three R&D indicators and two of their three human capital indicators belong to the top third of all industries; or, as 'low-knowledge' if two of their three R&D indicators and two of their three human capital indicators belong to the bottom third. All remaining sectors are classified as 'medium-knowledge' sectors. In the case of certain service sectors that lack R&D data, however, the classification is made solely on the basis of their human capital content. On this basis, for example, management consulting services is included in the 'high-knowledge' category, 'even though it has relatively low R&D personnel content' to qualify it as belonging to this group (Lee and Has, 1995: 8).[32]

A positive association between 'high knowledge intensity' in human resources and the extensive acquisition and use of 'high technology' capital goods is supported by research on innovative service sectors. Chapter 3, section 3.1 argued, under Hypotheses 2 and 4, that some services, such as those in the financial, insurance, real-estate and business services (FIRB) sector, are among the largest users of technological process innovations, primarily information technologies. This can lead to a large direct labour saving. Over the past decade, however, it has become increasingly clear that some branches and segments of financial services utilize information technology differently (Casadio, 1995; OECD, 1986). In this alternative strategy, there is a strong emphasis on using new process technology in combination with more highly qualified human resources in order to deliver new service products, so that 'a long term orientated training and recruitment policy is of paramount importance' (Bilderbeek and Buitelaar, 1992: 29).

Thus the educational demands of labour are increased over time in this case.

Service sectors investing heavily in human capital should properly be regarded as 'knowledge intensive' in the absence of any evidence of expenditures on 'formal R&D'. Here, we therefore consider service sectors with a large proportion of highly educated people to be equivalent to sectors with a high 'R&D intensity'. Rather than referring to 'R&D intensity' in such service sectors, we refer instead to their 'knowledge intensity'.[33]

Hypothesis 15   Formal R&D is not important for the development of new services.

'Formal' R&D is not entirely absent in the service sector and, it can be argued, makes a significant contribution to the development of new service products in some sectors. During the late 1980s, R&D expenditures in services increased at twice the rate of manufacturing R&D in the USA (Pollack, 1991). It has been argued that if small-business R&D activities were counted and software development were reclassified as R&D, the measure of service sector R&D would rise by a factor of two or three (Soete and Verspagen, 1991). However, the analysis of employment gains in the fastest-growing segments of the service sector – FIRB (financial, insurance, real-estate and business services) and CSPS (community, social and personal services)[34] – indicates that 'the overwhelming bulk of employment gains ... are due to increases in domestic final demand' (OECD, 1994b: 157). Product innovation – that is, the development of new services – may well have played an important part in the increase in final demand, but no clear link with formal R&D can be established.

The development of new services, however, may depend strongly on capacities to carry out 'informal R&D', or search activities.[35] These capacities, in turn, may be determined largely by a firm's or a sector's human capital content. The management consulting services sector is a case in point. As part of FIRB, management consulting services have probably experienced strong increases in employment across the OECD.[36] And as argued above, a significant part of these employment gains has probably been due to increasing demand for new service products. This is as opposed to an expansion of the demand for existing services, which is more likely to be the case in CSPS.[37] As the management consulting services sector has been included in the 'knowledge-intensive' (or 'high-tech') category, even though it ranks low on all indicators of R&D activity, this implies that human capital investment in such service sectors is, to a large extent, tied to the development of new service products.

Support for this proposition is provided by a recent Canadian analysis of the relationships between human capital investment and innovation in three sectors: manufacturing, dynamic services and traditional services (Baldwin, 1995).[38] In this study, management consulting services were identified as belonging to the 'dynamic' services sector.

The term 'dynamic services' originated with a major study of *Employment in the Service Economy* carried out by the Economic Council of Canada (1991). That study divided the entire service sector into two major groups: 'dynamic' and 'traditional' services. The two categories of services were distinguished from one another primarily on the basis of labour force characteristics – for example, salient differences in occupational composition, skill levels and wage rates (ibid.: 93, 139). However, examples of the kinds of sectors included in these two categories clearly indicate that they can also be distinguished from one another on the basis of the markets that they serve. The 'traditional services' category includes both the entire CSPS sector and any other service sectors, such as retail trade, restaurants and hotels, that primarily serve 'consumer' markets made up of individuals and households. The 'dynamic services' category includes both FIRB and any other service sectors, such as communication, transport and wholesale trade, serving commercial markets that are either entirely made up of, or are dominated by, businesses and other organizations. These points are made clear in the following quotation from the aforementioned Canadian study of human capital investment and innovation:

> The traditional services sector encompasses industries like retail outlets, personal services, education, health services, and accommodation. The dynamic services sector consists of finance, communication and utilities, real estate, transportation services, wholesale trade and business services. (Baldwin, 1995: 15)

The sectoral analysis of human capital development and innovation presented in the Canadian study revealed that, in both traditional and dynamic services, 'the primary value of the product lies in ... the service of the worker' (ibid.: 18). For this reason there is a strong link in both kinds of service sectors between human capital investment and innovation strategies focused on market development. Human capital investments in both dynamic and traditional services are, in other words, geared to product-innovation strategies. Generally, service firms develop such strategies 'in order to compete by offering highly tailored products' (ibid.). In dynamic service industries, however, the innovation strategies focus less exclusively on product 'quality' strategies, and concentrate more broadly on 'enhancements to all the factors of production' (ibid.: 23). Thereby, 'technological innovation ... is complemented by innovation in the form of human capital advancements' (ibid.).

These findings imply a greater emphasis on incremental product innovation (or the refinement of existing products) in traditional services – and a stronger emphasis on the development of new service products in dynamic services such as management consulting.[39]

Hypothesis 16　　There is a correlation between knowledge-intensive service sectors and service sectors with a great deal of product innovation.

If 'knowledge-intensive' service sectors are equated with those having a large proportion of highly educated people, there is some evidence to suggest that a link can be established between this 'knowledge intensity' and product innovation. One theoretical basis for making this link is suggested by the thesis that information technology has begun, or at least has the potential, to reverse the product cycle in service industries (Barass, 1986).

According to the 'reverse product cycle' (RPC) theory of service-sector innovation, heavy investment in service industries in new process technologies (acquired from the investment goods sector) tends, over time, to reverse the pattern of the 'normal' product cycle (from an initial concentration on significant product innovation to a later concentration on incremental process innovations) found in manufacturing industries (Utterback and Abernathy, 1975). Thus some service sectors instead progress from process to product innovation. The eventual result is that changes in technology initially dominated by labour-displacing technical process innovations later become predominantly employment generating and labour enhancing. This occurs through the development of product innovations that follow the initial process innovations and subsequently become the main focus of innovative activity (Barass, 1990).

The RPC theory describes a three-stage model of development. In the first stage, initiated by user firms' adoption of new process technology, process innovations are aimed at reducing costs and increasing the efficiency of production. Thus the innovation process is characterized by labour-saving technical change. R&D activities on the part of adopting firms are expected to be minimal (Hauknes, 1996: 114), and the priority given to developing cost-efficient 'back office' functions suggests a likely de-skilling of the workforce as a whole (Gallouj, 1994).

In the second stage of the RPC model, the focus shifts to quality improvements and from 'back' to 'front' office. There is a transition towards product innovation, although this tends to be incremental in nature, involving the improvement of existing products based on the new combinations made possible by new process technology. As quality improvements lead to market growth, there is a tendency towards a more thorough restructuring of production arrangements and the scope of product innovations becomes progressively more radical, with greater emphasis on systematic R&D. In industries such as software development, this stage of development has been characterized by an increasing emphasis on development of highly qualified personnel (Miles, 1987).

The third stage of the RPC model completes the transition towards a primary focus on product innovation. It is typified by a shift in the locus of delivery from point of production to point of consumption, improved flexibility and information for customers, and new producer–user relations (Barass, 1990). At this stage, development of a diverse stock of highly qualified human resources across a broad range of occupations reaches its highest level. One reason for this is that 'the knowledge base of the industry has now fully incorporated the technology and it is to be expected that the industry is a significant employer of relevant science and technology specialists' (Hauknes, 1996: 114). However, an equally important considera-tion is the increasing strategic importance of user–producer relations. A wide variety of highly skilled personnel is required to support innovative efforts aimed at diversification of service products through interfirm collaboration and infrastructure development (Tinnilä and Vepsäläinen, 1995). For these reasons, the RPC model expects that at the third stage of development there will be a strong positive association between high 'knowledge intensity' in services (as defined in Hypothesis 14) and extensive product innovation.

The RPC model was originally developed as a means of analysing and interpreting the impacts of information technology on the financial services sector. There may now be more current examples within the same sector. The recent emergence of Internet banking services suggests that 'stage 2' of the RPC may now have been reached again, and that the initial cycle is being repeated, with a qualitatively different process innovation that combines both information and telecommunications technologies.

The RPC model has been criticized on several grounds. Some authors argue that it is limited in scope to the description of a specific phase of the development of information technologies, and that this phase may not be repeated (Buzzachi, Colombo and Mariotti, 1995). This may be a weak criticism. The RPC model makes provision for a fourth 'maturity' stage in which the developmental cycle is completed and may eventually be restarted by new process technologies. This may now be occurring, as we have suggested above, through use of the Internet. Moreover, the non-repetition argument refers primarily to institutional and organizational factors, such as regulatory regimes and forms of business organization.[40]

Other critics have pointed to the RPC model's limited sectoral scope, arguing that it may not be generalizable beyond the financial services and other services with extensive 'back office' functions (Petit, 1990). Even accepting this criticism, however, the RPC model would still be applicable to a very broad range of service sectors, including many of those within the ICT (information and communications technologies) category, which encompasses transport and communication services, as well as the FIRB sector (OECD, 1996b). Considering the emergence of commercial applications of the Internet, it would be especially applicable in the case of communications industries (Miles, 1996).[41] A recent analysis of the health-care sector also indicates that standardization of existing services can provide the basis for the development of new specializations and transformation towards a more diversified health-care system as a whole (Herzlinger, 1997).

Finally, it has been argued that the RPC model expresses a strong technological determinism and does not give adequate consideration to 'the influence of social and economic factors' in the shaping of technology and the definition of 'innovative paradigms' in the service industries (Hauknes, 1996).

Although the RPC model has limited generalizability and explanatory power, there appears to be some agreement that this theoretical model does capture many of the essential connections between 'knowledge intensity' and product innovation in certain service sectors – most notably in banking and other financial services (Baba and Takai, 1990; Fincham et al., 1994). Moreover, as pointed out above, the RPC model is more generally applicable to much, if not all, of the ICT category of services – and particularly the information and communications services.[42] The recent emergence of Internet-based businesses underlines this point. Here, too, the widespread use of new process technology has led to the flowering of new service products.

We can also point to 'non-technological' – that is, social and economic – reasons for a strong association between 'knowledge intensity' and product innovation. Many industries in the service sector, it should be noted, have not only experienced extensive and rapid change in process technologies within the recent past, but also significant institutional change through the deregulation of existing markets and the creation of new ones. These developments have also stimulated product innovation and with it the demand for greater possibility to engage in search activities through more diverse and more highly qualified personnel.

One segment within the service sector where this dynamic is readily apparent is the knowledge-intensive business services (KIBS) grouping located within FIRB (Miles et al., 1995). This highly knowledge-intensive component of FIRB has recently experienced extensive change in the nature of the services it provides to other sectors. The restructuring of many firms and industries, involving an 'outsourcing' of KIBS functions, together with the opening up of new markets, has made KIBS an increasingly more prominent component of innovation networks (Hauknes and Miles, 1996). This has been especially the case for science and technology (S&T) services. The emergence and growth of a European market for these services have been closely linked with product innovation, in the form of the creation of new types of 'network' linkages with clients (Spriano, 1989). Thus social, organizational and economic factors, as well as technological factors, may affect the linkage between 'knowledge intensity' and 'product innovation' in services.

Hypothesis 17 Service sectors characterized by a high degree of product innovation are also characterized by rapid market growth.

Productivity and productivity growth in the service sector are difficult to measure (Baily and Gordon, 1988) and more difficult to explain (Brynjolfsson, 1991). We should therefore be cautious about accepting accounts of rapid employment growth in capital-intensive service sectors such as FIRB that refer to their 'lagging' productivity relative to manufacturing (for example, OECD, 1994b: 160). Such explanations of increases in service-sector employment are suspect and remain open to question.

This type of explanation typically refers to the difficulty of automating or making significant technical improvements to the efficiency of many services – a circumstance which seriously limits their potential for making improvements in productivity (Baumol, Blackman and Wolff, 1989). Even though it is sometimes admitted in the same sentence that their apparently small gains in productivity 'may partly reflect measurement problems' (OECD, 1998a: 95), CSPS services are often cited as prime examples in such arguments about sluggish productivity growth in services. However, we have already referred (in Chapter 3, section 3.1) to empirical research that identifies a large scope for gains in productivity through the rationalization of service production in CSPS 'segments' such as health care (Herzlinger, 1997).

Such evidence leads us to consider that the problems of measuring productivity and productivity growth in services may be the main reason for continued observations of a 'productivity paradox' in the service sector. As OECD analysts note for ICT-using industries, especially those in services, much of the growth in gross output is 'hard to capture in traditional output statistics' (OECD, 1998a: box 4.1). There are also difficulties with input-related measures. Due to the rate and intensity of investment in ICT, leading to consistent undermeasurement of ICT goods inputs, 'insufficient weight is given to technical improvements embodied in capital goods and too much to disembodied technical change' (ibid.). In contrast to data based on standard measurement practices, there is now empirical research demonstrating that ICT capital goods have increased their contribution to output and labour productivity over time (Stiroh, 1999). However, output measures pose a more serious problem – largely because services differ from goods in that the 'product' often does not exist as a separate entity and cannot be produced independently of the client, or consuming unit, which the service product acts to improve or transform in some way (Hill, 1997).

At the same time, rapid market growth cannot be adequately explained simply in terms of productivity increases and hence increased demand for existing products which have become cheaper. As the aforementioned RPC thesis indicates, there has been a close connection between market growth and production of new products in the case of FIRB. This would appear to be characteristic of other ICT service sectors as well.[43] In this connection, it is interesting to note that one of the major drawbacks of even the most sophisticated output measures, especially as applied to services, is that 'adjusting for quality' is extremely difficult (OECD, 1998a: box 4.2). Thus assessments of productivity growth based on such measures cannot fully take into account the growth of markets based on qualitative changes in products – that is, the development of partly or entirely new products.

The FIRB sector as a whole, and some segments (for example, health care) of the CSPS sector are among the heaviest private acquirers and users of advanced process technology. In an inventory of the industries making the greatest use of equipment-embodied technology in ten OECD countries, 'Service sectors typically occupy four out of the five top spots in the list of most countries' (Papaconstantinou, Sakurai and Wyckoff, 1995: 19 and table 2). Additional and more detailed findings include the following points:

> *Social and personal services*, an industry category covering, among other [things], equipment purchases by the health industry, is prominent and appears in the top 5 technology user industries in 8 out of 10 countries. The ... real estate and business services ... also show up as important users of technology. (Ibid.)

These parts of the FIRB and CSPS sectors are also characterized by rapidly expanding markets. Moreover, they have experienced a considerable upgrading of qualification requirements in recent years, and are currently strong investors in human capital (OECD, 1996b: 88–91). As noted previously, the growth of demand in their markets cannot be directly attributed to changes in (process) technology. It might have a more immediate connection with product innovation. This can be inferred from a more general pattern of employment growth within services driven by increased demands for information, more complex forms of industrial organization, and the tailoring of production to specific consumers (Sakurai, Ionnidis and Papaconstantinou, 1996). Arguably, the markets for FIRB and CSPS services could not have grown so rapidly if these changes in the nature of demand for services had not been matched by corresponding changes in the design of service products, sometimes involving the creation of wholly new services.

The rapid growth of markets and output for FIRB services may be due in large part to a rapid liberalization of financial markets resulting in increased demand. However, there is reason to view a significant part of this sector's growth as the result of changing input–output relationships – including technological process investments – which deepen its linkage with other sectors (OECD, 1994b: 145). Such linkages often involve the creation of new service products, as in the case of the rapidly expanding area of 'producer' or 'business services'.

An extensive study of the British FIRB sector during the 1980s and 1990s provides further insight (Fincham et al., 1994). It is well known that the British financial services sector underwent rapid expansion during this period, with important consequences for the national economy in terms of economic growth and employment growth. There was also considerable structural change in the sector, in terms of fluid market boundaries and shifting relations among firms and subsectors within the sector as a whole.

In this context, 'IT (Information Technology) played a major role in meeting these challenges and underpinned new services and operations' (Fincham et al., 1994: 7). However, it was the 'new services and operations', rather than the process technology on which they were based, that eventually became the major focus of competitive innovation strategies geared to the creation and expansion of new markets. The pattern of development, over time, was from an initial concentration on mastering new process innovations to a later strategic focus on the development of new product innovations:

> More recently, the development of IT networks has enabled distributed access to central records and has facilitated the earlier capture of data, opening up greater choice in the design and conduct of financial activities. The possibility of further centralisation ... is now matched by the possibility of integrating distributed activities and improving the quality of service. Also, growing emphasis on marketing and cross-selling has led to the recognition of internally generated information as a resource ...
>
> These trends have suggested the value of redistributing tasks to the branch, the point of interface with the customer. In particular, the development of integrated databases of customer accounts has been seen as a means of converting branches into financial 'supermarkets', delivering a range of products; while IT networks have created new methods of service delivery like EFTPOS (Electronic Funds Transfer at Point-of-Sale) and home banking. (Fincham et al., 1994: 8)

As indicated, there is much evidence that product innovation and market growth are closely related in the service sectors. As the examples of new financial service products presented immediately above suggest, there is sometimes a close relation between a new good and a new service. This will be discussed further under the next hypothesis. For the FIRB sector, in particular, this relation has already been discussed in terms of a 'reverse product cycle' (RPC) model, which we outlined under Hypothesis 16.

Hypothesis 18   The service sectors where there is a close relation between a new good and a new service are, generally speaking, more innovative than others.

Discussions under preceding hypotheses have already pointed to close relations between new services and new goods. Some further examples can be given here. Home banking requires the development of new IT and Internet goods. Mobile phone calls require mobile phones. Video-on-demand requires TV sets and data-com networks. Computer maintenance assumes the existence of computers. In all these cases the new good has led to the emergence of product innovation in services. Some services might, however, be quite independent of new material goods, for example, legal advice, hotel room cleaning, and provision of most kinds of education. The general conclusion with regard to the relations between material goods innovations and intangible service innovations is that although service innovations can, in principle, be independent of goods innovations, they often depend on them. Moreover, there can often be a strong interdependence between the two kinds of product innovations. In such cases, new goods and new services are equally dependent on one another so that the good might be useless without the development of the service, and vice versa – for example, mobile telephones. When new goods and services are dependent upon each other, it is the dynamic links between them that are important.

A general example of this close relationship between new goods and new services is increasing recognition throughout the OECD countries of the importance for job creation and economic growth of the development of new services based on new information infrastructures and multimedia technologies (OECD, 1996b: ch. 6). In this emerging field, there is a very close connection between new goods and new services. Miles (1996) provides an insightful overview of this complementarity. He maintains that 'by increasing the network capabilities for transmitting and processing information' – which will involve extensive innovation in both capital and consumer goods – 'the groundwork for expansion of new services is being laid' (ibid.: 115).

For a more specific example, we can refer to the twin development of mobile telephones and mobile telephone network services. The emergence of mobile telephony clearly illustrates the complementarity of new goods and new services in what is generally recognized as one of the fastest-growing and most innovative markets for information and communication services. The mobile communication service market has experienced extremely rapid growth. With over 44 million subscribers in the OECD area at the end of 1994, and with more than 1.2 million subscribers being added per month, its rate of growth in 1994 was double that of 1992 (OECD/ICCP, 1996). The innovation profile for mobile communications, as for the communications industry in general, is also extremely high (Kelly, 1995; Mercer Management Consultants, 1994). In 1997, there were about 170 million analogue and digital cellular phone subscribers in the OECD countries alone (OECD, 1999: 66). Moreover, growth rates for products such as cellular phones have continued to be very significant. From 1997 to 2000, the projected annual growth in demand for digital cellular telephone services has been estimated at a rate of about 30 per cent (Escher, 1997: 1).

Growth in the mobile 'share' of all telecommunications traffic is perhaps the best indicator of the rapid and expansive development of mobile telephony. In 1995, it was projected that the majority of new telephone subscriptions would be mobile based after 1997, and that 'by the year 2005, the majority of teletraffic would be related to a wireless terminal' (Rapeli, 1995: 20). It was also observed that, 'While the telephones/population density for fixed phones may not exceed an average of 50 percent, personal mobile telecommunications, in all forms, promise to reach nearly 80 percent of Europe's population' (DaSilva and Fernandes, 1995: 14). These projections concerning future growth were based on the patterns of growth associated with existing technologies in mobile telecommunications. New, 'third-generation' technologies for mobile telecommunications, such as the UMTS standard, have been conceived as a means of extending this growth trajectory even further.

The development of mobile communications within the country of Finland provides further indications of this industry's rapid growth and high innovation profile. The Finnish telecommunications sector is the first major knowledge-based industrial development block in Finland and the fastest-growing one, now in the process of becoming the most important block (succeeding the historically dominant 'forest' block) (Rouvinen, 1996).[44] Finland is a major telecommunications equipment exporter and its most significant products in this sector – in terms of export value, share of total exports, and share of OECD markets – are mobile and fixed interactive networks and mobile telephone handsets. Mobile telephone handsets, moreover, experienced particularly rapid growth during the 1990s (ibid.).

The Finnish case also yields rich historical insights into the extent to which the growth of mobile telecommunications has depended on the complementarity between innovations in goods and services. The major Finnish firm in the global market for mobile telephones and telecommunications equipment in general is the Nokia Group. The formation of the Nokia Group took place through a series of mergers, collaboration agreements and joint ventures occurring over a period of several decades (Koivusalo, 1995; Mäenpää and Luukkainen, 1994). Although many of the firms involved diversified out of unrelated sectors like rubber products and forestry, it was of particular and vital importance that the creation of the Nokia Group brought together innovative firms with distinctive competencies in both telecommunications equipment manufacturing and specialized computer and data-processing services. The telecommunications equipment-producing firms, however, had extensive experience of close cooperation with the Finnish PTT and other leading telecommunications service providers, and these relationships were further developed by Nokia.

Reviewing this history from an SI perspective, Palmberg (1998) highlights the 'technology-push' effects resulting from these linkages among telecommunications equipment producers. However, he also draws attention to the importance to Nokia's success of 'demand-pull', which took the form of close interaction with various local and private operators, the PTT, and other private- and public-sector actors (ibid.). Palmberg concludes that in the case of Nokia, public-sector demand for various telecommunications infrastructure equipment was instrumental in enabling the company to acquire a broad knowledge base in telecommunications (ibid.). After the first five years of mobile telephone development, though, linkages to private service providers became the most important for Nokia, reflecting a shift towards greater demand from private-sector users. A concomitant development was the shift from national to international markets.

Hypothesis 19   There is rapid growth in service sectors where there is a close relation between new process technologies and new service products.

As with the previous hypothesis, evidence comes from specific sectors. The FIRB sector in services shows a correlation between rapid growth relative to other services and a high level of 'knowledge intensity'. Furthermore, the UK evidence cited in relation to Hypothesis 17 indicates the link between FIRB's exceptionally rapid and sustained growth, on the one hand, and the development of new service products based upon new process technologies (IT products), on the other.

Moreover, the high growth and innovation performance of the FIRB sector internationally is both a consequence and a cause of close relations between new investment goods, used as innovative process technologies, and new service product innovations developed on this basis. Since financial services is one of the largest business users of IT, 'the sector's sizeable presence in the market-place for IT products has given it significant influence over technological developments and trends ... [and] the sector has funded research and development and been an active contributor to technological innovations' (Fincham et al., 1994: 151). In other words, firms in financial services have influenced the development of IT goods in a process of user–producer interaction.

The pattern of innovative activity that has characterized the rapid growth of this sector, therefore, has been a 'virtuous' relationship between the growing diversification of new process technologies and new service products:

> Thus, as the range of IT applications in financial services grows ever wider, they are becoming steadily more complex and the expertise necessary for their design and implementation increases in variety. The demand this places on in-house IT expertise is partly offset by a continuous process of commodification, in which innovations become available as packaged software. Even here, however, in-house IT expertise remains important for the almost inevitable task of customisation. (Fincham et al., 1994: 167)

More broadly, the larger category of ICT (information and communications technologies)-based services (of which FIRB is a part) appears to reflect this dynamic as well (OECD, 1996b: ch. 2). The ICT-based services category as defined here includes transport and communications services, finance and insurance, real-estate and business services (ibid.: 39). Thus this category incorporates services (such as all FIRB services) that are characterized by rapid growth and/or high levels of innovative activity.

One way to determine whether such linkages between new goods and new services have a positive influence on economic growth within particular sectors is to measure the contribution of new goods to total factor productivity (TFP) increases in those service sectors characterized by extensive development of new services. This type of analysis has been carried out for the linkage between ICT goods and services in the OECD study just cited. The analysis was based on a comparison of historical trends in ten countries.[45] It involved calculations of the 'estimated contribution of both domestic and imported embodied technology [that is, ICT process technology embodying R&D investments] to TFP [total factor productivity] growth in [the] ICT segment of services, here defined to include transport and telecommunications services, finance and insurance and real estate and business services' (OECD, 1996b: 39, graph 2.8). The study obtained the following general results:

> On average … the estimated rate of return of embodied R&D on TFP growth was 130 percent in the 1970s and 190 percent in the 1980s. The principal sources of such diffusion-based productivity gains were investment in R&D-intensive equipment and foreign procurement through imports. The effect of capital investment on productivity growth in services gives one of the most robust results in the analysis: the rate of return on capital-embodied R&D exceeded 200 percent in the 1980s. (Ibid.: 39)

Further results of this analysis showed that domestically produced R&D-intensive goods tended to be more important than imports of such goods for raising productivity in the service sectors studied. This was especially the case in the USA, Japan and (to a lesser extent) Germany. The results also indicated that 'between the 1970s and 1980s, the impact of domestic embodied technology increased in every country except the United Kingdom and France and particularly strongly in the United States, Japan and Germany, due perhaps to increasing domestic linkages with ICT manufacturers in the procurement of advanced products' (ibid.: 40–41). More specific results, in terms of effects on TFP, were reported as follows:

> Because ICT services have strong linkages with ICT manufacturers (defined to include computers, scientific instruments, communications equipment and semi-conductors), the estimated impact of acquired technology on ICT services was 0.8 percentage points on average across ... ten [OECD] countries in both the 1970s and the 1980s, of which 0.3 from domestic producers and 0.5 from foreign ones. (Ibid.: 41)

Here, the linkage between new process technologies and new services is extremely pronounced, and has had a significant positive impact on TFP growth. The 'virtuous' link between new service products and new process technologies can thus involve interactive relationships between users and producers, or other types of interactions within a system of innovation, in which closer relationships tend to have more positive effects.

4.3   SUMMARY AND FUTURE RESEARCH QUESTIONS

The foregoing discussion of product innovations has distinguished between material goods and intangible services to classify product innovations and to analyse their impacts on employment.

Section 4.1 discussed product innovations in material goods. It argued that the direct employment effect of such innovations is positive. Evidence on the linkages between R&D intensity, economic growth and the generation of employment within manufacturing sectors, both across the OECD and for particular countries, was reviewed and discussed. The empirical evidence shows that employment growth in manufacturing has been most pronounced in 'high-tech' sectors with high levels of R&D intensity and also high rates of product innovation. Historically, those countries with a relatively high degree of 'technological specialization' in sectors with these characteristics have enjoyed superior rates of economic growth and job creation. Increased employment in these 'growth' sectors has been based on productivity gains that differ in nature from productivity gains based on process innovations. In productivity increases associated with new products, the physical output of labour is not increased (as it is in process innovations). However, a larger share of existing economic 'welfare' is appropriated by the economic unit(s) associated with production of the new goods.

Section 4.2 discussed product innovations in intangible services. It began by drawing parallels to the identification, in section 4.1, of 'high-tech' sectors as 'growth sectors' characterized by high rates of both product innovation and job creation. The preceding section focused strongly on the classification of certain manufacturing sectors as 'high-technology', based on their level of R&D intensity (see also Chapter 2, section 2.4). Section 4.2 sought to develop a similar category for service sectors. It made the case that 'knowledge-intensive' service sectors – that is, those whose workforces are characterized by the highest levels of advanced educational qualifications – can be regarded as functionally equivalent counterparts, in services, of the 'high-tech' manufacturing sectors. This argument was based on evidence for exceptionally high levels in these service sectors of innovative activity, though it also noted that most of this activity falls outside the description of 'formal R&D'. The evidence reviewed also supported the contention that in 'knowledge-intensive' service sectors, as in 'high-tech' (or 'R&D-intensive') manufacturing sectors, high levels of product innovation have a strong positive impact on economic growth and increases in employment.

Section 4.2 also discussed and reviewed evidence concerning dynamic complementarities between new goods and new services. For example, new material goods produced by 'high-tech' manufacturing sectors have initially been used as technical process innovations in 'knowledge-intensive' service sectors. But these technical process innovations have subsequently provided the basis for new services, that is, service product innovations. The examples used pointed to empirical evidence for close linkages and interactive relationships between 'high-tech' manufacturing sectors and 'knowledge-intensive' service sectors such as FIRB. Both these sectors tend to be 'growth sectors', and the complementarities between them can contribute to a 'virtuous cycle' of economic growth and employment creation. In particular, FIRB, by supplying a major market for IT, has exercised considerable influence on the development of this technology by manufacturers. Conversely, IT has made significant contributions to TFP growth in FIRB and similar service sectors.

The complex relationship between new goods and new services motivates the following broad but relevant questions for future research.

Questions

1. What proportion of all services is dependent upon goods in the sense discussed above?
2. What proportion of all new services is independent of new goods?

To our knowledge, such basic questions have not been pursued very far in the existing research literature. Moreover, it is beyond the scope of the present work to expand upon these questions. We can, however, pose an additional question.

The evidence that we have reviewed concerning the virtuous relationship between innovative goods-producing and services-producing sectors provides a basis for the following research question:

3. Is product innovation most rapid in those service sectors that have a close relation to innovative manufacturing sectors?

While we consider these to be important questions, we do not expect that it will be easy to answer them. We have, for example, reviewed some evidence in our discussion under Hypothesis 18 that appears to support an affirmative answer to Question 3. However, most of the evidence concerned only one innovative service sector with a particularly close relationship to an innovative manufacturing sector.[46]

To provide a more conclusive answer to Question 3, we would need to examine not only a broader range of service sectors meeting this description but also service sectors in which there is no close or direct linkage with innovative manufacturing sectors. The most compelling answers would, of course, be provided by statistical research covering service sectors with both 'weak' and 'strong' links to manufacturing sectors.

The distinction between these two types of service sectors is, however, difficult to operationalize. There is, for example, no well-defined category of 'technology-intensive' service sectors. Most of the statistical approaches that have been used to distinguish particularly 'technology-intensive' categories of services within the service sector as a whole have not managed to include all services that are 'technology intensive'. The 'ICT' category discussed under Hypotheses 16 and 19 is a case in point. It excludes the health services sector, which – as discussed under Hypothesis 17 – is one of the greatest purchasers and users in services of new technology.

Our concluding questions are primarily concerned with services-producing, rather than goods-producing, sectors. As we noted at the beginning of section 4.2, there are a number of 'intractable measurement problems' associated with the study of service sectors. Consequently, there are serious limitations to what can be accomplished with existing sources of statistical data.

Given these considerations, the most appropriate way to begin answering such questions might be with detailed case-study research directed towards the operationalization and refinement of relevant theories and concepts. These might include, for example, the RPC model of innovation in service sectors described under Hypothesis 16, the category of 'knowledge-intensive' services proposed under Hypothesis 14, and the concept of 'informal R&D' discussed under Hypothesis 15. As to the designs of such case studies, these might usefully address developments within specific sectors and countries, following the example of the pioneering studies reviewed in the discussions of Hypotheses 17 and 18.

NOTES

1. Hence our concept of product innovation here includes diffusion.
2. Katsoulacos (1984) introduced a distinction between 'horizontal' and 'vertical' forms of 'product differentiation', or, in other words, product innovation. The former term refers to the creation of new products in new markets – that is, new products which do not substitute for existing ones. The latter term refers to the creation of new products for existing markets – that is, new products which substitute for existing products. The former are 'radical' product innovations, and the latter 'incremental' ones.
3. Depending on how one counts, this figure is between 75 and 90 per cent for Sweden (SCB, 1991: table 4). In 1985, 68 per cent of industrial R&D was spent on the development of new products and product changes in the USA. The figure for Japan was 36 per cent (Mansfield, 1988: 1771). The rest of industrial R&D was in all three countries spent on the development of new processes and process changes. Recent evidence on business enterprise R&D expenditure indicates a shift to more short-term research in order to reduce product development time and cost (OECD, 1998a).
4. One important explanation of the variation in R&D intensity among sectors suggests that the R&D intensity of any given sector is determined by two key variables: (1) technological opportunities, and (2) the ability to appropriate returns from new developments. The former determines the productivity of R&D; the latter determines the fraction of returns from R&D that the innovator is able to retain (Klevorick et al., 1995).
5. An R&D-intensive sector has a high ratio between R&D expenditures and production value or value added. See the definitions given in Chapter 2, section 2.4.
6. These authors use 'high technology' and 'technologically sophisticated' as interchangeable terms to describe machinery and equipment produced by R&D-intensive manufacturing industries. They briefly identify the main clusters of service (and other) sectors making use of such machinery and equipment in the following summary account of diffusion patterns:

> Certain types of technology tend to gravitate to certain sectors: information technology to HT [high-technology] manufacturing, communication services and finance, insurance and real estate; transportation technology to transportation services; consumers goods technology to wholesale and retail trade; materials technology to agriculture, and to MT [medium-technology] and LT [low-technology] manufacturing; and fabrication technology to mining, utilities and construction. (Ibid.: 4)

7. It should be noted, however, that there are a number of problems concerning the reliability of data from the first CIS survey. Some countries had very low response rates – of the order of 20 per cent to 30 per cent – and about half of the firms included in the CIS database were Italian.
8. The engineering industry constitutes 40–50 per cent of total industry in many OECD countries.
9. The arguments are presented under Hypothesis 13.
10. These authors also explain in a footnote that 'This is also confirmed at the industry level' (ibid.: note 6).

11. Sweden is a case in point. It has had one of the highest R&D intensities among the OECD countries for decades – but a lower economic growth than the OECD average between 1973 and the late 1990s. For an analysis of how R&D is used in Sweden, see McKelvey and Edquist (1997).

12. Here, the term 'growth sector' is used to refer to sectors 'where value added and employment have both increased', whereas the term 'sector in restructuring' refers to sectors that have experienced 'growth in production and fall in employment' (Pianta, Evangelista and Perani, 1996).

13. Other factors often mentioned are globalization and liberalization, which have made markets function more efficiently, a skilful macroeconomic policy and new incentive systems. However, new technologies are generally claimed to be the most important factor behind the 'new economy'.

14. Of course, the manufacturing and service sectors relevant at a certain point in time must be specified in detail to make empirical analyses and specific policy design possible.

15. The authors elaborate this explanation as follows:

> At the sector level we find that process innovations are far less favourable to employment than product innovation, whereas we find the opposite at the firm level. We can solve the puzzle with the following explanation. Process innovation generates job creation in the firms that perform it, but at the expense of their competitors. It does not enlarge the market size, but only the market share of its performer. On the other hand, product innovation does not increase so much the sales of the firm, but it does not harm so much the competitors. Substitution with existing goods on the market is lower. (Greenan and Guellec, 1996: 23)

16. However, labour productivity growth can of course occur through increased intensity of other factors, for example capital, increased intensity of work, and so on.

17. In the introduction to Part II, it was stated that the most common measure of productivity is labour productivity, defined as the ratio between production (measured as production value or value added) and labour input (measured as number of employed or number of hours worked).

18. For the period 1963–73 the annual productivity growth in Sweden was 3.4 per cent, but after correction for market form this growth was only 1.9 per cent. For the period 1963–87 the difference was smaller; productivity growth decreased from 2.0 to 1.4 per cent per year (Hansson, 1991).

19. The argument in this paragraph is compatible with the argument that prices go down when productivity increases because of a lower cost of production, thanks to process innovation.

20. If the measured productivity increase is caused by quality improvements (of a constant physical amount of goods), then the 'welfare' of the world has increased thanks to increased quality (but a higher price has also been paid for these different, or better, goods).

21. Again, this concerns productivity as it is measured, that is, in price-based value terms.

22. The only exceptions are Printing and Publishing as well as Plastics Products.

23. If comparable data up till now had been available, this difference would probably have been even larger.

24. In other words, employment would have increased by 14 per cent in Swedish industry as a whole if Sweden had performed as the OECD as a whole did on average in the growth sectors.

25. Although decreasing, total unemployment was still 7.7 per cent in Sweden in April 2000.

26. Hence there is a severe structural problem with regard to product innovation in Swedish industry. Under Hypothesis 8 we saw that Sweden has been very advanced with regard to the diffusion of process innovations – which foster productivity and competitiveness, but reduce employment in those sectors where they are introduced.

27. The calculations presented below are based on the STAN database (OECD, 1995c) and have been carried out by Charles Edquist and Harald Edquist. The figures for the EU include those 11 countries for which data are available on the STAN database, that is, Austria, Denmark, Finland, France, Germany, Greece, Italy, the Netherlands, Spain, Sweden and the UK.

28. In other words, R&D in services is an important but inadequately conceptualized and under-studied topic. In this respect services are similar to organizational process innovations, as discussed in Chapter 2, section 2.3.

29. However, it would also be important to find out whether these human resources are used for the development of new service products, for process innovations, or for other purposes.

30. It was also developed as an alternative to another approach that seeks to include services in the identification of high-technology sectors by using a definition of 'total technological intensity' based on the ratio of *all* high-technology inputs to production outputs (Papaconstantinou, Sakurai and Wyckoff, 1995). The definition of 'total technological intensity' includes both 'direct' inputs, in the form of technological expenditure on internal R&D, and 'indirect' inputs, in the form of R&D-intensive intermediate and investment goods ('embodied R&D') purchased from other sectors (ibid.: 26). Such a definition excludes 'human capital'. It 'may be used to define knowledge-using industries, but it cannot be used to define knowledge-producing industries' (Lee and Has, 1995: 6).

31. The three indicators of R&D activity are: R&D intensity, the proportion of R&D personnel to total employment, and the proportion of professional (university degree-holding) R&D personnel to total employment. The three indicators of human capital content are: the ratio of workers with post-secondary education to total employment, the ratio of workers with trade-vocational and non-university-degree post-secondary education to total employment, and the ratio of employed scientists and engineers to total employment (Lee and Has, 1995: 6).

32. Here, 'relatively low R&D personnel content' means that there is a comparatively low proportion of employees formally classified as R&D personnel according to standard categories for collecting R&D data. For example, consultancies tend to employ relatively few scientists and engineers and few positions in consultancies are designated as 'R&D' employment.

33. This approach, as noted above, is consistent with the 'knowledge intensity' definition used to identify 'R&D-intensive' sectors (in both services and manufacturing) and to explain their disproportionately strong contribution to the creation of private-sector employment (Department of Finance, 1992).

34. These sectors were defined and described in the discussion under Hypothesis 2 in Chapter 3, section 3.1.

35. The distinction between 'informal R&D' and 'formal R&D' is associated with a number of problems. It is difficult to separate 'informal R&D' from other activities that do not fall into the category of 'formal R&D' as defined, for example, in the OECD's *Oslo Manual* (OECD, 1996c: 68). However, it remains important to take the possibility of search activities and 'informal' R&D into account. This is because 'technologies are also developed outside the formal R&D system through, for example, learning by doing, learning by using, and learning by interacting' (Edquist, 1997a: 17).

36. While we do not have comparative employment data for the management consulting services sector, the data indicating large employment gains for FIRB in OECD countries can be disaggregated into two subsectors: one subsector of FIRB comprises finance and insurance, and the other consists of real-estate and business services. The data further indicate that the subsector including business services (and therefore also management consulting) has led employment growth in several countries (OECD, 1994b: 142, table 4.8).

37. The OECD employment data indicate that employment growth in most service sectors has been demand driven (that is, driven by domestic final demand or exports). However, in FIRB, together with some other sectors, employment 'also gained from changing input–output coefficients ... notably, more intensive use of business services by industry' (OECD, 1994b: 142, table 4.8). This finding implies the development of new relations of inter-dependency and interaction between FIRB and other sectors, leading to the development of new services. However, there is no similar finding for CSPS.

38. The sectoral classification used in this study is based on earlier work by the Economic Council of Canada, which distinguished between traditional and dynamic services on the basis of labour force characteristics (Economic Council of Canada, 1991). In this scheme, 'dynamic' services correspond closely to those identified as 'high-knowledge' service

industries, and the management consulting services industry appears in both classifications (Economic Council of Canada, 1991: 93; Lee and Has, 1995: 8).

39. In dynamic services, especially, where innovation tends to involve complementarity between investments in human capital and investments in other 'factors of production', such as new kinds of capital goods, the development of new service products may be partly based on the acquisition and use of new process technologies. Examples of such complementarity in dynamic services between new goods and new service products are discussed in relation to the following three hypotheses. See, especially, the discussion under Hypothesis 16.

40. The supporting evidence for this criticism refers to the lack of any clear relationship between lags in the adoption of new financial services and lags in the adoption of mainframe computer technologies (Buzzachi, Colombo and Mariotti, 1995). This lack of relationship in turn is interpreted as the result of 'a shift in power relations between the centralised, staff-based IT structures built up in the "mainframe" regime, and the decentralised management-based structures of the [other] regime' (Hauknes, 1996: 116). However, such conflicts and their effects on patterns of technology adoption and development have occurred only in some nations (UK) but not in others (for example, Japan) (Baba and Takai, 1990).

41. See also the discussion of telecommunications under Hypothesis 17.

42. For further discussion, see OECD (1996b: ch. 5).

43. See under Hypotheses 15 and 18.

44. The term 'development block', as used here, refers to a set of enterprises and industries coupled together by strong quantitative and qualitative linkages of interactive learning and commodity flows (McKelvey, 1994). The concept was originally developed by the Swedish economic historian, E. Dahmén (1988).

45. These countries were: the USA, Japan, Germany, France, Italy, the UK, Canada, Australia, Denmark and the Netherlands. The time period was the 1970s and 1980s.

46. For further evidence, dealing with a broader range of sectors, we refer readers to the recent work of Rinaldo Evangelista (Evangelista, 2000). His findings point to 'diversified patterns of innovation in services ... [as] ... an important starting point for the analysis of the impact of innovation on employment' (ibid.: 144).

5. Dynamic and secondary effects of systemic interaction

The preceding chapters have mainly examined the immediate or direct effects of product and process innovation on employment. The direct effects of process innovation were shown to be job destruction, and of product innovation, job creation. This chapter moves on to the more dynamic aspects of the interactions of these two types of innovation within the economy as an interrelated system. We will investigate the extent to which their direct effects are counteracted by other employment effects.

First, compensation effects related to process innovation are considered in section 5.1. Compensation mechanisms are those which mitigate the negative effect on employment of process innovations and which are directly linked to it. The 'theoretical' discussion here forms a counterpart to the more 'empirical' discussion of process innovations and employment in Chapter 3 and, in particular, section 3.1.

Subsequently, sections 5.2 and 5.3 discuss two dynamic aspects of product innovation, namely, substitution between products, and whether a product innovation is later used as a process innovation. These dynamic aspects of systemic interaction partly offset the immediate employment-generating effect of product innovation and could perhaps alternatively be labelled 'negative compensation effects'. These counteracting factors are much less discussed in the literature than the compensation mechanisms related to process innovation. In section 5.4 we also refer to dynamic complementarities between goods and services as a basis for product innovation and job creation in services.

5.1 COMPENSATION MECHANISMS IN PROCESS INNOVATIONS

The topic of compensation mechanisms, briefly introduced in Chapter 3, section 3.1, can be revisited by exploring the mainstream economic thinking about process innovations and their beneficial longer-term, aggregate and dynamic effects on employment. When time is introduced in standard economic theory, it becomes possible to identify various compensation mechanisms that may balance the immediate labour savings – per unit of output – caused by the technological process innovation. These mechanisms are called compensatory if the effect is caused by the innovation rather than by other economic or social factors.

5.1.1 Compensation Effects

The most important compensation mechanism would be activated if demand – and therefore output – increased.[1] A rise in demand might be (a) exogenous to process innovation – if, for example, demand increased because of macro-economic policies, or devaluations.[2] Alternatively, it might be (b) a consequence of the process innovation itself. The resulting cost savings could then lead to a lower price of the product and demand could increase given certain price elasticities. Only in this second case could a compensation mechanism, in the strict sense, be said to be operating.

Price reduction due to process innovation may lead to demand increases by two main mechanisms, namely, (1) increased competitiveness, and (2) increased global demand.

In the first case, the lower price could lead to increased competitiveness of the firm, region, or country where the process innovation was introduced. In this way, the firm (region or country) would appropriate market share from other firms (regions or countries). The increased demand for production from the same unit would occur at the expense of other units, and demand would not be increased globally. If, in this way, global demand for the product is constant (in volume), then the labour-saving process innovation leads to a decrease in employment in the production of that product.

Hence, a firm may conquer market shares through process innovations, but if global demand for the product is constant, the aggregate result for all firms producing the product is that labour is saved. This is true for a specific sector or for the production of a specific product – if the world as a whole is taken into account.[3] This highlights the importance of the level of aggregation in the analysis of compensation. The employment consequences of process innovations vary greatly at the different levels. A firm or nation may gain jobs, but that sector in the global economy as a whole does not.

Alternatively, lower prices due to process improvements could lead to a global demand increase for the product in question. In this case, the initial labour saving caused by the process innovation can be (more than) compensated for through market growth, and thus the initial job-displacement effect may be offset. Under some conditions this compensation occurs at the sector or product level in a global sense; that is, the total world market for the product increases.[4]

Whether or not there is a global increase in demand for labour because of the price reduction in this case depends on the price elasticity of demand and the income elasticity of demand for the commodity. If the price elasticity is less than one, there may be a reduction in demand; if it is unity, demand may not be affected; and if it is larger than one, there may be a demand increase, thanks to the reduced price caused by the process innovation. However, whether a price elasticity of unity will result in an unaffected labour demand, or whether price elasticities of less or more than one will result, respectively, in negative and positive effects on demand, depends on certain special circumstances.[5] The compensation effect that is activated by price elasticities may be called the *price effect* on demand.

Moreover, the increased productivity caused by the process innovation might increase incomes and consumption – *if* wages are increased with productivity increases. Then each commodity in the economy will be affected in relation to the income elasticity of demand for the commodity. This may be called the *income effect* on demand (Reati, 1996: 3). The importance of the income effect depends also on the share of total output represented by the commodity for which the price decreased. If this share is small, the income effect will also be small. If the share were small for most products, we could therefore disregard the income effect. We could obviously not do so if the prices of many or all products were reduced due to process innovations at the same time.

The size of income elasticities is a less central issue, but can also be important, depending on how many sectors of the economy are affected by fairly rapid productivity increases.[6] The crucial issue for employment then becomes the size of the price elasticities. What then *are* these elasticities? Let us concentrate on consumer products (defined in Chapter 2, section 2.3), for which data about elasticities are available.

A comprehensive study by Bosworth (1987) concerning consumer products in five countries shows that price elasticity of demand is less than one for most consumer products except for luxury commodities.[7] The author summarizes the findings on price and income elasticities as follows:

> The results ... indicate that the models of final demand yield results broadly in agreement with a priori expectations. These are perhaps typified by the results for Belgium in Table 5. The table (almost) divides into two: with basic necessities (e.g., food, drink, housing and perhaps clothing) and habit forming goods (e.g., tobacco and perhaps certain types of drink) associated with low Ep [price elasticity] and Ey [income elasticity]; and luxury items (e.g., durables, services and expenditures abroad) associated with high Ep [price elasticity] and Ey [income elasticity].
>
> The main exception to this simple categorisation appears to be recreation (with a relatively low Ep but high Ey). With certain differences, similar results are apparent for the United Kingdom and the United States. It seems fairly certain that consumer tastes and behaviour are sufficiently alike across industrialised countries to lead to similar results in other countries. (Ibid.: 163)

Thus the main exception to the rule of low price elasticities for most consumer products is shown to be luxury items. Moreover – with the exception of 'recreation' – there is generally a strong correlation between low price elasticity and low income elasticity. For nearly all the types of consumer products studied by Bosworth (1987), price elasticities are reported to be below unity. His study also found that income elasticity of demand is less than one in the majority of cases. Income elasticities were very high only for consumer durables.[8]

Further evidence comes from a Swedish study, which analysed price elasticities of demand for a variety of consumer goods and services (Finansdepartementet, 1987: table 2.13).[9] This study indicated that the price elasticities for consumer durables (as well as those for consumer services) do not normally exceed unity (ibid.).

The Swedish evidence on income elasticity differs somewhat from that on price elasticity. The Swedish study indicated, for example, that the income elasticities for a number of consumer goods (for example, beverages and tobacco, apparel, leisure products, and furniture and domestic furnishings) and services (for example, transportation) are usually greater than one (ibid.).

The Swedish study's evidence is generally consistent with that produced by Bosworth (1987). Very few commodities are shown to have high price elasticities. Moreover, income elasticities are shown to be high only for certain consumer goods and services that may be considered, at least to some extent, as 'luxuries'.[10]

According to a third source, it appears that the main exception to the consistent pattern of price elasticities below unity may be in the case of *new* consumer durables (Parker, 1992: table 3). For 12 categories of consumer durables in which price was found to be a significant factor in diffusion patterns over the course of the 'adoption life cycle' (that is, the product life cycle), this study found that price elasticities greater than one are predominantly located in the early stage of the life cycle (ibid.).[11] The study concludes that 'As products become necessities, elasticities generally fall or are close to zero throughout the adoption life cycle' (ibid.: 366). This implies that consumer products that are new first appear as costly luxuries. Some enjoy increasing demand as prices fall, eventually becoming so widely produced and used that they are necessities. Others remain luxuries, and may continue to command high prices.

We do not have price elasticity evidence on other types of products, such as investment or intermediate products. It is therefore difficult to know the dynamic effects of process innovations on the relative demand for these categories of products. However, other types of evidence are available. The previously cited findings concerning price elasticities are reinforced by the results obtained by Vivarelli (1995) from econometric tests based on Italian and US data (ibid.: chs 8 and 9).

The empirical study carried out by Vivarelli was not directly concerned with the measurement of price elasticities, but it did address the price effect on demand, which the author discussed as the compensation mechanism 'via decrease in prices' (ibid.: 29–30, 64). Consequently, the results can be used to draw inferences concerning the extent to which price elasticities, combined with other conditions (such as the extent of competition) that are essential to the price effect on demand, actually compensate for the immediate labour-reducing effects of technological process innovation. Similarly, the results of this study are also relevant for an evaluation of the income effect on demand.

Vivarelli's study of the Italian and US economies employed a macro-economic model, constructed to analyse not only the immediate but also the second- and third-order relations between innovation and employment at the level of national economies. The model was therefore not confined to the study of particular products or economic sectors. Moreover, the model was not designed for making forecasts of the employment effects of technological (process and product) innovation, based on particular assumptions about compensation effects and the supporting conditions and mechanisms that operate to realize these effects. The model was instead 'an open formulation with interpretive purposes' in which 'relationships have to be tested with historical data' (ibid.: 107).

In order to test all the relevant relationships specified in economic theory, Vivarelli's model incorporates several different compensation mechanisms, including the mechanism 'via decreased prices' corresponding (as noted above) to the price effect on demand (ibid.: chs 3, 5 and 7). Regarding the price effect on demand, Vivarelli states that the a priori neoclassical assumption of perfect competition 'is quite arbitrary' (ibid.: 64). He continues: 'If oligopolistic rigidity is assumed, the whole compensation mechanism remains inactive, any argument about the demand elasticity is beside the point, and compensation of no effect' (ibid.).

Vivarelli's model recognizes that the compensation mechanism 'via decreased prices' 'implies an increase in purchasing power, hence in consumption and ... in demand and production' (ibid.: 112). At the same time, the model accounts for three possible hindrances to full compensation via this mechanism: (a) an insufficient expenditure of increased purchasing power on immediate consumption, or 'propensity to consume'; (b) a fall in macro purchasing power, due to the immediate labour-saving effects of technological process innovation; and (c) the negative consequences for 'effective demand' that may be realized through the operation of another compensation mechanism, 'via decrease in real wages' (ibid.).

The 'income effect on demand' was also addressed by Vivarelli, although not as a compensation mechanism *per se* but rather as a 'complementary force'(ibid.: 61). This force comes into effect when productivity gains due to the cost reductions achieved through technological change are shared between employers and workers, resulting in increased profits and real wages. With the condition of 'immediate expenditure', it follows that compensation via the 'income effect on demand' 'operates both through "new investments" and "new consumption"' (ibid.).

Accordingly, Vivarelli's model uses two separate equations to describe the distribution in productivity gains between employers and workers. One represents a precondition for compensation 'via new investment'. The other indicates both the possibility of 'an increase in final demand due to the participation of workers in the distribution of the "fruits of technical progress"' and conditions (such as short-term effects of compensation 'via decreases in wages') that can prevent such participation (ibid.: 114–15).

Vivarelli's study found, for both the Italian and US data sets, that productivity gains resulting from labour-saving process innovations 'are eventually translated into decreasing prices and these in turn involve an increase in aggregate demand' (ibid.: 163). However, the author then went on to make the following statement:

> The critical point is that the increased purchasing power is only partially spent in the form of additional consumption: in view of the fact that we deal with rates of change, the 'propensity to consume' is far less than the usual 0.7–0.9 value. According to our estimates [it] ranges from 0.4 in the USA to 0.5 in Italy ... Generally, the [compensation] mechanism via decrease in prices is very effective but it seems to ensure only partial compensation in both economic systems (Ibid.)

Concerning the 'income effect' on demand, Vivarelli found for the USA that 'compensation "via additional incomes" also fails' to offset technological unemployment (ibid.). He states that 'there is no clear evidence at all that productivity gains involve significant increases in wages and hence in consumption' (ibid.). The evidence for Italy is somewhat different, though. This kind of compensation 'works very well in the Italian context', compared with the USA (ibid.).

This difference between the two countries, however, is explained by a high level of unionization and 'corporatist' wage regulation in the Italian labour market, and the absence of such conditions in the US labour market. 'Only in a "flexible" and "competitive" labour market [is] unemployment strictly linked with the workers' bargaining power, whilst this is not the case in a very unionised and corporatist labour market' (ibid.).

In other words, 'income effects' compensate for technological unemployment only under 'exceptional' conditions. The more closely that labour markets approach 'ideal' conditions of competitiveness and flexibility, the less effective compensation 'via additional incomes' will be.[12] Thus, 'if real wages are mainly determined on a competitive labour market where unemployment matters, [compensation 'via additional incomes'] is likely to fail' (ibid.).

The obvious conclusion from the evidence provided by Vivarelli (1995), combined with the various observations that were made earlier (in this section) regarding price and income elasticities and their impacts on demand, is the following: for a given product or sector, the compensation effects are normally *not* large enough to compensate for the immediate decrease in employment caused by process innovations.[13] In other words, the net employment effect of process innovations is normally negative, although there might be exceptions.

Thus, even including second-order compensation effects, process innovations are labour saving in the majority of cases. This is consistent with the empirical fact that employment normally decreases in mature industrial sectors, which are largely the same sectors where process innovations dominate.

With respect to possible exceptions to this rule, we have already suggested that they may be more likely to occur in the case of *organizational*, rather than *technical*, process innovations. Chapter 3, section 3.2 distinguished between *labour-saving* and *capital-saving* organizational innovations. The former appears to be consistently negative in its immediate effects on employment. In other words, this type of organizational process innovation seems to operate in the same manner as technical process innovations. In that case, the negative immediate impact on employment is seldom effectively counteracted by those 'compensating mechanisms' that are directly related to process innovation. In contrast to the former type, though, the latter type of organizational innovation appears to have no direct effects on employment levels.

5.1.2 Long-term Net Compensation Effects[14]

We should not, of course, limit our discussion of 'compensation effects' to considering only the short-term net employment impacts of process innovation and how these effects are achieved through various compensation mechanisms. The long-term net effects should also be addressed. For example, the increased demand that may be created for a particular commodity through the introduction of labour-saving process innovations has two distinct components. Only one of these, the 'price effect on demand' linked to the price sensitivity of the product, can work in the short term. The other component, which can be called the 'long-term net compensation effect' on other goods and services, only operates over much longer periods of time.

A further reason for taking a long-term perspective on the operation of compensation mechanisms is that price elasticities of demand are generally considered to be smaller in the short run than in the long run. This is because consumer spending adjusts more fully over time to changes in relative prices. Habits, imperfect information and other sources of inertia act to delay the process of adjustment. Consequently, changes in the level of employment resulting from the price effect on demand related to the introduction of process innovation in a particular sector will vary according to the period of time during which adjustments are made to the resulting changes in prices.

We have already considered some evidence that points to considerable variation in price elasticities over longer-run periods of adjustment. For example, we have discussed findings concerning price elasticities over the course of the product life cycle. This evidence indicated high price elasticities (greater than one) in the early stages of the product life cycle, and a subsequent decline (to levels below unity) in later stages, once wide 'market penetration' has been achieved (Parker, 1992: table 3, 366).[15] The data used in this particular study were selected to capture, for particular consumer products, both the various identifiable stages of the product life cycle (from initial 'launching' to widespread diffusion in consumer markets) and the different adopter categories associated with each stage. Consequently, the data consisted of 'series covering multiple decades' and, moreover, 'the length of certain series often exceeds thirty years' (ibid.: 362).

The tendency that was reported for price elasticities to fall below unity at a relatively early point in the product life cycle is consistent with the other data we have examined. That evidence, some of which also covers multiple decades, indicates that the price elasticities of most consumer products tend to remain at a constantly low level for extended periods of time. Bosworth's (1987) study, for example, obtained this result using data that covered nearly three decades – that is, the 1960s, 1970s and early 1980s.

As the relative price of most commodities falls and eventually stabilizes at a low level over the longer term, the immediate 'price effect' on demand can give rise to a less direct 'long-term net compensation effect'. These developments have been summarized as follows:

> Raising efficiency in the production of one commodity lowers its price. Two consequences follow. First, the real incomes of all consumers increase. This is the process by which the benefits of technical change (i.e., rising real incomes) are distributed over the community. Second, because the real incomes of consumers rise, the demand for most goods in the economy rises. As a result, the demand for labour in most industries increases. These increases in the demand for labour provide job opportunities for the workers initially displaced by technological change. (Allen, 1986: 77–8)

Thus the initial net impact of a reduced demand for labour in sectors where technological process innovations have been introduced may eventually be counteracted over the longer term by increased labour demand in other sectors. The increased demand is supposed to arise from the higher real incomes of consumers. These consumers – with the possible exception of those who have become unemployed due to technological change – are assumed to benefit from the reduced price of one or more commodities that can be produced more efficiently, owing to the process innovation in question. Eventually, both the economy in general and the labour market in particular are expected to adapt. At that point, the initial and largely sector-specific impact of technological unemployment will have been reduced to minimal levels and labour will have shifted from the sectors in which displacement occurred to new sectors of employment.

If a sufficiently long-term historical perspective is adopted, it is of course possible to identify clear examples of a 'long-term net compensation effect' on employment resulting from initially labour-displacing process innovation. In such cases, employment-reducing process innovation in one sector of the economy is eventually compensated for more or less completely by the movement of labour into new or expanding sectors of the economy.[16] One of the most outstanding historical examples is the shift in the primary concentration of employment for the US labour force from agriculture to manufacturing and, more recently, into services (Boissot, 1995: 10, figure 1.1). However, this shift, as depicted in Figure 5.1, was only accomplished over a period of more than a century.

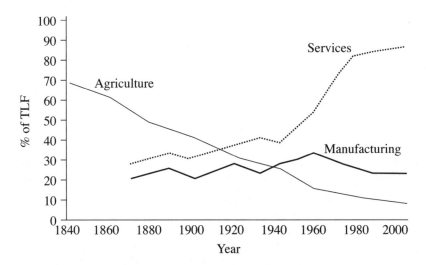

Source: Adapted from Boissot (1995: 10, figure 1.1).

Figure 5.1   Employment as percentage of total labour force

Thus the 'adjustment' process referred to in discussions of the 'long-term net compensation effect' of process innovation can cover extremely lengthy periods of time. Its pace and degree of success will, moreover, depend on the effectiveness of various mechanisms for labour market adjustment, including public and private income support and social insurance programmes designed to assist displaced workers. In contrast to the more immediate negative net employment impacts, the positive employment impacts of process innovation occur principally in the medium to longer term. They are also much more widely diffused throughout the economy. For these reasons, they are much more difficult to measure and identify.

In aggregate economic models of economic growth, technological change (which tends to be equated with process innovation) can only be observed by its effects on total factor productivity (TFP). This obscures many of the processes through which the positive employment impacts of process innovation are eventually realized. Recently, it has also given rise to an apparent 'productivity paradox' in which extensive technological changes – specifically, the introduction of information and communications technology (ICT) – have been associated with disproportionately small gains in TFP. As Lipsey (2000) has argued, however, this paradox may be largely the result of techniques of measurement and analysis that create confusion between changes in technology and its facilitating structure (ibid.: 50).

This argument follows David's (1990) thesis that the full impact of technological change on the economy is revealed only after the technology has been embodied in a facilitating structure of cooperating, or complementary, technologies and organizational structures. The development of an adequate facilitating structure usually requires a period of decades, and in the meantime no large productivity gains may be forthcoming from the 'core' technology or process innovation that was first introduced. Moreover, there is no basis for assuming that the economic results of a new technology will be directly proportional to the actual extent of technological change. Lipsey (2000) continues the argument as follows:

> Because aggregate models treat both technology and the facilitating structure as a black box, major changes in the facilitating structure are often misconstrued as being major changes in technology. ... [T]he point is as important as it is obvious ... Changes in technology, the facilitating structure and economic performance are separate phenomena. Related changes in these three, even if all driven by the same technological advance, do not have to be of similar magnitude. (Ibid.: 50)

In sum, there is nothing automatic about the process of economic adjustment to labour-displacing technological change and the various compensation mechanisms through which it acts to realize the benefits of process innovation. The achievement of a 'long-term net compensation effect' on employment, in the form of expanding employment in sectors of the economy other than that from which labour is initially displaced by technological change, is not assured. In the long run, its success depends on multiple adjustments in prices, wages, output and employment. In the middle run, there is considerable risk that these adjustments will not be complete, or will take place only very slowly. Under those conditions, the negative, sector-specific employment-reducing effects will dominate, and the contribution of the process innovation to economy-wide employment creation will be reduced or delayed.

Taken together, the fact that the 'long-term net compensation effect' on employment resulting from initially job-destroying process innovation is not 'guaranteed', the lengthy periods of time required for its completion, and the highly diffuse character of the processes through which such an effect is realized, all constitute a rationale for a number of related public policy interventions. The policies required, moreover, should be neither short-sighted nor narrowly conceived. Instead, they should adopt a long-term perspective and address a wide range of issues. Some essential features of appropriate policies have been discussed as follows:

> two global sets of measures have emerged (according to the OECD) which should be considered by the authorities in order to encourage the beneficial effects of advanced technologies. On the one hand, there are measures which centre upon encouraging the creation of, access to, and dissemination of increased technological knowledge. Increased public investment in financing research, as well as into the strengthening of private sector research, and collaboration between public research organisations and business, are important means which should be developed. At the same time, it is necessary to encourage policies which promote the development of human resources and support organisational change as ways of obtaining greater flexibility. Investment in human capital through education and on-going training of workers are core activities in the process of assimilating new technologies into the economic system, paying special attention to SMEs, for this and other policies. (Alaminos and Martinez, 1999: 34)

Policies implemented in the short and medium term can, moreover, have far-reaching consequences. Longer-term patterns of growth can be affected by the effectiveness of short- or medium-term adjustment processes. In other words, short- and medium-term developments 'matter', even from a long-term perspective. For example, the ineffective operation of compensation mechanisms in the short term may result – as we discuss below – in a systemic bias towards further labour-saving technological change and a tendency towards less employment-intensive forms of economic growth.

5.1.3 Technological Trajectories and the Employment Intensity of Growth

Compensation mechanisms related to process innovations have been dealt with in depth in the literature.[17] They will therefore not be further discussed here. We now turn, instead, to a relevant and related debate in the recent history of economic thought, about the widely alleged 'labour-saving bias' of technological change.

An ongoing controversy was initiated during the 1960s in reaction to Hicks's (1932) original position that compensation mechanisms, once activated, induce further labour-saving changes in production. That is, changes in factor prices 'spur' the development of process innovations that economize on labour as a 'particularly expensive' factor of production (ibid.: 24). In the 1960s, this position was challenged by Salter's (1966) objection that there is an absence of market signals indicating the relative 'expensiveness' of any particular factor. Hence 'The entrepreneur is interested in reducing costs in total, not particular costs such as labour or capital costs' (ibid.).

Subsequent debate on the factor-saving bias of technological change counterposed 'demand-pull' and 'scarcity-push' arguments. The 'demand-pull' thesis proposed that the direction of technological change is driven by 'wants' (Schmookler, 1966: 136). In contrast, the case for 'scarcity push' referred to 'the stimulating effects of bottle-necks and in particular to a scarcity of labour' on technical change (Habbakuk, 1962: 6). In the first of these approaches, technological unemployment is compensated for by the positive evolution of demand and production. In the second, labour-saving changes are undertaken to compensate for a situation of full employment. Both approaches reduce the relationship between technology and the economic system to 'a "one way" causal linkage from market forces to technical change', and neither adequately explains technological unemployment (Vivarelli, 1995: 13).

More recent work on the direction of technical change has underlined its internal logic of development, providing a basis for arguments that there is a 'two-way' relationship between technology and the economy: 'Although economic forces and motives have inevitably played a major role in shaping the direction of scientific progress, they have not acted within a vacuum ...' (Rosenberg, 1976: 13). On this basis, it has become possible to discern and explain the emergence of 'technological trajectories', which are cumulative and irreversible (Dosi, 1982: 158–61). They are irreversible partly because they are enforced by economic 'learning' about the greater profitability of remaining within a given technological regime (Stiglitz, 1987). Learning, knowledge and institutions may give firms incentives to follow one type of path of development rather than another. These paths are important because, as has been argued above, the sectoral specialization of a country will influence the relative growth in employment.

This evolutionary perspective becomes quite interesting because it provides a theoretical basis for the explanation of technological unemployment arising from 'technological trajectories' with a labour-saving bias (Nelson and Winter, 1982; Dosi, 1982: 155). According to this view, short-term market compensation mechanisms, such as labour market adjustment, will not fully counter the negative employment impacts of technological process innovations:

> An important conclusion follows from this overall assessment of 'induced innovation'. It is, that there is inherent plausibility in the Hicks inducement theory, biasing the long term direction of technical change in a labour-saving direction. Attempts to generate a reversal of this trend by temporary small reductions in the price of labour are extremely unlikely to be effective. (Freeman and Soete, 1987: 46)

There is a fairly direct parallel between 'technological trajectories' and 'growth patterns' – not only at the firm and sectoral levels, but also at the level of national economies. There are different types of technological trajectories and different types of economic growth. The reason why this is of such crucial importance is that 'technological trajectories' may be either labour saving or employment generating. Hence, national growth patterns, as policy makers now recognize, may have different levels of 'employment intensity' (Commission of the European Communities, 1994: 57–60). National growth patterns of low employment intensity can thus reflect the predominance of sectors in which the bias of technological change is labour saving. Preliminary research results indicate that this is typical of the European economy as a whole – as compared with the USA and, until recently, Japan.[18]

This type of growth pattern is evident, for example, in the case of Sweden (Edquist, 1990; Edquist and Texier, 1996). The Swedish pulp and paper industry provides a good illustration of a manufacturing sector where technological process innovations are important. Here very large investments, which involve process innovations and increased production, were made throughout 1995–96. But no new jobs were created after the investment period. These investments led to production growth but also reduced the number of jobs. Obviously the employment created through the increased production was smaller than the amount of labour saved through increased productivity induced by process innovation. In other words, economic growth does *not* necessarily imply more jobs! This is a revealing example of jobless growth.[19]

Manufacturing industries are often referred to for evidence, or counter-evidence, of this type of growth pattern, rather than service industries (Alexander, 1996: 308–9). This is partly because the greater exposure of manufacturing industries to international markets has tended, especially in recent years, to present particularly strong inducements for labour-saving technological change (Howell, 1996: 301–2).

However, technological process innovations are not limited to manufacturing, but are also increasingly important in service production. For example, computers and other IT equipment diffuse rapidly into some service sectors such as insurance and financial services. In fact, services are said to be responsible for the great bulk (even exceeding 80 per cent) of investment in new IT hardware (OECD, 1994b: 159; 1995a: 12). This might increase productivity (Griliches, 1992) and reduce employment substantially in these sectors.

In other service sectors – such as retail trade, hotels, cleaning and social services – technological process innovations might not be important at all. According to some analysts, the potential for labour saving and increased productivity because of technical change is simply not present in such sectors, which they therefore sometimes call 'stagnant sectors' (Baumol, Blackman and Wolff, 1989).

On average, however, increases in labour productivity due to process innovations are often said to be faster in goods production than in service production. If that is correct, process-related job destruction is larger in manufacturing than in service production. On the basis of this assumption, and in relation to the foregoing discussion, we can pose a number of research questions.

Questions

1. Are there manufacturing sectors in which there is comparatively little (that is, a relatively low rate of) job destruction associated with process innovation?
2. Are there service sectors in which the opposite pattern is found – that is, where, compared to services in general, there is an exceptionally high level (or rate) of job loss associated with process innovation?
3. What is the nature of the relationships, if any, between these 'outliers' in services and manufacturing?

Research carried out along these lines would add greatly to our knowledge of the dynamics of 'labour-saving' and 'employment-generating' technological trajectories in different sectors and nations and the differences between them.

Having argued for a theoretical perspective of technological trajectories and growth patterns that may be either labour saving or employment generating, the discussion has returned to the implications for the relations between innovation and growth. The first section of this chapter has considered the second- and third-order compensation effects of process innovation on employment. The next sections consider questions related to 'second-order' effects of product innovation on employment. It is necessary to consider these effects for both process and product innovations, so that we can begin to grasp the dynamic effects of economic systems.

5.2 COUNTERACTING MECHANISMS IN PRODUCT INNOVATIONS: SUBSTITUTION

Chapter 4 concluded that both new goods and new services have an immediate job-creating employment effect. Whether the net effect on employment is positive or negative depends, however, on certain other counteracting factors related to the character of the new products. These are counteracting mechanisms in the sense that they are dynamic or second-order effects, rather than immediate ones.

The first counteracting mechanism discussed here is the degree of substitution between products.[20] If the new product *satisfies a completely new kind of demand or serves a new function*, the production of the new product contributes to increased net employment. Examples are private automobiles, penicillin, black and white TVs, telefaxes and sporting material.[21] If a product is new to the world, total employment increases. If an existing product begins to be produced in a new country, region or company, that is, if the production of the new product diffuses, then employment grows in the country (region, company, and so on) where production is initiated. In this latter case, employment may, of course, decrease somewhere else; that is, the geographical division of labour is changing. Whether employment increases or decreases in that other geographical region depends, however, on the overall rate of market growth globally.

If the new product *functionally replaces an old one*, either increased or reduced employment may result. Examples are personal computers replacing typewriters, computer-controlled machine tools replacing manually controlled ones and HDTVs replacing colour TVs. The net employment effect then depends largely on two factors: first, whether the demand for satisfying the function changes when the new product replaces the old one; and second, the labour intensity of the process technology used for producing the new product, as compared with the old one.

Substitution is, of course, normally a matter of degree. Even a brand-new artefact such as the black and white TV involves some degree of substitution for a good or a service, for example, going to the cinema less. Although systematic evidence is scarce, we assume that product innovations tend to be employment creating in most cases, even when the substitution effect is taken into account. However, there are, of course, some exceptions to this.

These and related issues were earlier addressed by Kuznets (1972), who sought to distinguish between 'cost-reducing' and 'demand-creating' innovations.[22] 'Cost-reducing' innovation, Kuznets argued, tends to 'reduce the real costs of production but leave the product basically the same, except for minor changes in quality'. In contrast, 'demand-creating' innovation 'creates an entirely new production function, corresponding to the new product' (ibid.: 432). Hence it corresponds to our discussion of new products.

Setting aside the difficulties involved in differentiating a new product from quality changes in an old one, Kuznets remarked on the proposed dichotomy that 'the distinction depends on specificity in the definition of the product' (ibid.: 433). For example, if a new synthetic material such as nylon were thought of not as a particular commodity, but rather as simply another light, washable fabric, then it would appear to be an innovation that reduced the real cost of a 'known' type of product, and not a truly new product. A perspective utilizing only the most generic product categories, despite their relevance to the issue of substitution, could thus overlook new products that created and satisfied genuinely new demands:

> this wider view of need categories ... must not obliterate real differences between old and new products ... A tractor is only another version of a workhorse, but it does not originate in the agricultural sector; its production is subject to constraints unlike those of the production of workhorses; and its performance is vastly different. ... The demand-creating, new product type of technological innovation has a far wider range than the definition of a few broad groups of human needs suggests. (Ibid.)

We will also conclude this section with a number of questions to which the answers can be provided primarily through empirical research. Because of the absence of empirical work in this field, we cannot address them fully here. Instead, we raise points about how this might be done in future research.

Questions

1. Which kinds of new goods or services replace old ones and which kinds serve new functions? To what degrees? Can taxonomies be created?
2. In the case of replacement, does the demand for satisfying the function change because of the new product's performance?
3. Is the labour intensity of the process technology lower or higher for the production of specific new products than for the old ones? Is there a general trend?
4. Do the answers to these questions vary between new goods and new services?

In research directed towards answering these questions, it will be useful to bear in mind the above-cited remarks by Kuznets (1972). In particular, it will be important, in the identification of 'new products' and the determination of the degree to which they substitute for old ones (Question 1), to observe the need for definitional specificity. Essential elements in the specification of products should include the technological bases of products, their sectors of origin and use, their broader historical and geographical locations within the economic system, and the transformations of consumption and investment patterns which they involve. These specifications will also be relevant for the design of research seeking to establish the nature of relationships between demand and performance (Question 2).

Kuznets offers further insights that may assist the design of research into the relationships between the labour intensity of production processes and the degree of product innovation (Question 3), and possible differences between new goods and new services (Question 4). Most importantly, he draws attention to possible complementarities among sectors and their dynamic effects on the economy as a whole. With reference to production processes, he remarks that a major technological innovation of the cost-reducing type may not only affect production by 'permit[ting] a larger final output with the same or a lesser input of resources' (ibid.: 436). It may also have 'an additional major effect on the structure, and possibly the volume of ultimate consumption, through changes in the conditions of participation ... in the production process' (ibid.).

With reference to those innovations that do not replace existing products and can instead be considered to belong entirely to the class of demand-creating, new product innovations, he writes:

> even the technological innovations that create new consumer goods differ substantially in magnitude, depending on the weight and magnitude of the consumption component and the elasticity of its response. Thus innovations that determine the location of ultimate consumers on the land affect the demand for housing and all related equipment, a substantial category in the total consumption outlay; and they may lead to complementary changes in the services needed to maintain residences and household equipment. By contrast, even technologically sophisticated changes in the chemical provenance of clothing materials, while leading to the expansion of synthetic fabrics at the expense of cotton and other vegetable fibre textiles, will hardly have repercussions that substantially transform the structure, or perceptibly augment the volume of household consumption as measured in the national economic accounts. In general, if a significantly large component of household consumption is comprised of low-cost, efficiently produced goods, with a low price elasticity of demand, even technically significant changes in it are not likely to have much economic effect. (ibid.: 436–7)

In part, these remarks draw attention to the important issue of price elasticities of demand, which we discussed in section 5.1. But they also touch upon the substitution of new production inputs for old ones and the economic effects of substitutive and other relationships between new consumer goods and new consumer services. We address some of these issues in the following sections.

5.3 COUNTERACTING MECHANISMS IN PRODUCT INNOVATIONS: PRODUCT TO PROCESS INNOVATION

This section investigates the dynamic relationships between product and process innovations over time. These relationships involve the operation of mechanisms that counteract the immediate employment effects of product innovation and process innovation. Only after we have accounted for the combined operation of such mechanisms – that is, how they may interact to influence employment, in either the same or different directions – can we speak of the net employment effects of innovation. To do this, it is necessary to move beyond considering 'process' and 'product' innovations in isolation from one another.

Some innovations make two different kinds of 'appearances' in the economy. They are product innovations when produced because they are sold in market transactions, but when they are later used by the buyer(s) they become process innovations. In other words, some artefacts can play the roles of both job-creating product innovations and job-destroying process innovations. This is a second important factor counteracting the employment-generation effects of some product innovations.

Chapter 2, section 2.3 presented a classification of products and product innovations into three categories: consumer products, investment products, and intermediate products. These categories are useful in helping to specify what kinds of products and product innovations can play the 'double role' referred to above. The classification, which applies to both goods and services, can be briefly recapitulated as follows:

Consumer products are goods and services that are consumed (by households) for their own sake to satisfy current wants.

Investment products are durable products that are intended to be used as factor inputs for further production-generating subsequent benefits.

Intermediate products are (economically) non-durable products used by firms to produce other products, rather than for final consumption.

These categories are useful for discussing 'second-order' employment effects of product innovations. This is because only one of these categories can have the second-order effect discussed here.

Only *investment* goods can play the double role of employment generation and labour displacement. Investment products are by definition purchased in order to be an input into the production process of goods and services. Therefore they increase labour productivity when used, which reduces employment. Consumer products and intermediate products never become process innovations. Therefore they do not serve as job destroyers in a second 'appearance'.

One important example of investment goods and their impacts on employment is robots. For industrial robots, the net employment effect is negative. In an earlier US study of industrial robots it was shown that for each job displaced only 0.32 jobs were created (Hunt, 1984).[23] A more recent German study reached a similar conclusion that an overall positive impact of industrial robots on employment is extremely unlikely (Meyer-Krahmer, 1989). It projected that only about two-thirds of the initial losses in employment would be made up for by indirect compensation effects (De Wit, 1991). More research is, of course, necessary to determine whether this conclusion can be generalized from robots to most other investment goods.

There are also investment services. Chapter 2, section 2.3 mentioned consultancy advice to firms with regard to building a process automation system as an example of an investment service product. Chapter 2, section 2.2 mentioned that the knowledge basis behind organizational innovations may sometimes be commodified and sold as consultancy services. However, only a small share of all service products become organizational process innovations. It seems fairly difficult to find important categories of services which can be labelled 'investment services', that is, which can serve as product as well as process innovations.[24] Most services that are sold to firms actually seem to be intermediate products and not investment products. The reason is that the majority of services sold to firms are not durable and can therefore function only as intermediate service products; only a minority have long durability and are therefore capable of functioning as 'investment services'.

Services have been defined as products which, in contrast to goods, are intangible, tend to be consumed simultaneously with their production, and create values which often satisfy non-physical needs (Hauknes, 1994: 8–9). If we accept this definition, it follows that most services will behave either like consumer products or, in the case that they are purchased by firms, like intermediate products. In other words, they will not function as investment goods.

There are, however, some services which are not adequately described by the definition above, the most important of these being the provision of knowledge (primarily through education and training) resulting in the formation of 'human capital'.[25] Human capital, by virtue of its durability and its capacity to generate continuing returns, has long been recognized by economists as a special kind of 'investment product' (Becker, 1975). It differs from other investment products, however, in that – due to its embodiment in individuals as 'knowledge carriers' – an investment in human capital is an investment in labour (Machlup, 1980).

Given a free labour market, employers cannot expect fully to recover the benefits of their investment in human capital, with the result that this type of investment has important 'public-good' qualities, and is most appropriately conceived as a 'collective production factor' (Streeck, 1989).[26] None the less, firms in some sectors and some countries seem more willing to invest in skills and training because of the high level of firm specificity of the skills required to carry out certain jobs. Thus education and training may be regarded as an example of an 'investment' product in services – albeit one which may behave differently from most investment goods products.

Another way to approach the question of which services act like investment products is through the various attempts to develop a classification of service sectors indicating linkages with other sectors and industries (see, for example, Delauney and Gadrey, 1992). A comparison of these classifications (Hauknes, 1996: ch. 3) indicates consensus supporting the widely acknowledged 'Singlemann' classification (Browning and Singlemann, 1978). This scheme, based on functional categorization, divides all industries (including manufacturing) into six broad sectors.[27] Of these, it identifies four sectors which are categories of service industries:

- distributive services,
- producer services,
- social services, and
- personal services.

When matched with the European NACE standard for industry classification, this subdivision of the service sector reveals that most, if not all, services which may be considered to have the economic properties of private 'investment products' are concentrated in the category of producer services (Hauknes, 1996: table 3.2). This classification and some of its main results have been reproduced in Table 5.1.

Regarding Table 5.1, we can see that most producer services (and a large part of the distributive services) are closely connected with business activities, as opposed to 'social' or 'personal' consumption activities. In other words, most producer (and many distributive) services are purchased by and for enterprises, rather than by or for individuals and households. Thereby, they may contribute to capital accumulation on the part of the enterprises purchasing them. In these respects, they correspond to our categories of 'intermediate' and 'investment' products. In most cases, however, they will be the former rather than the latter. As we argued earlier, this is because they are non-durable – that is, used rapidly, if not instantly – and are therefore incapable of generating continuing returns on investment.[28] Clearly, this is typically the case with distributive services such as transport and storage, communication and trade.

Table 5.1   The Singlemann classification scheme

Service sector	Service industries	NACE Rev. 1	
Distributive	● Transport & storage	I	60–63
	● Communication	I	64.2
	● Wholesale & retail trade	G	50–52, exc. 50.2, 50.4, 52.7
Producer	● Bank, insurance & other financial services	J	65–67
	● Real estate	K	70
	● Legal services	K	74.11
	● Accounting	K	74.12
	● Engineering & architectural services	K	72–74
	● Misc. business services		
Social	● Medical/health services & hospitals	N	85
	● Education	M	80
	● Postal services	I	64.1
	● Government	L	75
	● Other professional & social services		
Personal	● Hotels & restaurants	H	55
	● Repair services	G	50.2, 50.4, 52.7
	● Entertainment & recreation	O	92
	● Other personal services		

Source: Adapted from Hauknes (1996: table 3.2).

Given that most distributive services are intermediate products, 'investment' products in services – that is, services with the properties of durability and the capacity to generate continuing returns on investment – are more likely to be found among the producer services. However, not all producer services can be considered to possess the qualities of investment products. Some producer services – such as, for example, contract R&D and related science and technology (S&T) services – do have the properties of durability and the capacity to generate ongoing returns on investment.

Producer services of this kind, however, are a minority. Most, for example, legal and accounting services, do not have the same properties. For this reason, it has been argued that 'knowledge-intensive' producer or business services 'are primarily of relevance as intermediate inputs' (Hauknes, 1996: 48).

Earlier, we discussed the case of 'human capital', or education, as a service product possessing the qualities of an 'investment product' – that is, the properties of durability and the capacity to generate continuing returns on investment. However, we also stressed that there are appropriability problems associated with 'human capital', based on the fact that it is embodied in individual workers who remain free to move from one employer to another. For this reason, there are strong disincentives for firms to invest in 'human capital', particularly when it is of a 'general' character and thus highly transferable from one firm to another. This accounts for the 'public-good' qualities of human capital.

As a 'public good', human capital is usually oriented towards individuals, rather than firms, and is often paid for primarily by public rather than private expenditure, especially in the case of general education. These considerations are reflected in the Singlemann classification by the fact that education is classified – along with medical/health services, postal services and government services – as a social service. In our definitional scheme, social services are normally used by households or individuals and are therefore equivalent to 'consumption' products. If used by firms – for example, postal services – they may most often be equivalent to 'intermediate' products.

In a final reference to Table 5.1, we note that personal services correspond even more closely to our definitional category of 'consumption' products. That is, these services – including hotels and restaurants, entertainment and recreation, and so on – are consumed by households or individuals for their own sake in order to satisfy current wants.

In sum, we consider that even among the producer services, few services meet the definitional criteria of an 'investment product'. Since only a small part of the services produced are investment products, the production of services is a job destroyer to a smaller extent than goods production through the mechanism of being transformed from product innovations into process innovations.

This section has dealt with the dynamic relationships between product and process innovations over time and across economic sectors. It was established in the first section (5.1) of this chapter, as well as in earlier chapters, that product innovations that are later transformed into process innovations in manufacturing industries normally have a labour-saving (or employment-reducing) effect. The discussion here has indicated that it is only new products belonging to the class of 'investment products' that serve as job destroyers in a 'second appearance' – that is, when used as process innovations. Intermediate and consumer products do not demonstrate the same tendency, because of their different properties.

Only a small part of the services produced are investment products. Therefore the production of services is a job destroyer to a much smaller extent than goods production through the mechanism of being transformed from product innovations to process innovations. (It is also of relevance here that most job growth takes place in services.)

5.4   DYNAMIC IMPACTS OF SERVICES

Service sectors now account for the bulk of employment in the OECD countries – on average, for two out of every three jobs. They have been responsible for the bulk of job creation in these countries, particularly since the 1970s, when there was a marked acceleration in the shift from manufacturing to service employment (OECD, 1994b: 5). Service sectors, therefore, have come to be regarded as employment generating. Although the economic downturn of the early 1990s had some characteristics of a 'white-collar recession' in many countries (ibid.: 52–3), service sectors remained the leaders in job creation. They continued a long-term trend of employment growth in which, 'until now, the gains have exceeded the losses' (OECD 1996b: 73).[29]

The case of the primary 'employment leader' in services, CSPS (community, social and personal services), is especially instructive with respect to the superior job-creation capacity of consumer product innovations in services. Here we will briefly review some of the salient facts, first mentioned in Chapter 3, section 3.1, about the importance of CSPS for job creation in OECD countries. We will then revisit explanations, first cited in Chapter 4, section 4.2, for the phenomenon of job growth in CSPS. We do so as a prelude to developing an alternative explanation. The argument that we subsequently put forward challenges established theories about the dynamics of substitution between consumer goods and consumer services. We refer instead to dynamic complementarities between goods and services as a basis for product innovation and job creation in CSPS.

As first indicated in Chapter 3, section 3.1, CSPS accounted for 30 per cent of all OECD employment in 1991 and its rate of employment growth was ranked among the top five employment growth sectors during the 1970s and 1980s in nine of ten OECD countries (OECD, 1996b; Sakurai, 1995).[30] The exception to this pattern was Denmark. In other countries, CSPS was ranked first for employment growth in Canada, second in Japan and the UK, third in France and the Netherlands, fourth in Germany and fifth in the USA (Sakurai, 1995). Owing to the combined effects of its size and rapid rate of employment growth, CSPS is clearly the primary 'employment growth' sector in the OECD countries. As mentioned earlier in Chapter 4, section 4.2, the rapid growth and high employment gains of CSPS have been analysed as being 'due principally to strong domestic final demand growth, supported by the absence of labour productivity improvements' (ibid.).[31]

It might be inferred from this type of analysis that there has been no connection between innovation and the generation of employment in CSPS. However, such reasoning would have to assume that all innovation is equivalent to productivity-enhancing process innovations and would therefore fail to take product innovation into account. Arguably, *product innovation* has been a major source of employment growth in CSPS. An instructive example is the music sector – which, like other cultural and entertainment sectors, such as tourism, involves the production of 'services' as a necessary complement to the production of 'goods'. The phenomenal economic growth of the music sector during recent decades has been linked to extensive product innovation, in both goods and services (Andersen and Miles, 1999).

A basic argument concerning product innovation as an important source of employment growth in CSPS is developed in a recent account of the historical development of household or consumer services, which are generally equivalent to those service sectors grouped within CSPS (Illeris, 1996). This account reviews recent debate over the 'self-service society' thesis advanced in the early 1980s (Gershuny and Miles, 1983).[32] That thesis alleged that consumers were increasingly producing service products themselves within households through the use of purchased goods. This type of substitution for services by new consumer goods (that is, through their use as process innovations within households) was supposed to accomplish a shift in the production of services from the 'formal' (waged) economy to the 'informal' (non-wage) economy.

The 'self-service society' thesis described a process of change towards an economy in which consumer services would increasingly be 'self-produced' within households. It assumed that this transformation would be driven by the tendency of service products to increase in price relative to goods. This tendency, in turn, would be due to lower productivity growth in services production and the tendency of wages in the service sector to parallel those in the goods sector. These economic assumptions were derived from Baumol's (Baumol, 1967, 1985; Baumol, Blackman and Wolff, 1985; 1989) approach to the study of service-sector productivity, according to which personal services were classified as 'stagnant' and characterized as a 'cost disease'. From this perspective, personal services were supposed to resist productivity increases based on standardization and greater capital intensity because of the negative impact on service quality. Instead of increasing productivity, these services would be inclined to demand higher prices than the market would bear. Alternatively, their quality would decline. In either case, the effect in their primary market, households, would be an increase in the substitutability of these services by consumer goods.

Contrary to the 'self-service' thesis, there is now considerable evidence that households have come to demand more services over time. This is not only true for public services, for which 'there can be no doubt that they have increased so much in recent decades that the net result has been an externalisation of tasks from households to the formal economy' (Illeris, 1996). It is also true for service purchases by households from the private sector. There is extensive cross-country evidence that these purchases normally form an increasing share of total private consumption (ECOAnalyse, 1995; Elfring, 1988; Fontaine, 1987; Green, 1985). This means that the income elasticity of demand for these service products is high.

The evidence concerning rising consumption of private-sector services by households can be satisfactorily explained by economic and sociological theories of the development of consumer services which focus on transformations in the basic nature of households (Gadrey, 1986; Silver, 1987). These theories refer to the emergence of households less able to provide services internally, an increasing need for services due to societal change, the non-exclusivity (in some instances) of higher prices and lower productivity, and growing affluence leading to greater consumption of certain types of highly income-elastic leisure, health and similar services (Illeris, 1996).

According to these theories, there is in many cases a complementarity, rather than competition, between services and goods. This is the case, for example, in the case of private automobiles and automobile insurance. Alternatively, there can also be complementarity between service production in the formal and informal economy. This is more generally the case in most person-related services (care, health and education) – for which machines cannot function as complete substitutes and for which, also, households cannot provide the full range of services that they may require.[33] These complementarities thus mitigate the job-destroying substitution effects of consumer goods upon consumer services.

Moreover, the complementarities depend on the development, by service industries, of specialized skills not available within households (for example, medical assistance) and service products based on complex bodies of knowledge produced by systematic research into complicated patterns of market demand (for example, banking services) (Gadrey, 1992). Thus economic and employment growth based on complementarity between consumer goods and services can be seen to be the result of extensive product innovation within the household services (or CSPS) sector.

To summarize, the discussion of empirical evidence in this section has focused on those service sectors in which the greatest part of employment growth continues to be concentrated. In this connection, we have discussed specific dynamic characteristics of services, as well as dynamic relationships between goods and services.

In the previous section (5.3), our discussion of the service sectors suggested that product innovation in the service sectors is, on the whole, more employment generating than product innovation in manufacturing sectors. In that section, it was shown that few service product innovations belong to the category of 'investment products', which are job destroying in their second 'appearance'. There is a very different pattern in the case of product innovations in manufacturing.

However, as shown in this section (5.4), the employment-reducing substitution effects of new products are much less pronounced in service sectors than in manufacturing sectors. This is because, as demonstrated with reference to evidence concerning the CSPS sector, the relationship between new goods and new services tends primarily to be one of complementarity, rather than direct substitution.

Rather than substituting for household services and creating a 'self-service' society, new material goods that are consumed by households tend to create demands for new commodified household services associated with their use. Such demands, moreover, have risen steadily over time. The main effect of new consumer goods for consumption by households has therefore been to create employment in new household services that are sold on the market.

NOTES

1. Product innovation is also sometimes considered to be a compensation mechanism. However, in our view the only compensation mechanisms proper are those caused by the process innovation itself (see (b) below). Product innovations and exogenous demand increases have no direct causal link to the initial process innovation. They might certainly increase employment but are not compensation mechanisms in a strict sense. They constitute other important determinants of employment (which is certainly a multicausally determined variable).

2. This kind of demand increase will not be further discussed here.

3. In this respect, the sector of production is a particularly important level of analysis. The compensation effects of this kind of innovation that may be enjoyed by an individual firm are cancelled out at the global sectoral level, since employment compensation is gained at the expense of other firms in the same sector. In this sense, sectors represent worldwide 'closed' economies in which these 'competitive' compensation mechanisms cannot be said to operate. That is, international competition based on the reduction of labour costs through process innovations ultimately leads to an overall reduction of employment within a given sector. At the national, regional and firm levels, increases in employment resulting from this type of competition are simply the consequences of having appropriated a larger share of the global market.

4. For the analysis of these complex relations a general equilibrium analysis would certainly be useful. However, as we indicated in Chapter 1, such an analysis has not yet been successfully performed. Moreover, there are serious theoretical and conceptual problems associated with conducting this type of analysis with respect to innovation and employment. For example, 'general equilibrium' generally assumes both full employment and perfect competition.

5. Several considerations affect the value at which the price elasticity of demand will simply offset the immediate job-destruction effects of process innovation. The situation in which a

price elasticity of 'unity' has a neutral net effect on employment and just balances the negative direct consequences of process innovation on jobs has been discussed by Chennells and Van Reenen (1998) as a special case. This case also implies that a price elasticity of greater than one will have positive effects exceeding the immediate negative employment impact of process innovation, and that a price elasticity of less than one will have a negative net effect on employment. Conditions that are necessary in order for these effects to occur at the specified levels of price elasticity include perfect competition and no substitution between labour and capital (ibid.: appendix I).

6. When only one or a few sectors are affected by rapid productivity increases, there is only a small impact on the average productivity of the economy as a whole. However, the income effect becomes more important as more sectors exhibit rapid productivity growth.

7. The countries studied were: Belgium, France, Italy, the UK and the USA. The types of commodities for which price elasticities of demand were reported were primarily consumer products. These included both durable ('durables') and non-durable ('food and drink', 'tobacco', 'clothing', 'housing', and so on) goods, as well as services ('transport and communication', 'other services', and the like). For the most basic categories used, see, for example, Bosworth's (1987) table 5. For a more detailed breakdown, see his table 6.

8. See the discussion of this evidence by Reati (1996).

9. The consumer services studied included items such as cultural services, hygiene and health-care services, household services and transportation; the goods studied included both perishable items, such as groceries, (alcoholic) beverages and tobacco products, and durable ones, such as leisure products, furniture and domestic furnishings.

10. Other sources suggest that particularly in consumer services income elasticities may normally be greater than one. According to the recent OECD study of *Technology, Productivity and Job Creation*, 'Services are what are called "superior goods", goods whose income elasticity tends to exceed unity, so that a given percentage increase in incomes tends to result in a more than proportionate increase in the demand for services' (OECD, 1996b: 73).

11. The interpretation of these results proposes a distinction between products which can be classified as 'necessities, or categories having reached and maintained penetration levels exceeding 90%', and 'non-necessities'. For *necessities*, price elasticities may be high initially, but the pattern revealed in later stages of the life cycle is that 'elasticities are either constant, not statistically different from zero, or decline towards the later stages of the adoption life cycle'. For *non-necessities*, 'elasticities increase during one or all stages of the adoption life cycle (with the exception of ironers and room air conditioners, which have inconclusive dynamics)' (Parker, 1992: 365).

12. Vivarelli continues this comparative analysis to make the point that in a labour market such as that of the USA, which more closely approximates what are for standard economic theory 'ideal' conditions of 'flexibility' and 'competitiveness', the reduction of wages also fails to compensate for technological unemployment:

> If the labour market is flexible (as in the USA), the prevailing technological trajectory is not induced by real wage dynamics; if the labour market is more rigid (as in Italy), technology is sensitive to real wages but they are not appreciably influenced by the current level of unemployment. Finally, if the additional effect on demand is taken into account ..., a decrease in real wages may have recessionary effects on the output and total working time. All these observations lead to discarding this mechanism as a way of dealing with technological unemployment. (Vivarelli, 1995: 163)

13. The evidence from Vivarelli (1995) covers the full range of possible compensation mechanisms. In addition to compensation via (reduced) prices and (increased) incomes, Vivarelli (1995) also discusses compensation via new machines, via new investments and - as observed in note 3 - via decreases in wages (ibid.: 27–38). However, his analysis indicates that the most important of these compensation mechanisms is the price compensation mechanism. As noted above, he finds that it is only 'partially' effective. He also finds, as discussed earlier, that the income mechanism is effective only under 'special'

circumstances and that the wage mechanism is not effective. Finally, he makes a further observation that 'the mechanism via reinvestment of extra-profits ... is statistically significant', but argues that 'these new investments may in turn be the means to introduce labour-saving technologies' (ibid.: 166–7).

14. This section is partly based on recent work by Edquist and Riddell (2000).

15. On this basis, it can be concluded that for a given product at an early stage of the product life cycle, process innovation can be employment generating – that is, it can have a positive net effect on employment.

16. In such cases, however, it is also worth noting that mechanisms other than cost reductions and increases in real income attributable to process innovation may also be at work. For example, product innovation is necessary in order for 'new sectors' to be created. And, as argued extensively at other points in this book, product innovation is also strongly associated with the expansion of existing sectors. It may even provide the main basis for such expansion. For these reasons, the 'long-term net compensation effect' that may be associated with process innovation cannot be reduced to process innovation alone.

17. See, for example, Edquist (1994b), Freeman and Soete (1994), Palmer, Edquist and Jacobsson (1984) and Vivarelli (1995). Of these, the last-mentioned source is especially comprehensive.

18. Data on the growth patterns for Sweden and the EU in comparison with the USA and Japan were presented under Hypothesis 13 above.

19. In this paragraph we have carefully made a distinction between economic growth (equivalent to increased production) and productivity growth. See also the Preface to this book.

20. In section 5.3 we will discuss the case of when a new product becomes a new process innovation in a later 'appearance'.

21. Defence material may play a similar role in this respect; it is 'destroyed' when used.

22. This dichotomy corresponds roughly to our basic distinction between process and product innovations. Kuznets reasoned that 'demand-creating' innovation, involving the creation of new products, would tend to create employment, while the 'cost-reducing' innovation, involving changes to production processes that would shift the existing cost curve downwards, would tend to have the opposite effect.

23. This study, however, apparently did not take a number of compensation mechanisms into account. A Swedish study that used 'Hunt's estimate' made the following disclaimer:

> No assumptions have been made about increases in employment because the use of robots leads to better products at lower cost so that more of those products can be sold at lower prices. Nor have other compensation effects been taken into account. (Palmer, Edquist and Jacobsson, 1984: 31)

24. It must be kept in mind, however, that product innovations in manufacturing are often transformed into process technologies in the service sector, for example, information technologies. See Chapter 4, section 4.2.

25. Consultancy services, for example, can be viewed as being founded on human capital, to the extent that they are based primarily on the commodification of specialist knowledge.

26. The appropriability problems associated with investment in human capital, like those associated with investment in research, have been argued to result in 'under-investment'. See the previous discussion under Hypothesis 6 in Chapter 3, section 3.2.

27. Two of these sectors refer to manufacturing industries. They are the 'extractive' and 'transformative' sectors. The remaining four sectors refer to services.

28. See the discussion in Chapter 2, section 2.3.

29. The most 'recession-proof' segment of the service sector proved to be the one oriented primarily to consumer markets. This was, namely, CSPS (community, social and personal services), in which 'employment continued to expand quite rapidly ... often driven by growth in health services'. The most severe employment effects of the recession occurred in 'the cyclically sensitive sectors of transport and wholesale and retail trade' (OECD, 1994b: 52).

30. The statistics mentioned here refer only to private-sector services and exclude government-provided services. On this point, see also the discussion under Hypothesis 2 in Chapter 3, section 3.1.
31. For elaboration, see the discussion under Hypothesis 15 in Chapter 4, section 4.2.
32. As initially stated, in Chapter 2, section 2.1, the discussion of product innovations in this book deals only with products produced for the market, and not those produced within households (or firms) for direct internal use. To the extent that the 'self-service society' thesis is concerned with such innovations, it might be considered inappropriate for discussion here. However, the thesis – and the debate surrounding it – also deals with consumer goods produced for the market (commodities) and their substitution effects, not only within households, but also in relation to consumer services produced for the market. Moreover, the theories and evidence discussed are relevant to service-sector employment.
33. On these points, for example, see Gadrey (1988).

PART III

Summary, Conclusions and Policy Implications

Part II of this book reviewed existing research literature in relation to the theoretical approach and conceptual framework outlined in Part I. In the course of this review, the initial conceptual framework was refined by considering how it could be operationalized in relation to various hypotheses and research questions. Doing so also contributed to the further development of our theoretical approach, through 'appreciative' theorizing and the formulation of hypotheses.

Part III of this book is concerned with drawing together and summarizing the ideas, evidence and arguments presented in earlier chapters. Chapter 6 is devoted to developing conclusions on this basis. Subsequently, Chapter 7 outlines policy implications that follow from these conclusions.

6. Summary and conclusions

This chapter provides a summary of the empirical evidence in relation to our research questions, conceptual framework and theoretical basis. Moreover, it draws conclusions about the relations between different kinds of innovations and the creation or destruction of jobs.

Section 6.1 relates the concepts and categories first presented in Chapter 2 to the specific arguments that were developed to interpret the empirical evidence reviewed in Part II (Chapters 3, 4 and 5). This section is primarily concerned with demonstrating the relevance and usefulness of our analytical framework. However, the discussion has an empirical basis as well, which is indicated by brief references to the supporting evidence discussed under various hypotheses in Part II.

The second section (6.2) is more concerned with the further development of 'appreciative' theorizing. Here, we consolidate and systematize some elements of our theoretical perspective on innovations and employment. This is done by linking together arguments that were developed in relation to specific concepts and particular hypotheses (or sets of hypotheses) in Part II. The result is a more general argument about the employment consequences of different kinds of innovations and their relation to different kinds of growth.

Section 6.3 applies this argument to the empirical evidence reviewed in Part II. Three general propositions are presented and discussed in relation to relevant research findings. In this way, we develop empirically grounded conclusions. We also raise questions for future research and discuss relevant methodological concerns. This final section draws together the main points made in the book as a whole and leads up to the consideration of policy implications, which are subsequently presented in Chapter 7.

6.1   JUSTIFICATION OF ANALYTICAL FRAMEWORK

In mainstream economic theory, the notion of innovation is often assumed, more or less explicitly, to be limited to process innovations. It has been shown in the present work that the subject of innovation is extremely complex and heterogeneous. It is therefore useful to make analytical distinctions between different categories of innovations in order to analyse the effects on employment.

The initial analytical distinction proposed here is that between product and process innovations. More detailed distinctions have also been made between technological and organizational process innovations and between innovations in goods products and service products. There are several reasons for making these distinctions, and seven of the arguments follow.

1. The patterns of diffusion of technological product and process innovations are very different. For example, Chapter 4, section 4.1 showed that, historically, Swedish industry has been very good at diffusion of process innovations and bad at diffusion of product innovations, while the pattern has been the reverse for the USA. Japan has been good at both product and process diffusion (Edquist, 1989; Edquist and Jacobsson, 1988).

2. The determinants that can explain these differing patterns of diffusion are also radically different between the two categories of technological process and product innovations.[1] Determinants of the diffusion of process innovation include factors such as industry structure, relative factor prices, regional wage differentials, rate of unemployment and union attitudes. Determinants of product innovation include factors such as the propensity of firms to stay locked into 'core business' activities and differences in state policies (subsidies to old sectors versus incentives to diversification into new ones) and currency depreciations.

3. The types of innovations involved differ. Process innovations may be technological as well as organizational.[2] Product innovations may be goods or services.[3]

4. The consequences for employment differ sharply between product and process innovations. On the whole, product innovation creates employment and process innovation destroys employment – although there are counteracting forces in both cases. (We have pointed out, for example, that some process innovations can also be commodified and sold as product innovations, so that they have two 'appearances' in the economic system.) Counteracting forces will be discussed in more detail in section 6.2.

5. Technological process innovation, as pointed out in Chapter 3, section 3.1 and emphasized in Chapter 3, section 3.3, normally has the effect of reducing employment.[4] In Chapter 5, section 5.1, this was shown to be the normal direct effect, as well as the normal net effect, of process innovation. In contrast, product innovation (as shown in Chapter 4) is associated with job creation – even after counteracting forces are taken into account (as discussed in Chapter 5, sections 5.2, 5.3 and 5.4).[5]

The introductory section of Chapter 4 referred to the argument that 'in determining the effect of product innovation on the level of employment, the primary factor involved is the "welfare effect" implying generation of employment' (Katsoulacos, 1984). By 'welfare effect' is meant job creation and increased income resulting from (product) innovations. This can be counterposed to the 'displacement effect', by which is meant job losses induced by (process) innovations. Chapter 4 discussed a range of evidence supporting this argument.[6]

In addition to discussing compensation effects related to process innovation (in section 5.1), Chapter 5 took up the theme of conversion from product to process innovation (the 'second appearance'). Section 5.3 explicitly discussed the relations between process and product innovations. The discussion there identified 'investment products' as the only class of products that can play a double role in the economy as both process and product innovations. It indicated that their net employment effects – that is, their combined effects as products as well as processes – are generally negative, in contrast to other kinds of product innovations, that is, in intermediate and consumer products.

Whether or not product innovations become process innovations obviously has an effect on the balance between employment creation and destruction. We have argued that the negative employment effects of the conversion of product innovations into process innovations are likely to be more pronounced in manufacturing than in services. This is because service products are seldom transformed into process innovations. We have also shown that new services are more likely to complement than to compete with new goods, resulting in positive effects on employment.[7]

6. The consequences for productivity of the various kinds of innovations are different and work through different mechanisms. Chapter 3, section 3.1 demonstrated that process innovations tend to enhance productivity by reducing labour inputs, although section 3.2 pointed to some kinds of organizational process innovations as exceptions.[8] Chapter 4, section 4.1 demonstrated that the increased productivity growth associated with new products (particularly, new goods) has to do with changes in the numerator of the ratio between production and labour input represented by labour productivity.[9] In this sense, the productivity increase (associated with new goods) does not mean an increase in physical output but is rather an increase in productivity 'as measured'.[10]

7. An analytical distinction between product and process innovation is necessary to make it possible to study the relations between the two.[11] Our discussion has criticized the tendency of mainstream economic theory to assume that all innovations are forms of process innovation, on the grounds that this ignores product innovations as the main mechanism behind changes in the production structure and that the two kinds of innovation have contrary consequences for employment.

In addition to the product/process distinction, other variables were initially introduced. They were either related to the type of market concerned or to the intensity of search activities. To analyse the type of market, the categories of consumer, investment or intermediate product were used. These categories were important in relation to whether a new product could be sold and then later used as a process innovation. To analyse the intensity of search activities, the level of R&D intensity was used for manufacturing sectors. Subsequently applying these categories to service sectors required either reasoning about how services could be classified or about how to identify appropriate indicators for the intensity of search activities. As a counterpart to R&D intensity in manufacturing sectors, the proportion of highly educated personnel in the firm was proposed as a parallel measure within services. The categories of 'R&D-intensive' manufacturing sectors and 'knowledge-intensive' service sectors were considered to be particularly important for changes in the production structure and thereby for economic growth and employment.

All in all, the continuing elaboration of the conceptual framework has been quite an interesting and useful exercise in that it allows for a more nuanced analysis of the dynamics of sectors. In this respect, our taxonomies of innovation also enable us to grasp the patterns of change in different sectors. This helps us understand the trajectories, or patterns of growth, followed by different national economies, because national economies exhibit specialization in certain manufacturing and service sectors.

6.2   DIFFERENT KINDS OF GROWTH

The remainder of this chapter is devoted to the employment consequences of process and product innovations respectively. This section begins the discussion of employment consequences by first considering different kinds of growth – specifically productivity growth and economic growth – and their relative impacts on employment.

Politicians and mainstream economists often argue that 'more rapid growth' would solve or mitigate the unemployment problem. However, the relation between 'growth' and 'employment' is by no means simple and mechanical. Some kinds of growth create jobs, other kinds destroy jobs, and there is the phenomenon of 'jobless growth'. Economic growth does not automatically or always lead to employment growth, and productivity growth normally leads to fewer jobs if induced by process innovation. Therefore a general policy of growth will not necessarily create more jobs. Moreover, specializations at the firm, industry and national levels will influence future ability either to continue along, or to shift between, labour-saving and employment-generating growth trajectories. On the basis of arguments presented in this book, this section will try to outline a more detailed and differentiated understanding of the relations between 'growth' and 'employment' with reference to innovations. So, the main question here is: which kinds of 'growth' lead to more employment and which do not?

There are many problems associated with measuring productivity growth.[12] Analytically it is important to distinguish between quality changes in products, which are associated with productivity growth (as it is measured), and increased output in physical terms of the same products, which is associated with economic growth. The importance of these differences has led us to try to further clarify and distinguish productivity and economic growth and their relationships to employment, as summarized in the following points.

First, labour productivity is the ratio between production value (value added) and amount of employment. Productivity growth, which is associated with more of the same kind of output and produced by the same amount of input, leads to a reduction in the number of jobs (per unit of output).

Thus if output (value added) is constant, this kind of productivity growth means that the denominator (amount of employment) in this ratio decreases. The most important sources of this kind of productivity growth are techno-logical or organizational process innovations.[13] While compensation mechanisms can mitigate job losses, they can promote net employment gains only when growth in production (that is, demand) outstrips productivity growth.

If the general level of demand is kept constant and if the price elasticity of demand for the product is below unity, jobs (in the world economy as a whole, that is, in a closed economy) will probably be lost in the sector of production where the process innovation occurred. If the elasticity is above unity, the number of jobs will probably increase in that sector (in the world economy as a whole) in spite of the process innovation. The price elasticity is, however, normally below unity.[14]

Thus, on the whole, labour productivity growth associated with process innovations is labour saving, even in a net sense, that is, after the operation of compensation mechanisms. If there is an exogenous increase in demand for the product, jobs are of course created.[15] However, this is not the result of productivity growth but of increased output. Output and the number of jobs are increasing, but the number of jobs per unit of output is not increasing.[16]

Second, productivity growth associated with new kinds of output leads to job creation. This is the case of product innovation. Productivity growth of this kind reflects the quality improvements of output as well as the monopolism often associated with new products. It influences the numerator in the ratio between production value (value added) and amount of employment (that is, labour productivity), resulting in a higher price paid for the new products.[17]

The denominator (employment), however, is not directly influenced by productivity growth associated with product innovations. In other words, the amount of labour needed per unit of output does not decrease; labour is not saved through product innovation.

Instead, the production of new products influences production value (value added). Product innovations often lead to the establishment of new units of production, which means new investments and change in the production structure, and often more jobs as well as higher productivity.[18] New products that satisfy completely new kinds of demand or serve new functions contribute most to increased employment. This statement holds whether the product is new to the world, or new to a country, region or company, that is, if the production of a product diffuses. Thus the 'immediate' effect of a product innovation is to increase employment.

However, employment generation caused by product innovation can be counteracted through: (a) substitution between old and new products, and (b) new products becoming process innovations in a later 'appearance'.[19]

(a) If the new product functionally replaces an old one, either increased or reduced employment may result. The net employment effect depends on whether demand for satisfying the function changes when the new product replaces the old one, and whether there are changes in the labour intensity of the process used for producing the new product.[20]

(b) Some new products are transformed into process innovations in a second 'appearance'. These products generally lead to a net reduction in the number of jobs in the economy as a whole.[21] However, only investment products can play this double role over time. Therefore, the net employment-generating effects of consumer products and intermediate products tend to be larger than those of investment products.

Because the proportion of investment products is smaller in services than in goods, the production of services destroys jobs to a lesser extent than goods production as a result of this 'second appearance' mechanism. Product innovation in services is, in this respect, more employment generating than product innovation in goods production.[22]

Thus productivity growth associated with product innovations is not, on the whole, labour saving. On the contrary, new jobs are created, mostly through the development, production and use of new products that satisfy new needs and wants. Moreover, the demand for new products often grows more rapidly than for old products. This implies an increase in (production and) employment in some industrial sectors as well as in (some) service sectors.[23]

On average, technological process innovations seem to increase labour productivity faster in goods production than in service production. Therefore process-related job destruction seems to be larger in manufacturing than in services. In both cases, however, the variation between subsectors is large. A net increase in employment can be expected in some industrial sectors and in some service sectors (due to product innovation).[24]

The implications of these arguments are that the firms, regions and countries producing new products do so for markets that are often growing rapidly. Growing markets mean an increase in output (demand) which reinforces the intrinsic employment-creation effect of product innovations. Again, this effect is not primarily associated with productivity growth, but with economic growth.[25] Both manufacturing and service sectors can be roughly divided into those that are more R&D (knowledge) intensive and product oriented and those that concentrate less on R&D and are more process oriented.

In summary, firms, industries and national economies that specialize in sectors engaged heavily in product innovations generally create more employment than those that specialize in process innovations. The overall extent of employment creation or destruction depends on factors such as changes in market growth and in demand (price elasticity) as well as dynamic effects within the economic system. Product innovations that neither substitute for an existing product nor are later used as process innovations have the greatest positive effect on employment creation.

The overall conclusion from this summary is that it is useful and important – in an analysis of the relations between innovations and employment – to make a distinction between productivity growth and economic growth and to analyse whether these different kinds of growth emanate from process or product innovations. This goes far beyond statements such as 'a more rapid growth will solve or mitigate the employment problem'.

The distinctions proposed open up the possibility of pursuing a more elaborated analysis of the relations between growth, innovations and employment. With these distinctions it is possible to take the character of growth, its sources and its content into account. Economic growth does not automatically or always lead to employment growth! Therefore a general growth policy does not necessarily lead to employment growth.[26]

In spite of the effort here to make analytical distinctions between (productivity and economic) growth based on process and product innovations, it must be borne in mind that they are closely intertwined and that both of them occur all over the economy, that is, in all economic sectors. However, the extent to and frequency with which they occur varies significantly between sectors. In some economic sectors, product innovations dominate; others are dominated by process innovations. This means that the 'employment intensity of growth' varies between sectors. This intensity of growth is closely related to the balance between product and process innovations.[27]

The implication is that it is crucial for the employment situation in an economy whether its growth trajectory goes in the direction of sectors dominated by process innovations or by product innovations. If a time period, country, firm or region is characterized by process innovations, this constitutes a tendency to reduce employment, particularly in a closed economy. If product innovations dominate, there is an opposite tendency to generate employment.[28]

6.3   SOME GENERAL PROPOSITIONS

To formulate some conclusions, the main arguments and observations about the relationships between different types of innovations and employment can now be summarized in the form of three general propositions.

Proposition 1   The balance between product and process innovation differs sharply within manufacturing (that is, between industrial sectors) and also between different service sectors. Those sectors that generate most product innovations are the R&D-intensive sectors in manufacturing and the knowledge-intensive sectors in services.

In our discussion of technological process innovations we distinguished between 'technological trajectories' or 'growth patterns' that are labour saving and those that are employment generating.[29] We argued that national growth patterns with a relatively low employment intensity reflect the predominance of industrial sectors characterized by a labour-saving technological trajectory in which there is a primary concentration on process, rather than product, innovations. We presented evidence for this argument that referred primarily to manufacturing industries.[30] We also discussed related evidence (concerning the relationships between product innovation and rapid market growth) which dealt with service industries.[31] Our conclusion was that there is a similar, though less clear-cut, pattern in services.

The empirical research reviewed thus suggests that, in broad terms, there is a greater emphasis on the development of new products in more R&D-intensive industries and more emphasis on process improvements in less R&D-intensive industries.[32] In the R&D-intensive industries, the main focus, then, is on product innovation. The less R&D-intensive industries tend to concentrate on process innovation, largely through the acquisition of investment products. Within the manufacturing sector, the evidence is fairly straightforward. Here, a clear division has emerged between the 'high-tech' (R&D-intensive) industries, in which product innovation is predominant, and 'traditional' manufacturing industries, which concentrate on process innovation.

In the case of service industries, it is somewhat more difficult to make this kind of distinction. One of the main reasons for this difficulty is that it is much harder to identify service industries with a high level of R&D intensity, since formal R&D is less important for the development of new service products, and conventional measures of R&D intensity are less applicable to industries in the service sector.[33]

It is also more difficult to distinguish clearly between product and process innovation in the service industries. For this reason, one authority has argued for the specification of a third, hybrid category of 'delivery innovations', described as innovations in the delivery system (hence, partly process innovations) that lead to the creation of new markets (hence, partly product innovations) (Miles et al., 1995).[34] However, others have considered that the proposed category of 'delivery innovations' can be subsumed under that of 'process innovations'. On the basis of trial survey results, one pair of authors has argued that 'the distinction between product (service) and process innovations (including delivery innovations), even if less clear-cut compared to the manufacturing sector, is still useful in identifying different firms' innovative objectives and strategies' (Evangelista and Sirilli, 1995). We have adopted a similar position.[35]

Our approach (given these problems) has been to treat the introduction of new process technologies in service industries as an indicator of both process innovation and (possibly) product innovation. An extended explanation of the theoretical rationale for this approach, its implications and practical limitations, has been given.[36] We have also pointed to segments of the service sector where there appears to have been extensive product innovation which has not relied primarily on technological process innovations.[37] This second type of product innovation in services therefore implies a primary emphasis on investment in human capital, rather than capital equipment investment products. It may also be capital saving and have a neutral effect on employment.[38]

Our approach is consistent with the distinction that has been made between 'dynamic' and 'traditional' services.[39] In connection with this distinction, it has been shown that in traditional services there is a primary focus on incremental product innovation (product quality) based on improvements to human capital. In contrast, dynamic services show a stronger emphasis on the development of new products based on 'enhancements to all the factors of production' (Baldwin, 1995). Our approach also allows for the identification of service sectors in which there has been a more exclusive concentration on process innovation without a complementary emphasis on product innovation. This would appear to be the case, for example, in high-productivity service industries that are strong consumers of new process technologies, and which have expanding markets, but stable or declining levels of employment.[40]

Proposition 2　For the reasons stated in Proposition 1, the employment effects of innovation also differ between sectors. These effects may be counteracted, however, if the sectors in question are primarily producing investment products. Intermediate and consumer products – the bulk of what is produced in services, especially – have the least potential for the reduction of employment through substitution.

Our point of departure for the discussion under Proposition 1 was the distinction between labour-saving and employment-generating technological trajectories or growth patterns and the identification of sectors in which one or the other type of trajectory or growth pattern is evident. We argued, and reviewed supporting evidence, that in both manufacturing and services, sectors in which there is a strong primary emphasis on process innovation tend to be characterized by labour-saving growth patterns or technological trajectories, while the opposite is true of those sectors which have high levels of product innovation.

In manufacturing throughout the OECD countries, there has been a growing divergence between industries with high levels of product innovation and those concentrating on process innovation. The former industries are clearly the 'growth industries', and have experienced net gains in employment, while the latter tend to be 'declining' industries with net employment losses (Pianta, Evangelista and Perani, 1996). We have presented direct empirical evidence on this point.[41] We have also discussed related empirical evidence.[42] In addition, we have presented analytical arguments,[43] and, have supported these with basic theoretical arguments.[44] Thereby we have provided multiple forms of support for the proposition that there is a strong positive association between product innovation and employment growth.

Taken together, this body of argument and evidence provides the basis for a more complete explanation of the observation that the labour-saving effects of technological process innovations tend to vary widely between industrial sectors within both the goods-producing and services-producing sectors.[45] The compensation effects connected with productivity-enhancing process innovations are not normally large enough to make the net employment effect of process innovation positive, rather than negative.[46] Therefore the explanation of variation in the employment effects of process innovation must also take into consideration the positive effects of product innovation.[47]

In the service sector there is a similar pattern, although it is much less clear cut. For manufacturing, we have shown that product innovation is positively associated with R&D intensity and that there is a similar relationship between employment growth and product innovation.[48] For services, we have argued that 'formal R&D' is less important to product innovation and we have proposed alternative (proxy) measures of 'R&D intensity'. Specifically, we have proposed an alternative measure of 'knowledge intensity' as indicated by the educational level of the labour force.[49] Even on that basis, it has remained more difficult to establish clear linkages between knowledge intensity, product innovation and employment growth for the service sector.

Against this background, we have observed that both a 'knowledge-intensive' segment (FIRB) and a relatively less 'knowledge-intensive' (or more accurately, a more 'mixed') segment (CSPS) have acted as the main engines of employment growth in services (OECD, 1996b: 73). However, it must also be recognized that one of the most 'knowledge-intensive' industries within CSPS – that is, health care – has been the main driver of employment growth in this segment (OECD, 1994b: 52). Therefore, if 'knowledge intensity' is correlated with a higher capacity for, and performance of, product innovation, it is possible to discern in the services a pattern somewhat similar to that observed for manufacturing.[50] Nevertheless, the differences between service industries are less easily identified than in manufacturing.

Our proposed proxy of a high proportion of highly educated people as a measure of 'knowledge intensity' in services may require further specification in terms of how these 'human resources' are actually employed.[51] Conceivably, they could be employed in forms of technological process innovation whose overall effects on employment are negative. Some examples of this type of trajectory in service industries with relatively high 'knowledge intensity' have been discussed.[52] In other instances, a dual focus on process and product innovation might have mixed employment effects, as appears to have been the case in the FIRB segment of the service sector. On this point, we have discussed developments in the FIRB sector of services.[53]

Particularly interesting, in this connection, however, is the case of the CSPS sector in services, which has been a leading source of job creation throughout the OECD, both within services and within the whole economy (that is, all sectors). As we have pointed out, the primary focus of innovation in CSPS has been on the development of new products.[54] Moreover, these products are of a particular nature. They are primarily, if not exclusively, consumer products – which, as we have argued, have the greatest potential for the generation of employment, especially where there is little or no substitution for other goods or services. As we have demonstrated, many of these service products have also been developed to complement goods innovations that originally threatened to replace them.[55] For these reasons, the 'final demand' character of product innovations should also be taken into account in analyses of their employment effects.

Proposition 3 It is too blunt to argue that, since employment is decreasing in industry and increasing in services, it is only the 'service sector' that will be able to save the world from massive unemployment. R&D-intensive or knowledge-intensive sectors in both manufacturing and services will have positive effects on employment, particularly where there is dynamic interaction between new goods and new services.

The discussion under Propositions 1 and 2 (and under previous, related hypotheses) has indicated that certain service sectors and certain manufacturing sectors will be of far greater strategic importance to job creation than others. It has also shown that these industries – namely, the knowledge-intensive and R&D-intensive ones – share a number of important characteristics and have become increasingly interlinked, particularly across the boundary between goods-producing and services-producing sectors.

Our work is thus consistent with, and may also provide some explanation of, the finding in other research that 'knowledge-intensive industries', in both manufacturing and services, have dramatically higher rates of employment growth and have made a disproportionately large contribution to total employment growth (Department of Finance, 1992; OECD, 1994b). Our findings also point to the importance for employment growth of interaction between R&D-intensive goods- and knowledge-intensive services-producing sectors.

The sectors most important for the creation of employment, we have argued, are those engaged in the creation of new products and new markets. This has been demonstrated empirically with regard to manufacturing sectors.[56] With respect to the service sectors, we have shown, with reference to empirical evidence, that the most innovative and rapidly growing are those where there is a close correlation between new goods and new services – or, in other words, a close linkage between manufacturing and services.[57] Since service sectors, generally, will continue to be the main source of employment growth in OECD countries, it will be appropriate to dwell briefly on the importance of the interaction between new goods and new services for the development of new employment within the service sector.

Earlier, we discussed the especially positive effects on employment of new consumer products in both goods and services.[58] We focused this discussion on the growth of employment in the CSPS sector of services, which has been a main source of new employment in services throughout the OECD. In this context, we discussed the extent to which employment growth in CSPS has depended on the development of new service products – and, in turn, the extent to which this kind of innovation has grown out of the complex interaction between consumer goods and consumer services.

In another part of our discussion, we referred to the development of new service products based on the acquisition of new process technologies from IT industries in the capital goods sector.[59] The service sectors referred to in these discussions fall within the FIRB sector of services, which has been recognized as the second main source of service-sector employment growth in the OECD. In the discussion under Proposition 2 (and in previous related hypotheses), we have argued that much of the growth of employment in FIRB can be attributed to the employment-generating effects of this type of product innovation. Such product innovation counteracts the normally employment-reducing effects of extensive process innovation. We have, in addition, emphasized that the type of product innovation under discussion would not have been possible without the process innovations on which it has been based.

We have also referred to the development of mobile communications as a specific example of the 'virtuous' interaction between new consumer goods and new consumer services.[60] In particular, we have pointed to the incredibly rapid growth of the mobile communications industry. Here we will comment briefly on its implications for the growth of employment in services.

The development of communication infrastructures has been identified as one of the most strategically important bases for job creation in several OECD countries – notably, the USA and Japan (Imai, 1996). For example, Japanese authorities have estimated that 2.43 million jobs can be created in network-based service employment in the multi-media market by 2010 (Ministry of Posts and Telecommunications, 1994). Similarly, estimates in France have projected an increase in this type of employment of between 2.5 and 5 times the 1993 level (Breton, 1994). In addition to its potential for explosive growth, this indicates that the growth in communications service employment will be closely tied to growth in the infrastructure of telecommunications goods. Currently, the dynamic role of mobile telecommunications equipment production, as well as of services production in a restricted sense, is in the process of being taken over by fixed and mobile Internet communication (including voice communication).

As this example suggests, it is necessary to develop a more discriminating analysis of innovation–employment dynamics in particular sectors than available data now permit. In some manufacturing sectors employment increases rapidly. In some service sectors, employment is decreasing. For empirical research and analysis to be fruitful, manufacturing as well as service production will have to be disaggregated.[61]

To summarize, the discussion in this chapter has reviewed a conceptual framework for the type of disaggregated empirical analysis recommended above. Such a disaggregated analysis is also a necessary basis for specific conclusions with regard to innovation and employment policy. Although we have not actually conducted a detailed analysis of this kind, we have generated hypotheses based on both empirical evidence and conceptual/analytical thinking. We will proceed to consider policy implications in the final chapter (7) of this book.

NOTES

1. These differences are indicated under Hypothesis 8 in Chapter 4, section 4.1.
2. This was discussed in Chapter 2, section 2.2 and demonstrated in Chapter 3, sections 3.1 and 3.2. (See under Hypotheses 1 to 6.)
3. This was discussed in Chapter 2, section 2.1 and demonstrated in Chapter 4, sections 4.1 and 4.2. (See, specifically, under Hypotheses 7 to 19.)
4. The empirical basis for these claims was reviewed under Hypotheses 1 to 4.
5. Accordingly, 'If we abstract from product innovation, we abstract from the most important of factors counteracting stagnation and unemployment' (Lundvall, 1985: 28).
6. See under Hypotheses 7 to 19.
7. These points were made in Chapter 5, sections 5.3 and 5.4.
8. See Hypothesis 5.
9. On this point, see Hypothesis 11.
10. On this point, see Hypothesis 12.
11. This argument was introduced in Chapter 2.
12. See Chapter 4, section 4.1 and Chapter 5, section 5.1.
13. See Chapter 3, sections 3.1 and 3.2, and Chapter 5, section 5.1.
14. See Chapter 5, section 5.1.
15. The case of increases in exogenous demand points to the crucial importance of coordination between innovation policies and macroeconomic policies, including fiscal, monetary and exchange rate policies. Macroeconomic stability is important for innovation processes and for investment more generally – and therefore for economic growth and employment creation. However, it seems extremely difficult to solve problems of low growth and high unemployment through innovation policy if macroeconomic policies are excessively strict.
16. See Chapter 3, section 3.3 and Chapter 5, section 5.1.
17. This kind of productivity growth (as measured) is not 'real' (in physical terms), but it matters to the welfare of the members of the unit producing the innovation. It increases their welfare since they appropriate a larger share of global output. See Chapter 4, section 4.1.
18. See Chapter 4, sections 4.1 and 4.3, and Chapter 5, section 5.2.
19. See Chapter 5, sections 5.2 and 5.3.
20. See Chapter 5, section 5.2.
21. See Chapter 5, section 5.3.
22. See Chapter 5, section 5.3.
23. See Chapter 4, sections 4.1 and 4.2.
24. See Chapter 4, section 4.3 and Chapter 5, section 5.2.
25. See Chapter 4, section 4.1 and Chapter 5, section 5.1.
26. See under Propositions 1 to 3 in the following section, 6.3.
27. It would be of great value to estimate these intensities in various economic sectors.
28. See under Propositions 1 and 2 in the following section, 6.3.
29. See Chapter 3, section 3.3 and Chapter 5, section 5.1.
30. See under Hypotheses 9, 10 and 13.
31. See under Hypotheses 16 to 19.
32. See, in particular, the discussion under Hypotheses 7 and 15.
33. On this point, see the discussion under Hypothesis 14.
34. A recent 'delivery innovation' that will probably be of great importance is electronic trade.
35. See the discussion in Chapter 2, sections 2.1 and 2.2 and under Hypothesis 15.
36. See the discussion under Hypothesis 16.
37. See, in particular, the discussion in Chapter 5, section 5.4 of household or consumer services.
38. On these points, see the discussions under Hypothesis 15 and in Chapter 5, section 5.3, as well as related discussions under Hypotheses 5 and 6.
39. This was referred to in the discussion under Hypothesis 15.
40. Examples of such industries were discussed under Hypothesis 4.
41. See the discussions under Hypotheses 10 and 13.
42. See the discussions under Hypotheses 7 to 9.

43. See the discussions under Hypotheses 11 and 12.
44. See the introduction to Chapter 4.
45. See the discussion under Hypotheses 1 and 2.
46. This was argued in Chapter 5, section 5.1.
47. See Chapter 3, section 3.3 and the introduction to Chapter 4.
48. See the discussions under Hypotheses 7 and 13, respectively.
49. See the discussions under Hypotheses 15 and 14, respectively.
50. See the discussion under Hypotheses 7 to 10, 14 and 15.
51. See our discussion of Hypothesis 14.
52. See under Hypothesis 4.
53. See under Hypotheses 4, 16, 17 and 19.
54. See Chapter 5, section 5.4.
55. See Chapter 5, section 5.3.
56. See the discussion under Hypotheses 7 to 13.
57. See the discussion under Hypotheses 16 to 19, and in Chapter 5, section 5.4.
58. See Chapter 5, section 5.3.
59. See the discussion under Hypotheses 16, 17 and 19.
60. See the discussion under Hypothesis 18.
61. It is not very useful to work at the levels of 'industry' and 'services'. Disaggregation has, of course, already been done much more frequently for industrial sectors than for service sectors – because of the sharp differences with regard to the availability of statistical data at disaggregated levels. The challenge is to do it also for services – which constitutes 70–80 per cent of production in advanced economies.

7. Implications for public policy and firm strategy

In this chapter we develop implications for public policies and also for the strategies of firms, based on the theoretical perspective, arguments and empirical evidence presented in earlier chapters of this book. The idea of innovation policy is introduced in section 7.1. Section 7.2 goes on to consider the reasons for public policy intervention. Subsequently, sections 7.3 and 7.4 discuss, respectively, the need for selectivity in innovation policy and both general and specific policy implications of the systems of innovation approach. A specific focus on innovation policy for employment creation is developed in section 7.5. Section 7.6 presents some of the main policy alternatives or options that have been suggested by theoretical and empirical work on the economics of innovation. Finally, section 7.7 deals briefly with implications for the management of innovation in firms.

7.1 INTRODUCTION

Both governments and firms are important actors that can at times influence the direction and rate of future innovations. The systems of innovation (SI) approach emphasizes that the creation and diffusion of new knowledge of economic value, that is, innovations, is a process which involves more than individual firms or other organizations. This implies that government can have a role in stimulating change beyond creating the institutions that allow the market to function. At the same time, the SI approach assumes that firms are the main actors that develop and implement innovations. Accordingly, this chapter addresses both public policy and, to a lesser extent, the strategies of firms.

Innovation policy is public action that influences technical change and other kinds of innovations. It includes elements of research and development (R&D) policy, technology policy, infrastructure policy, regional policy and education policy. At the same time, innovation policy is a part of what is often called industrial policy. Industrial policy is, however, a term that is burdened with a lot of dead wood in many countries because of vain efforts to provide public support for old and dying industries. The term 'innovation policy' is naturally associated with change, flexibility, dynamism and the future. Innovation policy should serve as midwife; not provide support towards the end of life.

Conceptualizing SI as systems in which interactions between organizations are crucial and in which institutions 'matter' has important implications for the development of firm strategies and public policies (McKelvey, 1997). From this perspective, government policy might be a question of supporting inter-actions in a system if these interactions do not function well spontaneously. This may enable economic actors to perceive existing technical and economic opportunities or create new ones. Directly or indirectly, government policy may help stimulate firms to act and plan on innovation opportunities. Certain characteristics of the firm and/or the sector will also influence this process, such as type of knowledge specialization, rate of innovation, changes in market demand and so forth. The definition of innovation policy thus goes beyond the traditional orientation of R&D policy, which mainly stimulates basic science as a public good.

The main reason for discussing innovation policy in broader terms is that the creation and diffusion of knowledge of economic value is a complex process where many different aspects are important. Perceived innovation opportunities may be tried and found to be dead-ends or avenues for successful development. The perception of innovation opportunities and the creation of new ones are activities carried out by individual firms, in relationships with other firm and non-firm organizations. Firms act, and react, to changes in markets, knowledge, technology and so forth. Governments may be able to take actions that influence the creation and diffusion of knowledge and thereby the production structure in the economy. This might include stimulating interactions among firms and promoting the development of various kinds of new knowledge, ranging from basic research without imme-diate commercial applications to inventions that are of direct economic value.

7.2 REASONS FOR PUBLIC POLICY INTERVENTION[1]

First, we want to point out that the market mechanism and capitalist firms best fulfil most economic functions in a modern society.[2] Usually, markets coordinate the behaviour and resources of private and public actors in a smooth and flexible manner. This concerns production of most goods and also a large proportion of service production. It is also true for many innovations, particularly incremental ones. Most of them occur spontaneously, through the actions of firms and in collaboration projects between firms. This is, however, less true for radical innovations, especially in the early stages of the development of new fields of technology.

Sometimes there are reasons to complement – or correct – markets and firm behaviour through public intervention. This is true in the areas of law, education, environment, infrastructure, social security, income distribution, research, radical innovations and the like. In some of these fields there is no market mechanism at all and the functions are fulfilled through other mechanisms, for example, regulation. In others, the market mechanism has for decades been complemented by public intervention in most industrial countries.

What, then, are the reasons for public policy intervention in a market economy? Regarding technical change and other kinds of innovations, two conditions must be met to justify public intervention in a market economy:

1. The market mechanism and private actors must fail to achieve the objectives formulated. A *problem* must exist (see below).
2. The state (national, regional and local government) and its public agencies must also have the *ability* to solve or mitigate the problem.

Let us discuss these two conditions in more depth.

First a 'problem' occurs when market forces and private actors do not automatically realize certain objectives.[3] Such problems can be identified through analysis (see section 7.4.2). Without them, there are no reasons for public intervention. This is in keeping with the principle that innovation policy should complement the market, not replace or duplicate it.

We use the term 'problem' and not 'market failure' because our approach differs from that of traditional economics. 'Market failure' in traditional economic theory implies a comparison between conditions in the real world (empirical facts) and an ideal or optimal system. However, innovation processes have evolutionary characteristics. The system never achieves equilibrium and the notion of optimality is irrelevant. Hence comparisons between an existing system and an ideal or optimal system are not possible. Thereby the notion of 'market failure' loses its meaning and applicability.

Since it is not meaningful to use the market failure approach in innovation policy design (Edquist, 1994b: sections 3.1 and 5), it is necessary to reduce the degree of formality and rigour normally expected when formulating economic policy. Therefore, when we speak of a 'problem' we do so on an empirical basis and in a pragmatic way, not referring to a formal model. This approach is more useful, since there is no alternative to a pragmatic basis for innovation policy design (Edquist, 1993b: 28).

Second, if the public sector does not have the ability to solve or mitigate a problem, there should be no intervention, since the result would be a failure. We spoke above about 'considering' intervention if a problem exists. This condition is an attempt to ensure that political failures are avoided to the largest extent possible. Adding this condition means that the existence of a 'problem', which is not automatically solved by market forces and private actors, is a necessary but not sufficient condition for intervention.[4]

Of course, it is not possible to determine beforehand – *ex ante* – whether or not public intervention can solve the problem.[5] The decision to intervene or not must thus be based upon whether it is likely or not that intervention can mitigate the problem. However, this likelihood is often difficult to calculate. Hence decisions must frequently be taken in a situation of uncertainty.[6] One can afterwards – *ex post* – determine through evaluations whether the problem was solved or mitigated. If this did not occur, we can speak of a political failure – something which can never be completely avoided in innovation policy because of the uncertainty involved. Such failures must, however, be exceptions and not the rule. In order to determine the success or failure of a given policy intervention through an evaluation, the objectives of the policy must have been clearly formulated – *ex ante*.

There may be two reasons why public intervention cannot solve or mitigate a problem. It might not be at all possible to solve the problem at a political level. Or the state might first need to develop its ability to solve the problem. A detailed analysis of the problems and their causes may, for example, be a necessary means of acquiring this ability.[7] The creation of new organizations and institutions to carry out the intervention might also be necessary; that is, new policy instruments might need to be created.[8]

There are two main categories of policies to solve or mitigate 'problems':

(a) The state may use *non-market mechanisms*. This is mainly a matter of using regulation instead of relying on the mechanisms of supply and demand. The kinds of regulation particularly related to innovation activities include the creation of technical standards, public subsidies to firm R&D, and tax incentives to R&D or innovation activities.

(b) Various public actions can improve the functioning of markets, or the state may create markets. The *improvement of markets* and how well they function is the objective of competition law and competition (antitrust or deregulation) policies.[9] One example of *market creation* in the area of inventions is the creation of intellectual property rights through the institution of a patent law that facilitates the selling and buying of technical knowledge.[10] Public policy supporting legal security or the formation of trust can also enhance the creation of markets. Another example is public technology procurement – to be discussed below.

In both cases (a) and (b), public policy is very much a matter of formulating the 'rules of the game' – that is, institutions. These rules might have nothing to do with markets (a) or they might be intended to create markets or make the functioning of markets more efficient (b).

Innovation policy can be proactive – and often should be! A 'problem-solving' policy might alternatively be called an 'opportunity-creating' policy.[11] One basic problem to be solved might be that uncertainty prevents new technologies from emerging. Hence public funding of basic R&D might be necessary because firms do not have the incentive to fund it. Training people and stimulating research in public organizations in certain fields could create new opportunities that would otherwise not be realized. We will revisit these kinds of innovation policies in section 7.4.1.[12]

The public creation of standards can also reduce uncertainty for firms. For example, the Nordic Mobile Telephony Standard (NMT 450) created by the Nordic PTTs in the 1970s and 1980s was absolutely crucial for the development of mobile telephony in the Nordic countries. NMT, a direct precursor of GSM, enabled firms such as Ericsson and Nokia to develop mobile systems – and later to assume global leadership in this field.[13]

A further example of policy leading to market creation is public technology procurement, that is, the public buying of technologies and systems that do not yet exist. Public technology procurement was used in combination with NMT 450 in Finland and Sweden to provoke Nokia and Ericsson to enter the new field of mobile telephony, which they were originally reluctant to do (Fridlund, 2000; Palmberg, 2000). Thus, as we discuss in section 7.4, public innovation policy might take the role of a 'midwife' in the emergence of new technology fields and whole production sectors.

7.3   SELECTIVITY IN INNOVATION POLICY

State intervention intended to improve the functioning of markets is often a matter of increasing the degree of competition – rather than increasing the rate of innovation.[14] This kind of policy can, in one sense, be argued to be 'general', since it tries to achieve the same thing everywhere. However, even this kind of competition policy has to be specific to certain sectors in certain countries or regions. The degree of competition has to be estimated, and if means to increase it are needed, they must be appropriately designed and implemented.

When markets are created by public action, the policy is also specific to certain functional areas, whether they concern inventions or the right to pollute. The creation of standards or specifications for public technology procurement is always technology or product specific.

Most public policy relies on non-market mechanisms and is selective in the sense that its consequences are not uniformly distributed among different activities. This follows from the first of the two conditions that constitute reasons for public intervention (see section 7.2): if a certain 'problem' is to be solved, it must be targeted in a selective manner.

This is, for example, true for devaluations. A devaluation of a country's currency (in a fixed exchange rate regime) means favouring export production and production exposed to competition from imports. Devaluations mean a preservation of the existing structure of production. They contribute to higher profits in established sectors while reducing the relative incentives to invest in new areas.

Public policy for basic research is also selective. Politicians and policy makers must, for example, allocate public research funds among fields of research. Someone must decide which fields of research shall be given priority. Should the funds be used for nuclear physics or biotechnology?[15] Regional policies are selective in a similar manner. Someone has to decide which regions to favour, why and how.

Hence it is not relevant to discuss whether or not innovation policy measures and instruments are selective in an absolute sense. It is only relevant to talk about degrees of selectivity. Public funding of basic research and direct support to specific companies can be seen as extremes in this respect.[16] Other innovation policy instruments are located in between them. To divide industry into two parts and favour one of them – for example, through devaluations – is, of course, less selective than providing direct support to specific firms.

It is natural that public policy – including innovation policy – is selective. Policy is a matter of governing, directly or through influencing the structure of incentives of other actors (and thereby their behaviour). To influence and govern is the *raison d'être* of politics and policy. The degree to which public policy meets its objectives is much more important than its degree of selectivity.

7.4 POLICY IMPLICATIONS OF THE SI APPROACH

The theoretical perspective that we use in this book, as explained in Chapter 1, is an SI approach. The SI approach has diffused rapidly in the academic world as well as in the realms of public innovation policy making and firm innovation strategy formulation.[17] This perspective encompasses all important factors influencing the development, diffusion and use of innovations as well as the relations among them. These factors can be studied in a national, regional or sectoral context; that is, national, regional and sectoral systems of innovation coexist and complement each other.

Generally, the SI approach synthesizes much of what we know today about innovation processes, their determinants and consequences.[18] It also resonates with the practical experience of policy makers and firm managers concerned with innovation. For example, the SI approach emphasizes that learning processes of various kinds, including formal education and R&D, are essential to innovation. As discussed later, in section 7.6, this emphasis is already present, though perhaps only implicitly, in most successful public policies and firm strategies for innovation.

7.4.1   Characteristics of the SI Approach and General Policy Implications

Chapter 1 provided a summary and overview of some general characteristics of the SI approach. These included an emphasis on the evolutionary character of innovation processes. From this standpoint an innovation system never achieves equilibrium and it is not possible to identify the potentially 'best' or 'optimal' technological trajectory to exploit. Similarly, we cannot specify an optimal or ideal system of innovation. As mentioned in section 7.2. above, this is different from the 'market failure approach', which implies a comparison between conditions in the real world and an ideal or optimal system. Since such comparisons are not possible in our approach, we have instead used the notion of 'problem', which was specified in section 7.2. In section 7.4.2, below, the notion of 'problem' will also be related to the idea of 'system failure'.

We can identify two main kinds of policy implications of the SI approach:

1. The SI approach contains *general* policy implications that can be derived from the characteristics of the approach. They are 'general' in the sense that they are of a 'signpost' character. In the rest of this section some further characteristics of the SI approach will be briefly mentioned and their general policy implications will be discussed.[19]
2. The SI approach provides a framework of analysis for identifying *specific* policy issues. It is helpful in identifying 'problems' that should be the object of policy and in specifying how innovation policies to solve or mitigate these problems could be designed. Such problem identification must be based upon comparisons between different existing systems – sectorally, geographically or historically defined. These issues will be addressed in section 7.4.2.

Organizations
As noted in Chapter 1, interaction and interdependence is one of the most fundamental characteristics of the SI approach. Innovations emerge in systems

where organizational actors and the relations among them are key elements. The importance of institutions and organizations is stressed in all versions of the SI approach (Edquist, 1997a; Edquist and Johnson, 1997).

The *organizations* with which innovating firms interact may often be other firms (suppliers, customers and competitors). Of particular importance are interfirm relations involving sustained interaction between users and producers of innovations. These are far more than arm's-length market relationships involving exchanges of only quantitative information about prices and volumes (see note 9). Firms may also interact with non-firm organizations such as universities, standard-setting agencies, research institutes, private foundations, financing organizations, schools, government agencies, policy organizations and so on.

A general policy implication is that such interaction should be targeted much more directly than is normally the case in innovation policy today.[20] Innovation policy should not only focus on the elements of systems, but also – and perhaps primarily – on the relations among them. For example, the long-term innovative performance of firms in science-based industries is strongly dependent upon the interactions of these firms with universities and research institutes. These interactions should be facilitated by means of policy – if they are not spontaneously functioning smoothly enough.

Organizations are consciously created formal structures with an explicit purpose. They are the players or actors in systems of innovation. Some organizations are created by public policy makers and can therefore serve as policy instruments; others are not. It is therefore important to study how firms and non-firm organizations interact with each other and how they perform in relation to innovations. In relation to this area of investigation, it should be emphasized that some of the key tasks of public policy are to create new organizations, to change some and to wipe out others.

Institutions

In Chapter 1 we stressed that from an SI perspective, institutions are the rules of the game; they shape the behaviour of firms and other organizations by constituting constraints and/or incentives for innovation (North, 1990). Some institutions are designed or created by public agencies, for example patent laws or (some) technical standards. They may serve as important innovation policy instruments. Others evolve spontaneously over extended periods of time, as do various kinds of social rules, habits or routines (Edquist and Johnson, 1997). Policy makers cannot directly influence them.

A general policy implication of this view of institutions is that a country or a region might need to redesign the institutional rules in the field of innovation and learning (that is, those that policy makers can influence). Of particular importance might be those institutional rules that influence interaction among firms and between firms and other organizations in the field of learning and innovation. Much innovation policy takes this form.

In any system of innovation it is important, from a policy point of view, to study whether the existing institutions are appropriate for promoting innovation. This dynamic perspective on institutional change is crucial in the SI approach, in both theory and practice. Not only organizational change, but also the evolution and design of new institutions have been very important in the successful development strategies of the newly industrialized countries of Asia as well as in the ongoing transformation of Eastern Europe.

Lock-in situations

In Chapter 1 we saw that the SI approach considers innovation processes to be evolutionary and path dependent. From this follows the danger of (negative) 'lock-in' to existing patterns of innovation, for example, trajectories leading to low growth, decreasing employment and so on. We also know that large-scale and radical technological shifts – that is, shifts to new trajectories – have rarely taken place without public intervention.[21]

There are strong arguments for early policy intervention and for supporting the emergence of new technological systems, which would facilitate transitions from dead-end trajectories for regions, countries and firms. Such intervention at an early stage in the product cycle has the potential for making a tremendous impact, as we saw in the case of the NMT 450 mobile telecommunications standard in section 7.2. Policy issues in this context concern how policy makers can help develop alternative patterns of learning and innovations and nurture emerging sectoral systems of innovation. A key issue here is the choice between supporting existing systems (with their historically accumulated knowledge bases) and supporting the development of radically new technologies and sectoral systems.[22]

Demand-side instruments

Another consequence of the interdependent and non-linear view that characterizes the SI approach, as discussed in Chapter 1, is that it is natural to bring in *demand* as an important determinant of innovation (Edquist and Hommen, 1999). This widens innovation policy to include 'demand-side' instruments. They include various institutions influencing suppliers from the angle of the product that is developed and produced. They also include public technology procurement (Edquist, Hommen and Tsipouri, 2000). (See also section 7.2.) Such procurement can trigger innovation, create a market, lead to the satisfaction of previously unsatisfied needs, and solve previously 'insoluble' socioeconomic problems.[23]

The SI approach stresses that many innovations emerge outside the formal R&D system, for example through learning processes immanent in ordinary economic activities (learning-by-doing, learning-by-using, learning-by-interacting and so on). In addition, innovations are not only developed but also produced, diffused and used. They also change during these processes. The general policy implication is that it is necessary to go beyond R&D as a determinant of innovation when designing innovation policies. (See section 7.1.)

The determinants of innovation – as seen by the SI approach – include not only economic factors, but also institutional and organizational factors (both discussed earlier), as well as political and social ones. It is obviously important to take all these different determinants into account when designing policies. As we will suggest in section 7.6, below, it is particularly important to integrate and coordinate policy areas such as R&D, education, regional policies and even macroeconomic policies.

Summing-up
The general policy implications of the SI approach discussed in this section can serve as rules of thumb, suggesting where to look for problems and possible solutions in innovation policy making. They can aid innovation policy makers to 'learn by doing'. Thus policy can be used to improve the functioning of systems of innovation without employing any notion of optimality. It remains important, though, to establish socioeconomic objectives such as economic growth and employment creation. (See section 7.2.) Such objectives can be achieved, for example, by creating incentives for changes in the production structure promoting sectors characterized by rapid growth and a high degree of employment creation.

The policy implications discussed in this section have been of a general character. They do not tell a policy maker exactly how to intervene in order to improve the functioning of a given system of innovation. The SI approach as such cannot answer these kinds of questions. Neither can any other approach or theory. However, in section 7.4.2 we will discuss how the SI approach can help in finding answers to system-specific questions.

7.4.2 Identifying Specific Policy Problems and Designing Specific Policies

As seen in section 7.4.1, certain general policy implications can be derived from the characteristics of the SI approach. However, this is not a sufficient basis for designing specific innovation policies. Here, we will indicate how the SI approach may serve as a framework for identifying problems that should be the object of policy and for designing specific innovation policies.

In section 7.2 we concluded that a necessary (but not sufficient) condition for public intervention in processes of innovation is that a 'problem' – which is not automatically solved by market forces and private actors – must exist. This means that neutral or general policies are normally irrelevant. (See section 7.3.) Substantial analytical and methodological capabilities are needed to identify 'problems'. Such capabilities are also needed to design policies that can mitigate the problems.

Problem identification by means of comparisons
There is no way to identify these problems specifically enough, for purposes of policy making, on the basis of theory alone. This is true for all existing theoretical perspectives and not only for the SI approach (Edquist, 1993b). Standard economic theory is not of much help when it comes to formulating and implementing specific R&D and innovation policies. It only provides general policy implications; for example, that basic research should sometimes be subsidized. The same is true for the SI approach, as we have seen in section 7.4.1.

The general policy implications of the SI approach are different from those of standard economic theory. This has to do with the fact that the characteristics of the two frameworks are very different. The SI approach shifts the focus away from actions at the level of individual, isolated units within the economy (firms, consumers) towards that of the collective under-pinnings of innovation. It addresses the overall system that creates and distributes knowledge, rather than its individual components.

Systems of innovation can be quite different from each other, for example, with regard to specialization of production, resources spent on R&D and so on. Further, R&D intensities vary greatly between countries. In addition, organizations and institutions constituting elements of the systems may be different. For example, research institutes and company-based research departments may be important organizations in one country while research universities may perform a similar function in another. Institutions such as laws, norms and values also differ considerably between national systems.

An important characteristic of the SI approach is that these differences are stressed, rather than abstracted from, as is the case in neoclassical economics. This makes it not only natural but also vital to compare different systems. Without such comparisons it is impossible to argue that one system is specialized in one or the other way, or that a system performs well – or badly.

Comparisons are the most important means for understanding what is good or bad, or what is a high or a low value for a variable in a system of innovation. However, as argued in section 7.2, we cannot specify an optimal or ideal system of innovation, since innovation processes have evolutionary charac-teristics. Therefore comparisons between an existing system and an ideal or optimal system are not possible. A 'problem' cannot be identified in this way.

The only possible system comparisons are between existing systems. Historically pre-existing systems can be compared with current ones, or different currently existing ones can be compared with each other.[24] Section 7.6 will specify dimensions in which national or regional systems might be compared with respect to their performance in specific technologies. Such comparisons should be genuinely empirical and very detailed. They would then be similar to what is often called 'benchmarking' at the firm level. Comparisons of this kind are crucial for policy purposes, for example to identify 'problems' that can be addressed by policy intervention.

Throughout the main text of this book we have provided examples of how comparative analysis can identify problems that should be subject to innovation policy. One such example was given in the discussion under Hypothesis 13, in section 4.1. There, it was shown that if employment in Swedish industry had grown as rapidly in the 'growth sectors' as in other OECD countries (on average) during 1975–91, then there would have been 125 000 more jobs created than the actual number of jobs in these sectors in Sweden in 1991. This comparison indicated that structural change in the direction of more knowledge-based activities had been considerably slower in Sweden, and the production structure more obsolescent, than in other developed countries. We argued that this was a major explanation for the fact that Sweden had an unemployment rate of about 10 per cent, meaning about 500 000 unemployed, in the late 1990s.[25]

Our empirical and comparative analysis thus identified a 'problem' in the Swedish national innovation system that should have been subject to public intervention.[26] The problem does not seem to have been solved spontaneously by market forces and private actors over a long period of time. However, it can only be solved by public agencies that have not only the will but also the ability to do so. This example demonstrates how explicitly comparative empirical analyses can be used to identify 'problems' as a basis for policy making in countries (and regions).

Causal explanation and policy design

Although it is a necessary condition for pursuing an innovation policy, identification of a 'problem' is certainly not a sufficient basis for designing specific policies; it is only a first step. The public sector must also have the ability to solve or mitigate the problem. In section 7.2, we mentioned that a detailed analysis of the problems and their causes might be necessary to develop this ability. We also suggested that new organizations and institutions might be required.

A symptomatic description of a problem only indicates *where* and *when* intervention is called for. It says nothing about *how* it should be pursued. In order to design appropriate innovation policy instruments it is necessary also to know the causes behind the problem identified, at least the most important ones. A causal analysis might also reveal that public intervention might be unlikely to solve the problem, due to lack of ability.

The combination of a symptom-describing (problem-identifying) analysis and a causal explanation may be called a 'diagnostic' analysis (Edquist, 1993b, 1994b). Such analysis can provide a basis for an efficient therapy or treatment, that is, a policy. Without a diagnosis it is impossible to know which prescriptions to make, and without timely prescriptions there is a risk that we will become pathologists, that is, that we will try to make the diagnosis after the patient has passed away.

However, satisfactory causal explanations in the social sciences are rare phenomena. Therefore an inability to explain in detail might not be a reason to abstain completely from intervention in the process of innovation. Because problems identified may sometimes be very severe – for the economy, for the environment or for social conditions – trial-and-error intervention may be appropriate. However, it is still necessary to have some clue about the most important causes behind a problem.

Within an SI framework an identification of the causes behind the problems is a matter of identifying functions that are missing or inappropriate and which lead to the 'problem' in terms of comparative performance. Let us label these deficient functions *system failures*. When we know the functional deficiencies behind a certain 'problem' (for example, low performance), we have identified a 'system failure'. The OECD has addressed what it calls 'systemic failures' and defined them as 'mismatches between the components of an innovation system' (OECD, 1998b: 102). Here, let us try to be somewhat more specific with regard to what a 'system failure' might be.

On the basis of the discussion of the characteristics of the SI approach in section 7.4.1, at least three main categories of systems failures can be mentioned:[27]

- organizations in the system of innovation might be inappropriate or missing,
- institutions may be inappropriate or missing, or
- interactions or links between these elements in the SI might be inappropriate or missing.[28]

In section 7.4.2, we pointed to an area of low performance of the Swedish economy which is likely to be closely associated with the functioning of the national system of innovation, that is, too little product innovation and insufficiently rapid change in the structure of production in the direction of a higher proportion of R&D-intensive goods in manufacturing production.[29] However, a detailed causal analysis of the problem identified is necessary to find out which kind of system failure is behind this problem.[30] Not until they know the character of the system failure do policy makers know whether to influence or change organizations, institutions, interactions between them – or something else.[31] Hence an identification of a problem should be supplemented with an analysis of its causes as a part of the analytical basis for the design of an innovation policy.

Summing-up

In summary, concrete empirical and comparative analyses are absolutely necessary for the design of specific policies in the fields of R&D and innovation. The SI approach is an analytical framework suited for such analyses. It is appropriate for this purpose because it places innovation at the very centre of focus and because it is able to capture differences between systems. In this way specific problems that should be objects of innovation policy can be identified.

In order to design specific policies, it is also important to identify the causes – or system failures – behind the problems. These problems and their causes do not come out of the SI approach as such, but from the empirical and comparative analyses that can be carried out with its help. There is no substitute for concrete analyses of concrete conditions in an effort to design innovation policy! However, the general policy implications of the SI approach, discussed in section 7.4.1, may be helpful as signposts in carrying out the empirical comparisons between systems of innovation.

7.5 PUBLIC INNOVATION POLICY FOR EMPLOYMENT CREATION

The degree of innovation opportunity should be a decisive criterion in designing innovation policy and, hence, in deciding to support certain areas or sectors. The feasibility of alternative directions for innovation must also be evaluated.[32] Although diverse types of innovations may be possible, dimensions such as distance to current knowledge and economic impact can be evaluated. For example, some types of innovation will be easier to make than others and some will have greater economic impact than others. Evaluation is important so that public policy does not remain 'blind' and support all alternatives in an indiscriminate way.[33] As emphasized in section 7.2, policy makers should identify objectives and create opportunities. In other words, they should develop selection criteria – such as the impact on economic growth and employment – while supporting the generation of novelty. Accordingly, 'Making these criteria explicit in terms of the economic and technical dimensions of innovation opportunities is a start towards informed decisions and policy-making' (McKelvey, 1997: 243).

The potential for employment generation is here considered a particularly important criterion for selecting among alternative pathways of innovation and economic development. Thus the most important conclusion of this book is that a reallocation of resources from sectors dominated by process to sectors dominated by product innovation should have a positive effect on employment. If the objective is to increase employment in the longer run, then government policy should focus on stimulating product innovations (or sectors where product innovations dominate). This is one of the most important policy implications of our analysis, as summarized in Chapter 6.

As argued throughout this book, sectors where product innovations dominate over process innovations are often new, high-tech sectors where the rate of growth is high. This is not to deny the possibility that there may be some very dynamic subsectors of low-tech sectors in which there may be a great deal of product innovation and employment generation.

A first broad recommendation for public policy is to identify and strengthen those manufacturing and service sectors where product innovations inherently dominate over process innovations (if reliance on private actors and the market mechanism does not suffice). As we have argued in this book, the relevant sectors are often those with a high R&D intensity and/or high educational level of the labour force, which tend to lead to product development and renewal.[34] The reason why these manufacturing and service sectors are more important than others in a longer-term, dynamic perspective is not that they are knowledge intensive *per se*.[35] Our point concerns their greater potential for carrying out innovations that can generate employment.

Firms in sectors dominated by product innovations often have more innovation opportunities than firms in other sectors, and thereby more potential for creating economic growth with jobs. They may be able to develop new products for which demand is expanding, rather than just focus on cutting costs of existing products. Thus it appears important for public policy to encourage change in the structure of production of the economy in the direction of new sectors (and/or renewal of existing sectors).[36] On the whole, these sectors are also characterized by higher productivity growth (as measured) and therefore they can carry higher wages and profits. They are also characterized by more rapid market growth than other sectors. If the firms in such sectors are successful, then a policy supporting their expansion would thereby increase employment in the long run in the economy, especially if these sectors are experiencing global expansion. This leads us to a broad recommendation for selective support of manufacturing and service sectors where product innovations dominate.

Before going further with this discussion, a countering point can be made about public policies which are *not* options for employment generation. In global capitalism, preventing innovation is not an option for protecting jobs. Thus encouraging product innovations must be sharply distinguished from a policy which contains any element of preventing technological or organizational process innovations.[37] Such a Luddite strategy of trying to protect employment by preventing process innovations will always fail in the long run because competition normally guarantees that potential increases in labour productivity are exploited in the long run. Even though process innovations normally increase labour productivity and reduce employment (per unit of output) in the short run,[38] they should not be prevented. Process innovations are absolutely necessary for increases in productivity and for the maintenance of competitiveness of firms, regions and countries.[39] Thus any policy that tries to give priority to immediate employment protection over productivity growth by preventing process innovation will ultimately fail. It might not only miss the policy objectives but it could even create serious social and economic problems by directing the economy into unsustainable, non-competitive behaviour.

This leads us into a complex, and unresolved, debate over the relative importance and ability of public policy to stimulate innovations as well as the relative ease with which firms, regions and nations can – or cannot – move beyond current specializations into new areas. Some of the basic terms of reference for this debate were reviewed in section 7.4.

It is common knowledge that product innovations often dominate over process innovations in many 'new' sectors of production and that, with increasing maturity of sectors, process innovations gradually become more important.[40] In a situation characterized by high unemployment, stimulating manufacturing sectors that are both R&D intensive and less process oriented is important for employment. Stimulating service sectors with a high level of product innovations and those with linkages to innovative manufacturing sectors is also important.[41]

Concepts such as 'lock-in' and 'structural change', as applied to firms and supporting organizations in both regions and countries, are useful for explaining their relative ability and willingness to change. Different regions and countries are specialized in different sectors and can therefore be seen to perform quite differently in terms of their ability to stimulate growth in R&D-intensive manufacturing and innovative service sectors. For example, the EU, including Sweden, has performed badly in this respect compared with the USA and Japan.[42]

In the EU as a whole, a growth pattern concentrating on process rather than product innovation has led to productivity growth – but not enough job creation. This is an important factor behind the fact that unemployment was, in the late 1990s, much higher in Europe (10 per cent) and Sweden (10 per cent) than in Japan (4–5 per cent) and the USA (3–4 per cent). Thus the different industrial and service specialization of countries has an impact on the potential for employment creation in a longer-term perspective. This means that public policy can attempt to dissolve situations of lock-in into sectors dominated by process innovations and to facilitate (or support) changes in the direction of sectors where product innovations dominate.

With respect to Europe, the employment situation strongly reinforces the recommendation for the policy just formulated. As analysed in the *OECD Jobs Study* (OECD, 1994a, 1994b, 1994c), European industry seems to have become locked into a trajectory, or growth pattern, which is dominantly labour saving, meaning that the employment intensity of growth is relatively low. This trend has continued for at least two decades now and seems not to be corrected spontaneously by market forces. This means that public policy supporting structural change in the direction of more R&D-intensive and less process-innovation-oriented sectors is called for more in the EU than in the USA and Japan. The present EU trajectory will lead to increasing competition with Eastern Europe and advanced developing countries. It will be increasingly difficult for EU economies to keep up, due to the mounting competition over price rather than quality and novelty.

On the whole, therefore, our conclusion is that public stimulation should often be targeted towards new sectors – or even towards sectors which do not yet exist. In both manufacturing and services, sectors with the greatest potential for employment growth will be those engaged in developing and producing new consumer products (goods and services) which are not transformed into (labour-saving) process technologies at a later time.[43]

Our emphasis that certain types of manufacturing and service sectors have larger positive effects on employment than others implies a certain selectivity in public policy. This goes against the view held by many economists that it does not matter what is produced, as long as something is produced and traded in international markets. To them, the relative efficiency of production – basically, productivity increases due to cost reductions – is what matters. The theoretical and analytical arguments presented in earlier chapters of this book show that while cost reductions are vital in competitive situations, the economic value of what is produced also matters. Sectors producing new products of high economic value will offer greater employment and growth, especially if the market for them is expanding internationally.

In our discussion of innovation policy for employment, we have emphasized production sectors where product innovation dominates and argued that these are often new sectors characterized by a high R&D intensity.

This certainly does not exclude the possibility that other sectors – for example, non-R&D-intensive sectors – may also contribute to employment growth. The reason is, of course, that product innovations also occur in other sectors – although they are less common there. These sectors may have high levels of embodied technologies, they may have extensive contacts with the scientific infrastructure, and so forth. However, this does not mean that they are R&D intensive in the OECD sense of this term. Based on the evidence reviewed in this book, we argue that the 'growth potential' of any given sector, in terms of production, productivity and employment, will probably depend critically on its performance with respect to product innovation.

Hence our overall recommendation for public policy to support the actions and capabilities of firms to move into sectors dominated by product innovation holds. However, changes must build upon existing patterns of production specialization, patterns of firm relationships, specialization of scientific and engineering knowledge, and so forth. Therefore our overall recommendation does not imply that public policy should ignore all other sectors. Their potential for employment-generating economic growth may be less than that of the sectors emphasized by us. Yet if public policy can potentially change the production structure towards growing markets and increasing productivity to sustain and/or develop employment, then doing so through innovation policy may be better than doing nothing.

7.6 POLICY AND STRATEGY OPTIONS

The inherently selective nature of public innovation policy (see section 7.3) implies that policy makers – and strategic decision makers in firms – need to identify options and choose among specific actions and agendas. The policy-making process does not end with such choices, of course. It also involves negotiation among various actors as well as the selection of specific instruments for implementation. Implementation, in particular, is a complex process that cannot be fully dealt with here. Nevertheless, our discussion in this section will have some general implications for the choice of instruments and strategies for implementation.

According to Metcalfe (1997), innovation policy should be formulated in relation to several important dimensions of the innovation process, and how relevant features of particular technologies differ within these dimensions. Thus specific aspects of technology are linked to key 'choices in … policy' (ibid.: 285). The remainder of this section employs the classification of policy options identified on this basis. The options are related to important aspects of technologies, the manner in which technological development takes place, and the economic settings within which that development occurs.

7.6.1   Development or Application?

One dimension in which decisions concerning a particular technology have to be made by various actors concerns the choice of whether to support *development* or *application* of a technology. This dichotomy is not identical to an earlier distinction drawn between *innovation* and *diffusion*, but follows from it. The latter scheme is now widely recognized as being inadequate, due to the accumulation of evidence that the innovation process does not end when the diffusion of a newly developed technology begins, but instead continues during the process of diffusion (Silverberg, 1990a, 1990b). In diffusion, adopters and users make important contributions to the design and performance capabilities of the technology (Amsalem, 1983; Bell and Scott-Kemmis, 1997; Metcalfe, 1988; Rosenberg, 1972, 1976; Voss, 1988). A network of adopters and users can even act as the developers, such as those involved in the Linux operating system, thereby blurring the distinction between users and developers (McKelvey, 2000, forthcoming).

Over time, it has become increasingly difficult for adopters of a new technology to realize economic gains from its further development merely by purchasing and applying it. With advanced, complex technologies that depend on high levels of R&D and diverse knowledge bases, improvements – especially those necessary to create new products – can no longer be easily achieved through simple 'learning-by-doing'. There has been a growing divergence between the development of 'production capacity' and the acquisition of 'technological capability'. The former can be defined as 'the resources used to produce industrial goods at given levels of efficiency and given input combinations'; the latter as 'the resources needed to manage technical change, including skills, knowledge and experience, and institutional structures and linkages' (Bell and Pavitt, 1997: 89). Increasingly, the acquisition of 'technological capability' has become the most important basis for economic growth (Dosi et al., 1988).

Empirical tests have indicated that national differences in technical efficiency cannot be fully explained by 'factor endowments' or 'entry barriers', but are also due to varying degrees of 'accumulated technological competence' (Fagerberg, 1988a, 1988b; Soete, 1981). Further, the most outstanding examples of growth in newly industrializing economies such as Taiwan and Korea have been strongly associated not only with the importation and use (application) of foreign production technology but also with the further development of such technology in terms of both process and product innovation. Such development has not been limited to incremental improve-ments in the efficiency of routine production. Instead, it has also involved the creation of new industrial facilities and new products. These initiatives have required the development of diverse engineering capabilities, strong reliance on business-financed R&D, and the synthesis of imitative and innovative activities (Bloom, 1992; Enos and Park, 1988; Ernst and O'Connor, 1992; Westphal, Kim and Dahlman, 1985).

7.6.2 Which Technologies - and Which Trajectories?

As noted earlier, in section 7.3, policy makers and firm strategists must also make choices about which problems to focus on. Decisions of this kind can be focused even further. The choices can be defined more narrowly by referring to alternative 'trajectories' in a given field of technology. Within a broad 'technological paradigm', there is often a relatively high level of uncertainty about which path would be the most productive to follow (Dosi, 1982; 1988). In contrast, the identification and selection of specific 'technological trajectories' - pathways for development that are based on particular design configurations, draw upon stable knowledge bases and provide frameworks for incremental improvement - can greatly reduce such uncertainty (ibid.). As we pointed out in section 7.2, one of the most important tasks of public innovation policy is counteracting uncertainty.

The choice of specific technological trajectories depends, first and foremost, on whether there are sufficient resources available for the pursuit of a given trajectory to constitute a realistic possibility for economic development and growth. Any given technology involves multiple forms of technical interdependency, occurring at several different levels of economic organization (Lipsey and Carlaw, 1998: 7). It follows that these interdependencies shape the possibilities for further development by determining which trajectories can be pursued under the constraints imposed by the availability or lack of necessary resources. Thus 'An improvement in one subsystem can only be adopted if the costs of engineering compatibility with the rest of the system keep the overall portfolio of changes economically feasible' (Metcalfe, 1997: 283).

In addition to these internal constraints of 'interrelatedness' within a given technological 'design configuration', its external relations to other technologies also pose problems of adjustment that are often discussed under the heading of 'technological complementarities'. 'One implication of these complementarities is that a change in one technology will typically induce changes in the physical make-up and economic value of many other technologies, as well as in existing R&D programmes' (Lipsey and Carlaw, 1998: 8). Therefore the choice of a specific trajectory of development in one technology field has to be made not only on the basis of immediate 'resource constraints' but also in view of the expected impacts on trajectories in other technology fields. These may, of course, present many new opportunities for the development and growth of a national economy as a whole. However, these opportunities may not be realized without policies aimed at the development of new bases of competitive advantage. These should take into account both the most fruitful directions for advance in key technologies and the most promising directions for the co-evolution of these technologies (Bell and Pavitt, 1997: 85).

7.6.3   Technology as Artefacts, Skills or Knowledge?

As implied by the discussion thus far, technology can be thought of not only in terms of artefacts, but also in terms of techniques or practical skills and in terms of knowledge – or, rather, a knowledge base comprising related bodies of applied scientific, technical and other knowledge (Layton, 1974). Policy makers should encourage other economic actors to consider which of these interdependent dimensions of a given technology should be the main focus of measures aimed at its development.

Technology as artefacts
We have already alluded to the limitations of policies that focus only on the artefact dimension of technology.[44] Such policies often assume that not only economic gains but also the skills and knowledge required for the further development of a given technology will follow automatically from buying machinery, installing it and learning how to operate it efficiently. Such assumptions might once have been valid for simpler technologies with less differentiated resource bases, smaller scales of production, and more direct relations between routine production activities and the competencies needed to make the technology and modify its design and performance capabilities.

However, increasing technological complexity and rising scales of production have meant that the conventional focus on investments in physical capital is no longer adequate to achieve economic growth based on technological development. This approach 'completely ignores the investment in intangible capital that is necessary not just to operate machines, but to "choose" them in the first place, to improve their performance, once acquired, to replicate them and further develop both them and the products they produce, and to lay the basis for higher value-added activities in future' (Bell and Pavitt, 1997: 85). Artefact-oriented strategies might compensate for some of these deficiencies, though, if they were directed less towards process innovation and more towards product innovation. Strategies for product innovation must address not only technical but also market uncertainties. Consequently, they are more attentive to relations between innovating firms and other key actors, such as financiers, shareholders and stakeholders. They are therefore also more concerned with the development and distribution of intangible capital, such as firm- and industry-specific knowledge among lenders and shareholders, and the 'enfranchisement' of stakeholders (Tylecote, 1998: 123–4).

Technology as skills

Policies oriented towards the 'skills' dimension of technology are primarily concerned with the development and coordination of human capital, both within and among firms and other organizations. Skill is not completely distinct from knowledge. Rather, it is equivalent to a particular kind of knowledge, often referred to as 'tacit' knowledge – which is, by definition, 'knowledge that can not be articulated' (Nelson and Winter, 1982: 76). Like tacit knowledge in general, skill cannot be readily codified and therefore cannot be replicated easily. Such knowledge is empirically based and acquired primarily through experience complemented by learning through observation and induction. Its transmission from one individual to others usually depends strongly on close contact and common understandings based on shared experience, which may or may not be verbalized (ibid.: 76–82).

All this implies that skill tends to be 'linked inextricably to specified activities carried out by specific organisations' (Metcalfe, 1997: 281). Moreover, because skill is embodied knowledge, it has usually been effectively 'carried' between organizations or countries only through the mobility of specially skilled individuals (Bruland, 1989; Henderson, 1965; Jeremy, 1981; Landes, 1969). In addition, the substantial bodies of tacit skill connected with product innovation and the management of technological change have been shown to be generally more costly and slow to transfer than those associated with the operation of specific kinds of machinery (Scott-Kemmis and Bell, 1988; Senker, 1992).

These considerations should be emphasized in approaching the development of technological skill. This concerns not only the build-up of 'know-how' and competence within particular organizations, but also the coordination and transfer of skills among a variety of organizations, within the overall framework of a broader 'technological division of labour'. In section 7.2 we suggested that public organizations might provide training in certain fields to create new opportunities that would otherwise not be realized. Here, we should add that unless it is possible for the skills provided in this way to be 'carried' from public organizations to private firms, those opportunities might still be lost.

Technology as knowledge

The 'knowledge' dimension of technology – or, more properly speaking, technology as codified or 'explicit' knowledge – is usually related primarily to R&D. R&D is carried out in both public research organizations, such as universities or public laboratories, and the R&D departments of firms (as well as in private organizations dedicated to carrying out contract research). Policy in this area is concerned with the appropriate division of labour and balance of expenditure among these various kinds of organizations. 'Systems perspectives' are useful in formulating such policy. Compared to approaches based on 'market failure' (see section 7.2), they have a 'greater potential for identifying where support should go' (Smith, 1998: 42).

At several points above, we have indicated that specific technologies can be conceived of in terms of a 'knowledge base'. The knowledge base of a technology comprises both tacit, or uncodified, and explicit, or codified, knowledge. The former kind of knowledge, as we have already noted, tends to be firm (or organization) specific. The latter, however, tends to be of a more generic – and, in this sense, 'public' – nature. 'Generic knowledge tends to be codified in applied scientific fields like electrical engineering, or materials science, or pharmacology, which are "about" technology' (Nelson, 1987: 76).

At the same time, generic technological knowledge tends to be less fully public and accessible than the general scientific knowledge base. It may be, for example, that the actors within a sector share a great deal of common knowledge that is codified and readily accessible, at least within that sector. However, not all of the knowledge that is codified may be equally accessible in the sense of belonging to the 'public domain'. Much of this knowledge may instead be 'proprietary', rather than 'public', due to the establishment of intellectual property rights to patents and so on.[45] The 'codification' of a technology thus corresponds to a combination of both private and public organizations which work together within an institutional framework to develop, conserve and transmit 'generic' knowledge. These elements constitute what has been called a 'technology infrastructure'. In addition to such obvious components as 'technical information, and research and test facilities', a technology infrastructure also includes less technically explicit elements, such as 'information relevant for strategic planning and market development, forums for joint-industry planning and collaboration, and assignment of intellectual property rights' (Tassey, 1991: 347).

From a 'systems' perspective, it is vital to understand the anatomy and operation of the technology infrastructure. 'Systems' approaches generally emphasize that knowledge is the crucial resource utilized by firms and industries in the process of innovation. It follows that both the identification of 'problems' and the development of capabilities for solving them on the part of policy makers (see section 7.2) depend critically upon mapping the technological knowledge base. This involves not only identifying and measuring relevant 'knowledge inputs', but also charting and analysing the interaction of different forms of knowledge and different kinds of organizations, which may be governed by different institutions.

In all of this, the codified knowledge base can provide a centrally important 'key' to the structure and operation of the broader 'knowledge base' of a technology and its supporting 'infrastructure'. 'Generic' knowledge about a given technology should not, therefore, be considered in isolation. Rather, it should be analysed in terms of its relation to, on the one hand, the vital activities and crucial skills and techniques of individuals and organizations, and, on the other, the organizational forms through which these and other elements of the knowledge base are produced and reproduced (Smith, 1998: 49–50). On this basis, it is possible to assess the specificities and dynamics of a 'knowledge system' and, thereby, to identify problems in the 'coordination' and 'flow' of economically useful knowledge (ibid.: 52–3).

7.6.4 Which Sectors?

As implied in the foregoing discussion, it is important to identify those specific elements of the 'technology infrastructure' that will be the main channels for the improvement of a given technology. Particular kinds of firms and supporting public organizations embody or 'carry' certain kinds of knowledge and operate according to specific institutional rules and principles. Their relative importance for a given technology can be assessed, as we have indicated, on the basis of an analysis of system specificities and dynamics that focuses especially on the evolution of the technological knowledge base. Such an analysis reveals that in different sectors the technological infrastructure may be constituted very differently, with profound implications for the identity of 'key actors'. In Italy, for example, these sectoral differences are so pronounced that the country has been described as having two largely separate 'systems of innovation'. On the one hand, there are localized networks of small firms that have successfully developed certain 'historical' specializations, supported primarily by local or regional public organizations. On the other hand, there is the somewhat less successful 'core R&D system' that includes large firms, universities, high-tech SMEs and major public research institutes (Malerba, 1993).

Sectoral differences are important in other countries, as well. Generally, sectors differ with respect to patterns in the development and spread of new technology. In some, such as agriculture, diffusion among small producing firms of process technologies developed by 'external' research organizations (often, though not always, based in the public sector) is the characteristic pattern (Griliches, 1957). In other sectors, such as civil aircraft production, pharmaceuticals and semiconductors, the spread of new technology occurs primarily through growth (at the expense of their competitors) of firms that successfully develop an innovative product (Charles River Associates, 1980; Mansfield, 1968; Phillips, 1971; Schwartzman, 1975). Generally, there appear to be no simple causal connections between sectoral characteristics such as 'industry structure' and rapid technical change and productivity growth. The strength of the knowledge base and the character of the institutional framework that supports R&D are also important determinants of innovative activity (Nelson, 1996: 36–9).

7.6.5   R&D or Other Learning Processes?

As we have stressed throughout this discussion, innovative activity consists of far more than R&D. And, as indicated above (in subsection 7.6.4), an insufficient level of R&D activity is not always the only or the main deficiency in economic 'learning' to be corrected in order to solve problems of technological innovation. Other possible reasons for learning failures affecting the performance of innovation include an inadequate level or range of advanced human capital, or an inadequate diffusion of technical and market knowledge to firms (Dosi and Malerba, 1996). It follows that innovation policy, instead of focusing only on R&D, should also address the support of less tangible learning processes. In any case, it should take them into full consideration.

Several learning processes other than R&D have been identified in the literature on innovation (Malerba, 1992). These include 'interactive learning' between firms and their customers or suppliers (Lundvall, 1985), 'learning by using' (Rosenberg, 1982) and 'learning by doing' (Arrow, 1962b). Firms may engage simultaneously, although to different degrees, in some or all of these types of learning processes, depending on their capabilities and the patterns of innovation characteristic of the technologies and economic sectors in which they are based. Their learning behaviour is thus related to a broader technological system, its knowledge base and its supporting 'technological infrastructure' (David and Foray, 1995). Generally, firms' ability to engage in learning is 'shaped by the structure, type, scale and communication processes between relevant knowledge-creating or knowledge-holding [organizations]' (Smith, 1998: 40).

Research on learning has indicated that, in agreement with our earlier discussion of the centrality of R&D to technological 'knowledge bases' (in subsection 7.6.4), R&D and other types of learning processes need not be considered as mutually exclusive activities. There can be important complementarities between these activities, as indicated by the notion of R&D as a key means of developing the 'absorptive capacity' of firms (Cohen and Levinthal, 1990). This argument has been elaborated as follows:

> Support of basic research not only generates new codified scientific knowledge, but has two additional effects. First, it develops tacit capabilities in solving complex problems in various scientific and technological realms. Second, it opens up linkages in research networks crossing firms and universities, which prove quite

important in the process of adaptation by firms to drastic changes. (Malerba, 1998: 7)

However, it is important to emphasize that this approach implies the coordination of support for R&D with support for complementary activities. It might therefore involve providing less support for R&D and more support for other kinds of learning, which operate through different mechanisms. One such complement is the development (via education) of advanced human capital, which is a necessary resource for firms to diversify into, or start up within, new technological fields (Mowery, 1995a; Rosenberg and Nelson, 1994). Another is diffusion policies, particularly those of a developmental nature, aimed at adoption and learning (Ergas, 1987; Mowery, 1995b).

7.6.6 International or National Policies?

A final dimension of technology with important implications for policy making is the extent to which a technology is international, rather than purely national, in terms of its production, distribution and transfer (Bartlett and Ghoshal, 1990; Dunning, 1992; Howells and Wood, 1993). In the case that a technology has been, or is being, internationalized, 'strategies developed by both government and business ... to generate technology are no longer based on a single country' (Archibugi and Michie, 1997: 4). Independent national policies may then have to be replaced by collaborative international policies. Another, different possibility is that national policy makers may become more explicitly aware of the policies of other countries, but without working directly with them. Rather, they may try to see where national policies can make a contribution relative to those of other countries. This second alternative emphasizes coordination, rather than collaboration. Whereas collaboration depends on more explicit and centralized decision making, coordination may occur more spontaneously and may change over time as different actors adapt or react to one anothers' initiatives.

Even in the present period of economic and technological 'globalization', there still remains some scope for national innovation policy measures that do not directly involve international collaboration. However, even these measures should take globalization into account. For examples, we can refer to developments in the area of technical standard setting (discussed earlier in section 7.2). The globalization of markets and technologies has created both opportunities and incentives for governments and public agencies to take a more passive approach to standards. Instead of defining standards, it is now often easier (if not necessary) for them to adopt (*de facto* or *de jure*) world standards and require firms to observe them (OECD, 1991). Moreover, setting a standard other than the world standard might place domestic firms in a poor competitive position. But government passivity regarding standards may do nothing to advantage domestic producers either. A superior strategy, therefore, is to adopt national standards that do not conflict with world standards and that also encourage compatibility among different variants of a given technology. Such standards refer to so-called 'gateway' technologies (Cohendet and Llerena, 1997). They allow for the importation (and adaptation) of foreign technologies and the export of complementary or equivalent domestic technologies, thus resolving a potential trade dilemma.

In addition to national policies of the 'coordinating' kind described above, 'collaborative' policies can also be used to build national competitive advantage. The internationalization of technology has brought the practice of directly subsidizing the innovative efforts of firms into serious question, since such policies can benefit domestic firms and their foreign competitors more or less equally. However, globalization has also increased the effectiveness of more indirect policies, whereby nations 'upgrade their infrastructure to attract technologically intensive activities' (Archibugi and Michie, 1997: 17). Some important lessons can be drawn from a recent discussion of how Japanese innovation policy has evolved over the past several decades (Fransman, 1997). Japan has responded to globalization in two ways:

> The first has been by internationalising its national co-operative R&D programmes while retaining their national objectives, while the second has involved establishing new fully internationalised programmes that are also oriented towards national objectives. ... although there are over time significant leakages of knowledge from the Japanese science and technology system, ... policies aimed at strengthening Japanese companies through these programmes are nonetheless appropriate. (Ibid.: 80)

The collaborative policies that have been followed in Japan, as well as the thinking behind them, are clearly relevant for large Western economies.

7.6.7 Summing-up

To summarize, this section has dealt with some of the options that can be identified in order to define and select among alternative courses of action in innovation policy. The discussion related specific kinds of policy options to relevant dimensions of the innovation process. It pointed out that, along these dimensions, different technologies vary greatly with respect to a number of key features. Some of the most important of those features were identified and exemplified in the discussion. An underlying theme of the discussion was that even 'specific' policies must be further adapted to particular contexts. Adaptation depends partly on relevant features of actors, institutions, development processes and other aspects of the technologies under consideration. It also depends on the contexts in which technologies are implemented. These contexts are often broadly conceived as sectoral, regional and national systems of innovation.

7.7 FIRM DIVERSITY AND INCENTIVES TO INNOVATE

As we have emphasized throughout this chapter, the interactions between firms and between firms and organizations are affected by both market forces and public innovation policies. In addition, the extent and type of interactions among actors in a system of innovation can vary according to differences in technologies and sectors. By providing technical and market information, interactions in a system of innovation can affect firms' incentives and disincentives to engage in innovations, which in turn affect the direction and rate of economic development. What firms choose to do – and how well they perform – matters for the overall economy. Economic growth arises mainly through innovation and its attenuated dynamics and occasional disruption, not through the static allocation of existing resources.

As indicated in sections 7.2 and 7.5, firms and other organizations interact in a variety of ways around, or in addition to, arm's-length market transactions. Public policy has the potential to affect longer-term trajectories of growth because market-based economies allocate resources both through market transactions as well as through other coordination mechanisms such as institutions, knowledge infrastructures and relationships. Firms, however, have not figured so prominently in the system of innovation analysis, as represented here and in the broader literature (see Edquist and McKelvey, 2000). Accordingly, much of the analysis in this book compares sectors and national economies, and much of this chapter discusses public policy. Public policy can affect the public, or collective, aspects of innovation through the other coordination mechanisms of institutions, knowledge infrastructures and relationships.

Yet individual firms clearly play a crucial role in developing, using and translating different types of knowledge into innovations. They are often organized in such a way as to become – and also remain – specialized in certain technical and product knowledge areas (Bell and Pavitt, 1997). Knowledge about technical and market opportunities plays a key role in stimulating firms to innovate. The firm may obtain knowledge about market and technical opportunities (or dead-ends) from a variety of other actors, such as suppliers, users and universities (McKelvey, 1997). All firms in a sector may know about (or have access to) some types of knowledge whereas only a few firms may know about other types of knowledge. In other words, the knowledge that is relevant and necessary for the firm to act upon innovation opportunities requires a combination of widely available, public knowledge and locally held, private and organizationally specific knowledge.

Both Nelson (1991, 1996) and Metcalfe (1998) argue that this diversity of firms – even in the same sector – is a micro-level fact which accords with the empirical evidence. Firms do not all act the same way at the same time, based on rational calculations. Instead, firms act based upon a combination of vision and competences, which leads to diversity among a population of competing firms. Over time, some firms within the population will be more successful and others less successful. Some firms may be successful because they individually 'got it right'. Other firms may be successful because they had access to the right types of knowledge through a series of other organizations, knowledge flows and relationships in a system of innovation.

This implies two points of relevance here. We discuss them immediately below.

1. The environment, or broader economic conditions, matter to the firm. The economic conditions can be conceptualized in terms of macro-level economic variables, such as the interest rate, as well as other relevant variables that influence the development and diffusion of new knowledge, such as the national investment in education.
2. If the objective of public policy is to increase overall employment, it will therefore be important to influence how decisions and actions are taken within individual firms. This can also be a means to implement public policy, albeit indirectly, by influencing the behaviour of firms. After all, firms generally do not set about to increase employment; rather, they sell products (goods and services) in order to survive, make profits and perhaps grow. Nevertheless, firms that succeed at selling products – particularly some types of goods and services – will create economic growth and employment as a side effect of going about their business. Therefore, a few words about firm behaviour and firm decision making in relation to innovations are in order.

The first implication from the analysis developed here is that firms, too, need to concentrate on developing product innovations, particularly knowledge-intensive products. Such products offer the highest returns, so that the firm can compete based on novel products of high quality, rather than on price. Much of the empirical material used in this book discusses trends in certain types of sectors, contrasting those dominated by product innovation with those dominated by process innovation.

The reason it is important to conclude by discussing firm behaviour and decision making about innovations is that just being in a sector does not automatically lead to benefits. The preceding analysis has the danger of leading firms in sectors dominated by product innovations to rest on their laurels – for example, to think that just being active there means that they are automatically superior to other types of firms. Similarly, policy makers might assume that having firms in certain sectors is enough to ensure competitive firms, longer-term economic growth and employment. This condition is certainly advantageous but it is not sufficient.

In practice, firms within the same sector can choose different strategies to compete. One might focus mostly on new product innovations – thereby increasing productivity through higher economic value – while another might focus mostly on new process innovations – thereby increasing productivity through reduced input costs. Some firms will be more successful than others, with relative success depending on how well they meet the pressures found through the market – for example, the level of sophistication and uniqueness of the product, rate of growth of the market and so on. The behaviour and decisions of the individual firm matter, of course, which is why public policy and firm-based collective action that influences institutions, knowledge flows and relationships can influence the innovative outcome.

Even firms in sectors dominated by process innovations can innovate through product innovations, thereby acquiring an edge over their competitors. Farmers, for instance, mostly sell commodity products for which cost is crucial, but some actively look for, and develop, niche markets where they can sell unique products.

The second implication is that the firm has to accept some level of risk as well as make judgements about the relative possibility of success. These judgements are made under conditions of true uncertainty about the future, and based on unsure perceptions about the potential market and potential technical advances in the innovation opportunity. Although every firm hopes that every attempt to innovate will succeed, the empirical evidence suggests that failure may be as much a part of innovation as success. Some things work and some things do not. Some things sell and some do not. For the firm, it is important to develop internal routines and knowledge structures that help gather information to evaluate the potential of innovations. Access to other firms and other organizations through knowledge flows and relationships can help supplement the internal innovation decisions. Taken together, they can help the firm move in new directions.

Even so, one problem with innovating from the perspective of the individual firm is that there are no guarantees of success. They may succeed. They may fail. If they are taking the risk of doing something radically new rather than just improving on the old, then the positive returns to success, as well as the costs of failing, will probably both be higher. It depends on how far the innovation is from the firm's current markets and current technical specializations – as well as how much the firm is already threatened by current market pressures. Deciding to innovate involves accepting some risks.[46]

A third implication, it follows, is that the most important current innovation activities in the firm are those which help the firm to learn in order to innovate in the future. One hypothesis is that the reason why R&D intensity and/or high educational levels are shown to be important at the sectoral level is that R&D can be interpreted as an investment enabling firms to prepare for the future. In this perspective, the most important outcomes of R&D are not just the resulting products but are instead the firm's capacity to monitor, use and further develop knowledge and technology for the future.

A fourth implication is that, because the external world is changing, firms need to have an internal ability to monitor what is going on and to respond by trying to identify, and create, new innovation opportunities. The firm needs a conscious innovation strategy, which goes beyond the traditional focus on R&D. Therefore the firm not only has to specialize today in certain strategically important kinds of core knowledge and products. It must also have in parallel the organizational capacity to switch into emerging areas with potential for growth and development.

Having a strategy to innovate does not mean, however, that it will be automatically implemented. Nor does it mean that implementation will necessarily be easy. It does, however, provide a benchmark against which new options and ideas can be compared. Having a conscious innovation strategy is usually better than having a random strategy or one that consists of waiting to see what might transpire and then reacting. Most managers are familiar with the modern success stories of product innovations and of growth sectors, yet most also know too little about failures in the same areas. Accepting the possibility of failure takes the firm one step closer to analysing why it could happen – and how to improve the possibility of innovating successfully in the future.

Implementing firm strategy to promote and evaluate product innovations will require systematic thinking about trade-offs. There are trade-offs in terms of potential risks and benefits, in terms of current firm abilities and future necessities, and in terms of the ability to master new challenges when technical and/or market dead-ends appear. Being flexible means continuing to evaluate internal firm decisions and competences against a changing environment.

As with all else, including science, the incentive structures should be analysed in terms of whether they promote or suppress creativity and innovation. Are people rewarded for continuing to do what they have always done? Or for thinking in new ways? This book is intended to stimulate the reader to think in new ways, especially about how and why employment increases or decreases with different types of innovations.

NOTES

1. Sections 7.1 to 7.4 are partly based upon Edquist (2001).
2. Capitalist firms include private firms, but also publicly owned firms, which function in a similar way.
3. We assume that the objectives are already determined by a political process. They do not necessarily have to be of an economic kind. They can also be social, environmental, ethical or military. They must, however, be specific and unambiguously formulated in relation to the current situation. With regard to innovation policy, the most common objectives are formulated in terms of economic growth, productivity growth or employment (Edquist, 1994a and 1994b: section 4).
4. As an alternative to calling for the fulfilment of these conditions for public intervention, one might argue that it should be discussed for each specific issue (from defence to bread production and radical innovation) whether markets and private actors or public actors can fulfil the objectives most efficiently – or if collaboration between them is called for.
5. This is especially the case with innovation. Here, by definition, it is highly unlikely that there will be any clear-cut precedents for the problem to be solved.
6. Economists and others often distinguish between 'risk' and 'uncertainty'. Risk can be calculated and insured against by such means as 'risk spreading'; uncertainty cannot. Moreover, since the degree of risk frequently cannot be determined in policy decisions concerning technological innovation, such decisions are often affected by uncertainty. 'In many cases we have uncertainty proper where no probability calculus can be applied; the experiments are one-off, they change the conditions for the next experiment and it is never possible to calculate completely the set of possible outcomes' (Metcalfe, 1997: 277).
7. Hence, it might be necessary to carry out a detailed comparative empirical analysis – see section 7.4.2.
8. Instruments might take the form of either reforms to institutions or the creation of new organizations. Institutions as used here constitute the 'rules of the game', for example laws, rules, habits, routines and so on. Organizations are the actors or players, the actions of which are shaped by (and shape) the rules. See North (1990) and Edquist and Johnson (1997).
9. However, markets are always institutionally embedded and there might be a contradiction between 'perfect competition' and innovation – especially product innovation. If a market is 'perfect', in the neoclassical sense, the only information exchanged between producers and users relates to products already existing in the market and it contains only quantitative information about price and volume. Anonymous relationships between buyer and seller are assumed. Producers have no information about potential user needs and users have no knowledge about the characteristics of new products. 'If the real economy was constituted by pure markets, product innovations would be haphazard and exceptional' (Lundvall, 1988: 350).
10. Paradoxically, then, a monopoly is created by law, in order to create a market for knowledge, that is, to make it possible to trade in knowledge. This has to do with the peculiar characteristics of knowledge as a commodity or a tradable product (Arrow, 1962a). It is hard to know the price of knowledge as a buyer, since you do not know what it is before the transaction. And if you know what it is you do not want to pay for it. In addition, knowledge is not worn out when used – unlike other products.
11. There might also be reasons to treat the solving of existing problems and the creation of future opportunities as two different situations calling for public intervention.
12. Obviously, the degree of uncertainty increases when the problems concern the future. Sometimes the problems may be very difficult to identify.
13. The NMT story is told in Fridlund (2000) and Palmberg (2000), as well as in McKelvey, Texier and Alm (1998).
14. As mentioned earlier, perfect competition might even reduce the rate of (product) innovation. Lundvall (1988: 350) argues that markets supporting product innovation are normally not pure, but institutionally embedded. If policy makers are trying to create conditions that resemble perfect competition in their rule making, it may therefore obstruct

product innovation. Elsewhere, we have shown that this applies to the rules governing public technology procurement created by the European Commission: 'too great a stress on "perfect competition" can undermine competitiveness' (Edquist, Hommen and Tsipouri, 2000: 307).

15. Such allocations are made every year, but the basis for choosing areas to support is seldom discussed explicitly and publicly.

16. Public funding of basic research is provided in all countries, but direct support to specific companies only in some. This is probably because direct support to individual firms has negative side effects, for which reason it should be avoided, to the largest extent possible.

17. For example, EU policy makers have adopted some elements of the SI approach, which is evident in the broader view of innovation policy that was expressed in the 1995 Green Paper on Innovation. Prime Ministers Paavo Lipponen (Finland) and Antonio Guiterres (Portugal) also used the concept of 'innovation system' when they were outlining the immediate future agenda of the EU in terms of 'a Europe of innovation and knowledge' (Letter to the Members of the European Council of 16 October 1999). The OECD also uses the approach intensively (for example, OECD, 1998b). The SI approach is also used as a framework for designing innovation policy at the national level in some EU member countries, for example, Finland and Ireland.

18. The first two books exclusively devoted to analyses of 'national systems of innovation' were Lundvall (1992) and Nelson (1993). However, Chris Freeman (1987) first used the expression in published form. Regional systems of innovation have been addressed, for example, in Braczyk, Cooke and Heidenreich (1998). Sectoral systems of innovation have been analysed in Carlsson (1995), Breschi and Malerba (1997) and Nelson and Mowery (1999). All these books – and others – are reviewed in the introduction to Edquist and McKelvey (2000), which is a collection of 43 central articles on systems of innovation of various kinds.

19. The discussion of the general characteristics of the SI approach is based upon the more detailed discussion in Edquist (1997a: 15–29).

20. For example, public technology procurement policies could be used more systematically to shape patterns of user–producer interaction. Or the knowledge infrastructure (including the system of intellectual property rights) could be used to develop R&D cooperation more fully and so on (Edquist et al., 1998).

21. Lipsey and Carlaw (1998) have shown this for the case of the USA.

22. A general remark related to this issue is that radical innovation and the emergence of new sectoral systems of innovation seem to be more of a 'problem' than reproduction and incremental innovation in established ones. There might be exceptions, though, particularly when established systems undergo profound technological shifts.

23. The mandate and problem-oriented approach of the EU Framework V Programme could also be mentioned here.

24. This includes comparisons with averages for more than one, or all, systems for certain variables. A final kind of comparison would be between a value for a certain variable in an existing system and some norm or goal. However, this would, of course, not be a comparison with another existing system, nor with an optimum.

25. It is often said that every new manufacturing job creates three to four service jobs; that is, 125 000 manufacturing jobs might mean 500 000 jobs in total.

26. A similar analysis identifying a 'problem' in Europe as a whole with regard to the structure of production has been carried out by Jan Fagerberg, Paoloo Guerreri and Bart Verspagen (1999).

27. Two of these three categories (organizations and interaction) were mentioned by Andersen, Metcalfe and Tether (2000), in their short discussion of system failures.

28. The interactions might, for example, lead to lock-in situations. This could be a consequence if conservative users with a weak technical competence put their suppliers at a competitive disadvantage, as a result of the interaction between the two (Lundvall, 1988).

29. There are, however, indications that the performance of the Swedish national system of innovation with respect to product innovation improved during the late 1990s and at the very beginning of the new millennium. Because of the time-lag with regard to the availability of

comparative data, this could not be shown in a systematic way at the time of writing.

30. Such a causal analysis was attempted in Edquist (1993b).

31. It should be mentioned that a certain system failure might be solved in several different ways, since, for example, different organizations may perform the same function, as mentioned in section 7.4.1. For example, research institutes and company-based research departments may, in one national system, perform the same function as research universities in another.

32. See the discussion of 'options' in section 7.6.

33. See section 7.3 for a discussion of selectivity in (innovation) policy.

34. See under Proposition 1 in Chapter 6, section 6.3.

35. Indeed, firms in most sectors of the economy have a high level of knowledge intensity, as measured in other terms, such as embodied technology in machines, and so forth.

36. See under Hypotheses 9 to 13 and 17 to 19.

37. It might be useful to distinguish between labour-saving and capital-saving types of organizational process innovations and a policy for increased employment should, of course, support the latter more than the former. Those kinds of organizational innovations which increase capital productivity (and are capital saving) without reducing employment are, of course, very interesting from an employment perspective. On the whole, however, we know much too little about organizational process innovations and their impact on productivity and employment. (See under Hypotheses 5 and 6.)

38. See under Hypotheses 1 to 4 and 5 and 6.

39. To indicate that a Luddite strategy is non-viable, it could be mentioned that any unemployment problem can be solved by a large enough decrease in productivity. Such a policy would, of course, be devastating for welfare, since productivity growth is the main source of increased material welfare in the long run.

40. This is, for example, the basis of the influential product cycle theory (Utterback and Abernathy, 1975).

41. There is a correlation between 'knowledge-intensive' service sectors and service sectors with a great deal of product innovation. Service sectors with a great deal of product innovation are also likely to be characterized by high productivity, high productivity growth (as measured) and by rapid market growth. The dynamics of goods production seems to be larger than that of service production. Therefore one could expect that product innovation is most rapid in those service sectors that have a close relation to innovative manufacturing sectors. These service sectors grow faster in terms of production as well as employment. (See under Hypotheses 16 to 19.)

42. See under Hypotheses 9 and 13.

43. See the discussion in Chapter 5, section 5.3 and Proposition 3 in Chapter 6, section 6.3.

44. See subsection 7.6.1.

45. See the earlier discussion concerning the creation of markets for technical knowledge through the institution of patent laws in section 7.2.

46. See the discussion of uncertainty and risk in section 7.2.

PART IV

Appendices

Appendix A   Defining and measuring product and process innovations

It is now widely accepted that a useful distinction between product and process innovation can be made, following Schumpeter's (1911: 66) original definitions. However, this idea still remains controversial in some circles (Archibugi, Evangelista and Simonetti, 1994).

Archibugi et al. argue that a major problem is diversity of definitions. They conclude that achieving greater clarity and consistency within clearly specified 'single' definitional approaches will be the most useful way of improving the measurement and analysis of product versus process innovation.

These authors base their argument that the operational distinction between product and process innovations remains elusive on a review of the different definitions that have been used for this purpose. (These are identified below.) Their review is combined with an empirical test of 'variation in the number of product and process innovations, according to the definition adopted' (ibid.: 7).[1]

Archibugi et al. identified several definitions distinguishing product and process innovations. These were simultaneously operationalized and applied to a database capable of accommodating this operation. Most (96.9 per cent) of the innovations examined were found to occupy a 'grey zone' between the categories of product and process innovation. In other words, for 96.9 per cent of the innovations, their classification into one or the other of these two categories was an arbitrary matter.

The 'grey zone' found by Archibugi et al. is produced by differences between the various methods of classification. The authors discuss the basic reasons for this high level of ambiguity in their initial presentation of the various definitions, which we now address. They identify four main definitional approaches:

1. *The 'interviewing' approach*, which relies on the subjective opinions of designated experts, who may be either (a) firm managers or (b) engineers. In both variants, a firm-level definition of innovation is used. According

to such a definition, the innovation in question need not be new to the world, to the national economy, or even to other firms in the same sector, but it must be newly produced (and, hence, a product innovation) or used (and, hence, a process innovation) by the firm that is investigated.

2. *The 'first-user' approach*, which seeks a more objective assessment by asking whether an innovation was first used within the innovating firm (hence, a process) or outside the producing firm (hence, a product). This approach also uses a firm-level definition of innovation, but brings in a market transaction.

3. *Sectoral approaches*, which classify innovations according to both their sector of production and their sector of use, and can identify as their units of analysis either subjects (an organization which both produces and uses the innovation) or objects (for example, a technological application in which the innovation is used). Three sectoral approaches are possible: (a) by subjects, (b) by objects, and (c) by objects and subjects.

4. *The 'final-demand' approach*, which distinguishes between innovations that are directed to consumers (and are thus classified as product innovations) and those that are used as either investment or inter-mediate products by other firms (and are thus classified as process innovations).

Regarding the four definitional approaches to distinguishing between product and process innovations, it can be seen that there are significant continuities and parallels, as well as important differences, among the first three. In contrast, the fourth ('final-demand') is unique among these approaches. Let us, therefore, begin by considering methodological problems connected with the first three approaches and how they might be resolved. Subsequently, we will address the fourth approach.

The first three approaches are, in effect, all 'locational' approaches. That is, they are all based on relating the economic location of a given innovation to the nature of its main use, as either product or process, in that location. (In the second, or 'first-user' approach, for example, the type of use is inferred from the location in which it occurs; by contrast, the first, or 'interviewing' approach, treats the type of use as an indicator of the innovation's primary location of use – that is, whether it remains 'inside' the firm as a process, or is sold 'outside' the firm as a product.[2])

These three approaches differ in terms of whether they use subjective or objective criteria for making this determination, and also in terms of the level of aggregation at which they identify economic locations – that is, firms versus sectors. Thus approaches 1 ('interviewing') and 2 ('first-user') are, respectively, subjective and objective approaches, but both are firm-level approaches.

Approach 3 ('sectoral') encompasses both subjective and objective approaches at the sectoral level. (Accordingly, the two basic sectoral approaches can be merged by insisting upon agreement between sector of production, sectoral technology classification and sector of use to identify process, as opposed to product, innovations.)

According to Archibugi et al. the chief methodological difficulty encountered with all locational approaches to distinguishing between product and process innovations is the problem of aggregation. Thus it is argued that the firm-level approach 'does not say anything at the macro-economic level' and that 'Aggregation of the results obtained for individual firms can generate misleading results' (ibid.: 10). Similarly, it is argued that 'All of the sectoral approaches are influenced heavily by the aggregation of the classification adopted: in the absence of sectoral disaggregation (i.e., if the economy is merged in one sector only) all of the innovations appear as processes, while the number of product innovations increases with the level of disaggregation of the classification adopted' (ibid.: 11).

These methodological difficulties are not insurmountable, especially when viewed in the context in which they have been identified. Archibugi et al. are quite explicit that the large 'grey zone' that they have identified between product and process innovations is largely an artefact of their own methodology (that is, the operationalization of multiple definitions). The methodology, in turn, is limited in its application to only one known database, which has the peculiar advantage of including measures of all the definitions reported and compared by these authors (ibid.: 8, 20).

Not surprisingly, Archibugi et al. reach the practical conclusion that achieving greater clarity and consistency within clearly specified 'single' definitional approaches will be the most useful way of improving the measurement and analysis of product versus process innovation since, 'despite some variability ... and the presence of outliers, empirical analyses using the same definitions achieved reasonably similar results' (ibid.: 21). They also admit quite readily that 'The majority of empirical research that we are aware of classified innovations according to the firm level approach' (ibid.: 17).

It follows from these considerations that for any individual definitional approach, the 'grey zone' identified by Archibugi et al. will remain a largely artificial problem – that is, a non-issue in practice. As for 'the majority of empirical research', it also follows from earlier observations about the limitations of the firm-level approach that the most important of the 'real' difficulties can be resolved by paying close attention to the problem of aggregation – that is, by clearly specifying and, if possible, comparing levels of aggregation in any analysis.

In this book, we counter the methodological difficulties considered thus far in this discussion by taking the following three steps:

1. We adopt (and explicate) a firm-level definition of the distinction between product and process innovation.
2. We use – primarily, if not exclusively – empirical analyses based on data collected through instruments using this definition (or very similar ones) as the main basis for the survey of research findings presented in this report. Both of these measures are facilitated by the fact that the main international organizations (for example, the European Commission and the OECD) responsible for collecting data and coordinating and sponsoring empirical research and analysis relevant to the purposes of this report have consistently used a 'firm-level' approach to the identification of process and product innovations. Moreover, this approach is similar in its terms of reference to the 'subjective' (that is, firm-centred) definition that we elaborate (European Commission, 1993: 2; OECD, 1996c: 9–10, 34–5).
3. Finally, we pay close attention to the problem of aggregation, distinguishing among – and where possible, comparing – results obtained from empirical analyses conducted at several distinct levels of aggregation: firms, industries, sectors and nations.

Let us now turn to a brief consideration of methodological problems associated with the fourth or 'final-demand' approach to distinguishing between product and process innovations. Unlike the 'locational' approaches discussed above, the 'final-demand' approach focuses on fundamentally different types of consumption. Thus, whether or not a given innovation is used inside or outside the originating firm or sector becomes here a relatively unimportant consideration.

What is of far more importance in the 'final-demand' approach is the nature or manner of its intended use or consumption. Thus a fundamental distinction is made between innovations, 'according to whether they are initially directed towards consumers or towards other firms' (Archibugi, Evangelista and Simonetti, 1994: 12). Implicit in this approach is the idea that product innovations might be most appropriately associated with production for consumer markets and process innovations with production of 'investment' or 'intermediate' products for other firms, since '[consumer products] are strongly influenced by exogenous shifts in demand, and [products for firms] are subject to direct linkages between suppliers and users' (ibid.).

Strictly speaking, however, the 'final-demand' approach does not establish a basic distinction between product and process innovations but only considers innovations as products of different types. Thus the definitional 'one-sidedness' of this approach represents a problem equivalent to that of 'aggregation' in locational approaches.

Just as the aggregation of all sectors into one generates the result that all innovations within an economy become process innovations, 'In the case of process innovations, the Final Demand approach shows the highest percentage of innovations, at 95.5 percent' (ibid.: 14). This result simply reflects the market distribution of innovations, but it also indicates why the 'final-demand' approach is a large contributor to the 'grey zone' – that is, it is not properly a distinction between process and product innovations.

In this book, we counter the methodological difficulties associated with the 'final-demand' approach by dealing with the question of whether and for what purposes innovations are destined for either 'consumer' or 'producer' use entirely under the heading of product innovation. More specifically, we consider the distinctions among product innovations as 'investment', 'intermediate' and 'consumer' products in relation to processes of 'substitution' and the extent to which products destined for consumption by other firms can become process innovations in a 'second appearance'. This discussion occurs in Chapter 5, sections 5.2, 5.3 and 5.4.

NOTES

1. The empirical data used in this test comprised a sample drawn from the SPRU database, which 'has the great advantage of allowing the measurement of all the definitions reported and the comparison of them; in other words, the differences that emerge cannot be attributed to differences in the data sources, but rather to the definitions adopted' (Archibugi, Evangelista and Simonetti, 1994: 8).
2. A quasi-objective variation on the 'interviewing' approach, employed in one national patenting office, uses expert opinion on the engineering characteristics of innovations to determine type of use, but still locates the innovations in specific firms (Ellis, 1980).

Appendix B   Organizational innovations

Our emphasis in this report on organizational changes as a type of process innovation draws attention to the interdependencies between organizational and technological innovation. It stems from the argument that 'A theory of technical change which ignores these interdependencies is no more helpful than a theory of economics which ignores the interdependencies of prices and quantities in the world economy' (Freeman, 1995). The main difficulty involved in incorporating a concept of organizational change into our broader concept of innovation is the problem of doing this in a systematic way, on the basis of well-specified categories that are congruent with the theoretical foundations of the SI approach (Edquist, 1997a: section 2.3.1).

This appendix goes beyond our central question of how different types of innovations are related to employment creation and destruction. Despite that, we include it because it introduces some interesting parallels and ways forward for analysing and discussing organizational innovations. It does so by discussing relevant, and partly related, theories in sociology and/or organizational theory that could be useful for analysing organizational innovations within an SI perspective. We include it mainly because of the pressing need for further studies of organizational process innovations and the relation between technological and organizational innovations. Thus the main aim here is to stimulate further research and the formulation of research questions.

There is, of course, a very broad and diffuse body of work on organizational change that is situated largely outside of the economics literature, in related fields such as management theory and economic sociology. However, even in those sub-disciplinary fields that are most closely concerned with the interdependencies between technological and organizational innovation, such as management studies in technology strategy, reviews of the literature have consistently pointed out conceptual weaknesses. It has been stated that 'the most basic categories and terminology ... have not yet been satisfactorily determined' (Kantrow, 1980) and (more recently) that 'the study of technology strategy is not a discipline with a well-developed internal motor of conceptual development' (Adler, 1989: 80). These considerations warn us against indiscriminate borrowing from theoretically eclectic and conceptually underdeveloped 'applied' research literatures.

Other bodies of organizational theory and research, however, appear to have a much higher degree of complementarity with, and potential for contribution to, the SI approach. The 'organizational ecology' approach in economic sociology is highly promising in this respect (Carroll and Hannan, 1995; Hannan and Freeman, 1989). This school of thought is based on evolutionary and institutionalist principles similar, if not identical, to those informing the SI approach, and concentrates on the same themes of the generation of novelty, the operation of selection environments, and the retention and transmission of information. Thus it views organizational innovation as a complex historical process in which 'few organisations succeed at transformation and imitation and ... selection serves as the driving force of long-term change' (Carroll and Hannan, 1995: 23).

The organizational ecology perspective shares the view of evolutionary economics that 'highly flexible adaptation to change is not likely to characterise the behaviour of individual firms' (Nelson and Winter, 1982: 134) and therefore draws attention to the tendency of existing organizations to exhibit 'structural inertia'. It suggests that those aspects of organizational forms in which such inertia is most pronounced are the several 'core' dimensions of organizational structure: 'stated goals, forms of authority, core technology and marketing strategy' (Hannan and Freeman, 1989: 79). This conceptualization of 'core structure' provides a basis for classifying and determining the relative importance of the many varieties of organizational change discussed in the management literature. It also generates categories of changes in organizational form that are congruent with the different types (organizational and technological changes in *processes*, and design and quality changes in *products*) of innovation considered by the SI approach. However, the integration of concepts drawn from 'organizational ecology' into the SI approach is clearly beyond the scope of this appendix.

Another avenue for the incorporation of elements of existing theory and research on organizational change into the SI approach is suggested by the strong emphasis on institutions of some authors working within this approach (Johnson, 1992). Their work draws attention to the important contribution of institutionalist economics to the SI approach (Hodgson, 1993). Institutional economics has its sociological counterpart in the 'new institutionalism' in organizational analysis (Powell and Dimaggio, 1991). No integration of these traditions has yet been attempted within the SI approach, although some authors consider it important for the SI approach to answer questions concerning 'the relations between institutions and organisations and between institutions and markets' (Edquist and Johnson, 1997: section 3.2.2). However, at least one chapter (5) in one of the foundational texts (Lundvall, 1992) of the SI approach has dealt with institutional aspects of organizational innovation (Gjerding, 1992).

The last-mentioned contribution draws attention to the special importance of firm-level organizational innovations of a particular type – namely, changes in the 'management system', which is defined as 'the common general organisational principles of a national system of innovation guiding the organisation of work at the factory level' (ibid., 1992: 95). This definition makes explicit an analytical focus implicit in some of the earliest writing on systems of innovation (Freeman, 1988).[1] In terms of extension to higher levels of aggregation, innovation in the 'management system' at the firm level can be linked to adaptations or transformations of the institutions that serve to coordinate activity in regional, national and international economies.

The 'management system', essentially, is the firm-level expression of an economy's 'governance system', which has been defined as 'the totality of institutional arrangements – including rules and rule-making agents – that regulate transactions inside and across the boundaries of an economic system' (Hollingsworth, Schmitter and Streeck, 1994: 5). Some authors working within the SI approach have expressed interest in exploring the implications of change in governance structures, because 'for the sake of innovation and sustained economic development, it matters who makes investment decisions, what types of decisions they make, and how returns generated by these investments are distributed' (Lazonick, O'Sullivan and Smith, 1996). It follows that the SI approach is at least peripherally concerned with how innovations in firm-level governance or management systems affect the manner in which 'The organisational structure of the enterprise plans and co-ordinates ... a collective learning process' (Lazonick, 1994: 190).

From the perspective of the evolutionary and institutionalist theories contributing to the SI approach, organizational innovation is viewed mainly as a matter of creating new routines or modifying existing ones (Baum and Singh, 1994; Hodgson, 1993; Nelson and Winter, 1982).[2] This often occurs through diffusion processes in which organizational innovations have not originated within firms. Rather, there is a deliberate transfer and subsequent adaptation of new 'routines' from one context to another, such as through the agency of external consultants (Niosi, 1996: 3). The postwar migration of total quality control (TQC) from the USA to Japan is a famous case in point (Juran, 1993; Main, 1994).

Organizational innovation remains difficult for authors working within the SI approach to measure and analyse. That is because, as we have observed in the main body of this book (Chapter 2, section 2.2), they are not based on formal R&D and are seldom appropriated through intellectual property rights – even though they are sometimes commodified in the form of consultancy services.

The assertion that organizational innovation is not based on formal R&D

may be viewed as questionable when the work of consultancy services specializing in areas such as 'organizational development' is taken into consideration. However, 'formal R&D', as the term is normally used, is a highly exclusive category. For example, software development (among other, similar activities) is only sometimes classified as formal R&D activity, with the result that statistics concerning service-sector R&D are greatly misleading (Soete and Verspagen, 1991). This is the case, despite the fact that authorities such as the *Oslo Manual* have adopted broad definitions of R&D as 'creative work undertaken on a systematic basis in order to increase the stock of knowledge, including knowledge of man [*sic*], culture and society' (OECD, 1996c: 43).

The practical qualification to such broad definitions is that only 'initial suggestions' have been made about how to modify a conventionally rigid definitional separation between 'technological' and 'organizational' change, so that most instruments for collecting data about innovation continue to exhibit a very strong technological bias (OECD, 1996c: annex 2). Therefore, organizational innovation is generally neglected in innovation surveys, and software development is regarded as a 'borderline case', which can be classified as R&D only 'as long as it involves making a scientific or technological advance and/or resolving scientific/technological uncertainty on a systematic basis' (ibid.: 43). 'Missed' by this 'scientific–technical' approach, of course, are instances where software development may use conventional technology to reconfigure knowledge, communication and organizational structures within firms, with important consequences for their economic performance.[3]

The diffusion of organizational innovations in the form of 'new routines' is not well understood. However, existing knowledge indicates that the pattern of diffusion is similar, in some respects, to that of technological process innovations (Niosi, 1996). Similarities include the following: large firms are usually the main originators, since they possess greater resources for experimentation. Certain industries have also served as the 'cradles' of organizational innovations later diffused to others – for example, the diffusion of 'Fordist' forms of production organization from the automotive manufacturing to others – indicating the importance of industry characteristics (Kenney and Florida, 1993; Spitz, 1988). Moreover, national environments and regulatory conditions can pose serious obstacles to diffusion, demonstrating that institutional patterns affect the direction and rate of organizational innovation (Niosi, 1995; Posthuma, 1992).[4]

The similarity of diffusion patterns between organizational innovations and technological process innovations (and the discrepancies between these patterns and the predictions of mainstream economic theory, which expects that there will be a standard diffusion pattern for any innovation in any given population of firms) can be partially explained by reference to problems of appropriability. There are common problems related to the importance of tacit knowledge, which has to be developed largely on a trial-and-error basis and makes it difficult for competitors to determine the value of an innovation. However, these problems are more pronounced in the case of organizational innovations. They therefore give rise to distinctive features in the pattern and mechanisms of diffusion for organizational innovations – particularly the greater importance of 'secrecy' as a means of appropriation, and the need for originating firms to diffuse innovations at their own costs in order to capture the full benefits (Niosi, 1996: 9–10).

Economists have long tended to assume that knowledge of technological innovations is easily codified (that is, rendered into an explicit form, capable of transmission) and is thus readily utilized – 'the sort of thing that can be recorded, stored at negligible cost, and referred to when needed' (Nelson and Winter, 1982: 61). These assumptions have proven to be rather weak in the case of many technological innovations (Von Hippel, 1994). Conversely, economists have tended to regard knowledge of organizational innovations (as part of the broader category of 'technical skills') as less codifiable (due to their more 'tacit' or 'context-bound' character) and, hence, less easily transmitted – except through the transfer of skilled personnel, who can serve as 'translators' of this knowledge between the context of one firm and that of another (Rosenberg, 1976: ch. 9). These assumptions have proven to be rather more sound.

The diffusion of the Japanese model of factory organization provides an instructive case in point. US auto manufacturers initially experienced great difficulty in replicating the organizational innovations assumed to be responsible for the economic success of their Japanese counterparts. These practices were eventually translated into the US context with relative ease by Japanese 'transplants' and 'joint ventures' with US manufacturers (Womack, Jones and Roos, 1990). What is significant in this example is not simply the obvious importance of tacit knowledge to the successful transfer of organizational innovations. It is also noteworthy that many of the organizational innovations characteristic of the Japanese model had to be diffused by the originators if their full benefits were to be captured. Large assembly firms, for example, must educate their suppliers in the use of JIT methods (Cusumano, 1985).

The example given above demonstrates that, just as supposedly transferable technological knowledge sometimes exhibits a fairly high level of 'stickiness' (Von Hippel, 1994), organizational knowledge is sometimes 'slippery' enough to be copied effectively. Moreover, it shows that there can be strong economic incentives for innovators to promote the imitation of new routines or organizational forms. Nevertheless, due to the difficulties of transferring this kind of information, even within firms, skilled 'translators' are often required for this purpose (Abo, 1994). Thus one of the most important mechanisms for the diffusion of organizational innovations among wholly independent firms is the flow of managers and technical personnel from one firm to another (Allen, 1977).

These considerations provide a basis for understanding how and why the process of copying is sometimes facilitated by organization consultants – who are then 'social carriers' of organizational knowledge. That is, such knowledge is embodied in them. Thus the knowledge basis behind organizational innovations may sometimes be sold as consultancy services. In such cases organizational innovations are commodified. Somewhat ironically, the purchase of such services is often required by firms to cope with the unanticipated effects of technological process innovations.[5]

There are indications that this phenomenon is becoming increasingly widespread, in conjunction with the rapid growth in recent years of 'industrial networks' – and, more particularly, of 'networks of innovators' (Freeman, 1991). As intermediary providers of less easily codified forms of knowledge – including technical skills and organizational 'know-how' – consultancies, design services, training and education services, and services bridging the gap between technology suppliers and users have an increasingly prominent role. In this connection, it has been argued that 'the information "explosion" poses major management problems' for firms, such that '[a] growing premium is now placed on effectively employing (external) technical and business expertise to guide organisations through continuous change' (KISIN, 1996: 10).

To summarize, the SI approach has shown some recognition that organizational innovations are sometimes not only important process innovations as such, but also vital for the development and use of technological innovations. It is also a fact that the study of organizational process innovations is neglected as compared to the study of technological ones. This is particularly true of the economics literature, although historical, sociological and organizational studies have much to offer in this respect (Clarke, 1987). However deficient our knowledge about technical change is, we have even less systematic knowledge about the emergence and diffusion of organizational innovations and their socioeconomic consequences. Because organizational innovations are likely to have major impacts on employment creation and destruction, and because organizational innovations can conceivably be studied across sectors and nations, the relations between organizational innovations and employment are important avenues for further research.

NOTES

1. Moreover, at the firm level of aggregation it clearly corresponds to organizational ecology's focus on changes in 'core structure' – particularly, those dimensions of core structure (for example, 'goals' and 'forms of authority') that may be identified with specifically organizational (as opposed to technological) innovation.

2. This novelty-generating process can produce either gradual variation marked by high levels of continuity, or discontinuous bursts of variety, depending on the features and operation of the relevant selection environments (Somit and Peterson, 1992). From the perspective of the firm, however, the process 'is far from coherent, logical and well-structured, but is best characterised by experimentation, tinkering and trial-and-error' (Niosi, 1996: 3).

3. An interesting case in point is that of management information systems (MIS) (Ciborra and Schneider, 1992). These authors discuss the example of the introduction of a standard computerized 'manufacturing resources planning' (MRP) system at an aircraft instruments plant. Implementation did not involve the creation of new software, merely the inputting of categories and data specific to the plant. The ostensible purpose was not to restructure the manufacturing system but to create a replica or 'simulation' of it. However, it was subsequently discovered that the system failed to produce the expected gains in efficiency because of 'poor fit' between the computer simulation and the actual process of production. To resolve this problem, organizational change was required. In particular, new organizational routines and new skills would have to be developed, in order for workers using the system 'to participate in a constant round of evaluation and decision-making' (ibid.: 275). Contrary to original expectations of a simple replication of the existing system via computer simulation, some organizational restructuring of the manufacturing system was needed.

4. In these respects, the diffusion of organizational innovations is better understood from an SI approach than from the perspective of standard economic theory, whose predictions of a standard diffusion pattern for any innovation in any given population of firms has been criticized for its overly restrictive assumptions (Davies, 1979).

5. Instances might include unsuccessful attempts to replicate organizational routines with computerized information systems. In such cases, consultants may be necessary to provide solutions to problems of incongruity or conflict between computer 'simulations' and highly resilient 'background assumptions and institutional arrangements' within organizations (Ciborra and Schneider, 1992: 270).

Appendix C   Taxonomies of innovation

The following discussion provides a brief overview of the main arguments and concepts used in developing taxonomies of various kinds of innovations. Our primary purpose in this discussion will be to explain the significance (and possible limitations) of the definitions of 'significant' and 'incremental' innovation that have been used in data collection instruments for much of the empirical research to which this report refers (European Commission, 1993; OECD, 1996c).

One basis for categorizing product innovations has been the distinction drawn by some theorists between 'generic' and 'non-generic' innovations (Freeman, 1974; Nelson and Winter, 1977, 1982). Generic innovations refer broadly to new 'systems' or classes of technology that have wide diffusion and economic consequences of major importance. Non-generic innovations refer to technological alternatives within these systems that are potentially substitutable for one another, and hence optional.

Related to the dichotomy between 'generic' and 'non-generic' innovations is a distinction between 'radical' and 'incremental' innovations – that is, between those involving basic changes in design and those involving only minor modifications. It has been argued, though, that 'Radical innovations are difficult to disentangle from generic innovations and it is therefore best to use radical and incremental as relative terms whose interpretation is anchored in agreed benchmarks of empirical examples' (Clarke, 1987: 35). The difficulty alluded to here arises because the term 'generic' has to do with the degree of *impact* in other sectors, while the term 'radical' refers to the degree of *change* in artefacts.

Specifying what is meant by a distinction between 'radical' and 'incremental' innovations is further complicated when different levels of analysis are introduced. In studies of technology development this differentiation of levels is usually accomplished through the disaggregation of technological systems into their subsystems or component parts. For example, the early development of the automobile as a 'generic' innovation has been shown to be associated with a host of 'radical' innovations in its subsystems (Abernathy, 1978). Examples of radical innovation at the subsystem level would include design choices in propulsion systems (steam versus internal combustion engines) and transmission systems (clutch-and-gearbox transmissions versus simple variable speed transmissions). With this type of analysis, however, it is not always possible to identify 'radical' innovations with 'generic' ones. For example, it has been demonstrated that continuous incremental innovation at the subsystemic level can, over time, result in significant changes to 'generic' technology systems (David, 1975: 174–91; Rosenberg, 1982).

One solution to this problem has been to distinguish more clearly between radical and incremental innovation by developing new categories of 'architectural' and 'modular' innovation (Henderson and Clark, 1990). In this scheme, a product innovation can be classified along two dimensions: (a) the impact on components, and (b) the impact on linkages between components – with impact itself being thought in terms of whether or not any basic change occurs. Accordingly, a radical innovation is conceived of as establishing a new 'dominant design' and thereby a new set of 'core design concepts' embodied in components that are linked together in a new 'architecture'.

In contrast, incremental innovation refers only to the further development of an established design, through improvements to individual components that change neither their core concepts nor the links between them. On this basis, we can also identify two additional possibilities. Where there is change only in the core design concepts for the components of a technology, but not in relationships between them, 'modular' innovation can be said to occur. The opposite case – that is, where there is change only in the linkages between components, but not in any of their underlying core design concepts – can be said to constitute 'architectural innovation'.

The additional categories of 'modular' and 'architectural' innovation are particularly useful in explaining why technical innovations involving seemingly modest changes to existing technology often have important consequences for firms and economies (Clark, 1987). Despite its explanatory power, however, there is little use in the empirical research literature of the approach to classification of product innovations with which these categories are associated. This classificatory approach is what might be referred to as an 'expert' definitional scheme, and as such remains difficult to operationalize for purposes of firm-level data collection. Responses to innovation surveys are usually supplied by managers who may or may not be expert in the engineering characteristics of a given technology.

Accordingly, the innovation surveys regularly conducted by bodies such as the EC and the OECD have continued to rely upon a conventional dichotomy between significant and incremental innovation. These terms, as used in the surveys, are consistent with the *Oslo Manual* distinction between 'a technologically new product' and 'a technologically improved product' (OECD, 1996c: 35). In EC innovation surveys, these categories have been translated, respectively, as '*significant innovation* ... involving radically new technologies, or ... combining existing technologies in new uses' and '*incremental innovation* ... enhanced ... through use of new components or materials ... [or] improved by partial changes to one or more of the subsystems' (European Commission, 1993: 2). Purely 'cosmetic' product changes are excluded by these terms.

References

Abernathy, W.J. (1978), *The Productivity Dilemma: Roadblock to innovation in the automobile industry*, Baltimore, MD: Johns Hopkins.

Abo, T. (1994), *Hybrid Factory*, New York: Oxford University Press.

Abramovitz, M. (1989), *Thinking about Growth*, New York: Cambridge University Press.

Abramovitz, M. (1993), 'The search for the sources of growth: Areas of ignorance, old and new', *Journal of Economic History*, **53** (2), 217-43.

Adler, P.S. (1989), 'Technology strategy: A guide to the literatures', in R.S. Rosenbloom and R.A. Burgelman (eds), *Research on Technological Innovation Management and Policy: A research annual*, vol. 4, Greenwich, CT: JAI Press, pp. 25-151.

Alaminos, J.D. and Martinez, S.B. (1999), 'The interrelation between technology and total employment: Some observations', *IPTS Report*, **34** (May), 30-35.

Alänge, S., Jacobsson, S. and Lindberg, P. (1996), *From Job-less Growth to Growth-with-less-jobs: Employment and equity impact of technical and organisational change*, Göteborg: Chalmers University of Technology, School of Technology Management and Economics.

Alexander, L. (1996), 'Technology, economic growth and employment: New research from the US Department of Commerce', in D. Foray and B.-Å. Lundvall (eds), *Employment and Growth in the Knowledge-based Economy*, Paris: OECD.

Allen, R.C. (1986), 'The impact of technical change on employment, wages and the distribution of skills: A historical perspective', in W.C. Riddell (ed.), *Adapting to Change: Labour market adjustment in Canada*, Toronto: University of Toronto Press, pp. 71-110.

Allen, T. (1977), *Managing the Flow of Technology*, Cambridge, MA: MIT Press.

Amsalem, M.A. (1983), *Technology Choice in Developing Countries: The textile and pulp and paper industries*, Cambridge, MA: MIT Press.

Andersen, B., Metcalfe, J.S. and Tether, B. (2000), 'Distributed innovation systems and instituted economic processes', in J.S. Metcalfe and I. Miles (eds), *Innovation Systems in the Service Economy*, Boston/Dordrecht/London: Kluwer Academic Publishers.

Andersen, B. and Miles, I. (1999), *Distributed Innovation Systems in Copyright Industries: Music in the knowledge-based service economy* (discussion paper), Manchester, UK: ESRC Centre for Research on Innovation and Competition (CRIC).

Aoki, M. (1990), 'A new paradigm of work organization and coordination?', in S. Marglin and J. Schor (eds), *The Golden Age of Capitalism: Reinterpreting the postwar experience*, Oxford: Clarendon Press.

Archibugi, D. (1989), *The Sectoral Structure of Innovative Activities*, Brighton: University of Sussex.

Archibugi, D. and Michie, J. (1997), 'Technological globalisation and national systems of innovation', in D. Archibugi and J. Michie (eds), *Technology, Globalisation and Economic Performance*, Cambridge: Cambridge University Press, pp. 1–23.

Archibugi, D., Casaratto, S. and Sirilli, G. (1987), 'Innovative activity, R&D and patenting: The evidence of the survey on innovation diffusion in Italy', *Science, Technology and Industry Review*, **2**, 135–50.

Archibugi, D., Evangelista, R. and Simonetti, R. (1994), 'On the definition and measurement of product and process innovations', in Y. Shinonoya and M. Perlman (eds), *Technology, Industries and Institutions: Studies in Schumpeterian perspectives*, Ann Arbor, MI: The University of Michigan Press.

Arrow, K. (1962a), 'Economic welfare and the allocation of resources for invention', in National Bureau Committee for Economic Research and Committee on Economic Growth of the Social Science Research Council (eds), *The Rate and Direction of Inventive Activity: Economic and social factors – A conference of the universities*, Princeton, NJ: Princeton University Press.

Arrow, K. (1962b), 'The economic implications of learning by doing', *Review of Economic Studies*, **XXIX** (80).

Assarsson, B. (1991), 'Kvalitetsförändringar och produktivitetsmåatt', in K. Eklund (ed.), *Hur mäta produktivitet? Expertrapport nr. 1 till Produktivitetsdelegationen*, Stockholm: Allmänna Förlaget, pp. 193–257.

Australian Manufacturing Council (1994), *Leading the Way: A study of best manufacturing practices in Australia and New Zealand*, Melbourne: Australian Manufacturing Council.

Baba, Y. and Takai, S. (1990), 'Information technology introduction in big banks: The case of Japan', in C. Freeman and L. Soete (eds), *New Explorations in the Economics of Technical Change*, London: Pinter Publishers.

Baily, M. and Gordon, R. (1988), 'The productivity slow-down, measurement issues and the explosion of computer power', *Brookings Papers on Economic Activity*, no. 2, Washington, DC: The Brookings Institution, pp. 347–431.

Baldwin, J. (1995), *Human Capital Development and Innovation: A sectoral analysis*, paper presented at the Conference on Implications of Knowledge-Based Growth for Micro-Economic Policies, Ottawa, 30-31 March.

Baldwin, J. and Johnson, J. (1995), 'Business strategies in more and less innovative firms in Canada', *Research Policy*, **24**.

Barass, R. (1986), 'Towards a theory of innovation in services', *Research Policy*, **15**, 161-73.

Barass, R. (1990), 'Interactive innovation in financial and business services: The vanguard of the service revolution', *Research Policy*, **19**, 215-37.

Barker, T. (1990), 'Sources of structural change for the U.K. service industries', *Economic Systems Research*, **2** (2), 173-83.

Bartlett, C.A. and Ghoshal, S. (1990), 'Managing innovation in transnational corporations', in C.A. Bartlett and G. Hedlund (eds), *Managing the Global Firm*, London: Routledge.

Baum, J. and Singh, J.V. (1994), *Evolutionary Dynamics of Organizations*, Oxford: Oxford University Press.

Baumol, W.J. (1967), 'Macroeconomics of unbalanced growth: The anatomy of urban crisis', *American Economic Review*, **57**, 415-26.

Baumol, W.J. (1985), 'Productivity policy and the service sector', in R.P. Inman (ed.), *Managing the Service Economy: Prospects and problems*, Cambridge: Cambridge University Press.

Baumol, W.J., Blackman, S. and Wolff, E. (1985), 'Unbalanced growth revisited: Asymptotic stagnancy and new evidence', *American Economic Review*, **75**, 806-17.

Baumol, W.J., Blackman, S. and Wolff, E. (1989), *Productivity and American Leadership: The long view*, Cambridge, MA: MIT Press.

Becker, G. (1975), *Human Capital*, New York: National Bureau of Economic Research.

Bell, M. and Pavitt, K. (1997), 'Technological accumulation and industrial growth: Contrasts between developed and developing countries', in D. Archibugi and J. Michie (eds), *Technology Globalisation and Economic Performance*, Cambridge: Cambridge University Press, pp. 83-137.

Bell, M. and Scott-Kemmis, D. (1997), 'The mythology of learning-by-doing in world war II airframe and ship production', *Industrial and Corporate Change*, **6**.

Betcherman, G., McMullen, K., Leckie, N. and Caron, C. (1994), *The Canadian Workplace in Transition: Final report*, Kingston, Ontario: Queen's University Industrial Relations Centre.

Bilderbeek, R. and Buitelaar, W. (1992), 'Bank computerization and organizational innovations: The long and winding road to the bank of the future', *New Technology, Work and Employment* (Spring), 54-60.

Blazecjak, J. (1991), 'Evaluation of the long-term effects of technological trends on the structure of employment', *Futures* (July–August), 594–604.

Bloom, M. (1992), *Technological Change in the Korean Electronics Industry*, Paris: OECD Development Centre.

Boissot, M. (1995), *Information Space: A framework for learning in organizations, institutions and culture*, London/New York: Routledge.

Bosworth, D. (1987), 'Prices, costs and elasticities of demand', in OECD (ed.), *Information Technology and Economic Prospects*, no. 12, Paris: OECD.

Braczyk, H.-J., Cooke, P. and Heidenreich, M. (1998), *Regional Innovation Systems: The role of governance in a globalised world*, London: UCL Press.

Breschi, S. and Malerba, F. (1997), 'Sectoral innovation systems, technological regimes, Schumpeterian dynamics and spatial boundaries', in C. Edquist (ed.), *Systems of Innovation: Technologies, organizations and institutions*, London: Pinter Publishers/Cassell Academic, pp. 130–156.

Breton, T. (1994), 'Les téléservices en France, quels marchés pour les autoroutes de l'information', *La Documentation Française*.

Brouwer, E., Kleinknecht, A. and Reijnen, J. (1993), 'Employment growth and innovation at the firm level', *Journal of Evolutionary Economics*, **3**, 153–9.

Browning, H. and Singlemann, J. (1978), 'The transformation of the U.S. labor force: The interaction of industries and occupations', *Politics and Society*, **8**, 481–509.

Bruland, K. (1989), *British Technology and European Industrialisation: The Norwegian textile industry in the mid-nineteenth century*, Cambridge: Cambridge University Press.

Brynjolfsson, E. (1991), *The Productivity of Information Technology: Review and assessment*, Cambridge, MA: Center for Coordination Science, Sloan School of Management, MIT.

Buzzachi, L., Colombo, M. and Mariotti, S. (1995), 'Technological regimes and innovation in services: The case of the Italian banking industry', *Research Policy*, **24**, 151–68.

Calvert, J., Ibarra, C., Patel, P. and Pavitt, K. (1996), *Innovation Outputs in European Industry: Analysis from CIS - Report to DG XIII (EIMS 93/52)*, Brighton: Science Policy Research Unit, University of Sussex.

Campbell, M. (1993), 'The employment effects of new technology and organisational change: An empirical study', *New Technology, Work and Employment*, **8** (2), 134–40.

Carlsson, B. (ed.) (1995), *Technological Systems and Economic Performance: The case of factory automation*, Dordrecht: Kluwer Academic Publishers.

Carlsson, B. and Stankiewicz, R. (1995), 'On the nature, function and composition of technological systems', in B. Carlsson (ed.), *Technological Systems and Economic Performance: The case of factory automation*, Dordrecht: Kluwer Academic Publishers.

Carroll, G. and Hannan, M.T. (eds) (1995), *Organizations in Industry: Strategy, structure and selection*, New York: Oxford University Press.

Casadio, C. (1995), *Evidence from Firm-level Case Studies: Motor vehicles, health care, financial services: Paper prepared for the OECD Secretariat by Insights Consulting*, Paris: OECD Secretariat.

Charles River Associates (1980), *Innovation, Competition, and Government Policy in the Semi-conductor Industry*, Lexington, MA: Lexington Books.

Chennells, L. and Van Reenen, J. (1998), *Technical Change and the Structure of Employment and Wages: A survey of the microeconomic evidence*, paper presented at the conference on 'Transition to the knowledge society: Policies and strategies for individual participation and learning', Vancouver, British Columbia, Canada, 5–6 November.

Ciborra, C.U. and Schneider, L.S. (1992), 'Transforming the routines and contexts of management, work and technology', in P.S. Adler (ed.), *Technology and the Future of Work*, New York: Oxford University Press, pp. 269–91.

Clark, K.B. (1987), 'Managing technology in international competition: The case of product development in response to foreign entry', in M. Spence and H. Hazard (eds), *International Competitiveness*, Cambridge, MA: Ballinger, pp. 27–74.

Clarke, P. (1987), *Anglo-American Innovation*, Berlin: Walter De Gruyter.

Cohen, W.M. and Levinthal, D.A. (1990), 'Absorptive capacity: A new perspective on learning and innovation', *Administrative Science Quarterly*, **35** (March), 128–52.

Cohendet, P. and Llerena, P. (1997), 'Learning, technical change and public policy: How to exploit and create diversity', in C. Edquist (ed.), *Systems of Innovation: Technologies, organisations and institutions*, London: Pinter Publishers/Cassell Academic.

Commission of the European Communities (1994), *Growth, Competitiveness, Employment: The challenges and ways forward into the 21st century – White paper*, Luxembourg: Office for Official Publications of the European Communities.

Cusumano, M. (1985), *The Japanese Automobile Industry: Technology and management at Nissan and Toyota*, Cambridge, MA: The Council of East Asian Studies of Harvard University.

Dahmén, E. (1988), '"Development blocks" in industrial economics', *Scandinavian Economic History Review*, **1**, 3–14.

DaSilva, J.S. and Fernandes, B.E. (1995), 'The European research program for advanced mobile systems: Addressing the needs of the European Community', *IEEE Personal Communications*, **2** (1), 14–19.

David, P. and Foray, D. (1995), 'Accessing and expanding the science and technology knowledge base', *STI Review*, **16**, 14–69.

David, P.A. (1975), *Technological Choice, Innovation and Economic Growth: Essays on American and British experience in the 19th century*, Cambridge: Cambridge University Press.

David, P.A. (1990), 'Computer and dynamo: The modern productivity paradox in a not too distant mirror', *American Economic Review*, **80** (2), 355–61.

Davies, S. (1979), *The Diffusion of Process Innovations*, Cambridge: Cambridge University Press.

De Meyer, A. (1994), *Manufacturing Delivers! But will that be enough?* Fontainebleau: INSEAD.

De Wit, R. (1991), *A Review of the Literature on Technological Change and Employment*, paper presented at the EEC conference on Macro-Economic and Sectoral Analysis of Future Employment and Training Perspectives in the New Information Technologies in the EC, Brussels, 17–18 October.

Delauney, J.-C. and Gadrey, J. (1992), *Services in Economic Thought: Three centuries of debate*, Dordrecht: Kluwer.

Denison, E. (1962), *The Sources of Growth and the Alternatives Before Us*, New York: Committee for Economic Development.

Department of Finance, Canada (1992), *Employment Growth in High-tech and High-knowledge Industries*, Ottawa: Department of Finance, Canada.

Dosi, G. (1982), 'Technological paradigms and technological trajectories', *Research Policy*, **11**, 147–63.

Dosi, G. (1988), 'The nature of the innovative process', in G. Dosi, C. Freeman, R. Nelson, G. Silverberg and L. Soete (eds), *Technical Change and Economic Theory*, London: Pinter Publishers.

Dosi, G. and Malerba, F. (eds) (1996), *Organisation and Strategy in the Evolution of the Enterprise*, Basingstoke: Macmillan.

Dosi, G., Freeman, C., Nelson, R., Silverberg, G. and Soete, L. (eds) (1988), *Technical Change and Economic Theory*, London: Pinter Publishers.

Dreher, C. (1996), *Measuring Innovations in Manufacturing: Diffusion, adopter potentials and characteristics of technical and organisational process innovations*, paper presented at the 'Innovation Measurement and Policies' International Conference of the European Commission (Eurostat DG XII), Luxembourg, 20–21 May.

Dreher, C., Fleig, J., Harnischfeger, M. and Klimmer, M. (1995), *Neue Produktionskonzepte in der Deutschen Industrie - Bestandsaufnahme, Analyse und wirtschaftspolitische Implikationen. Technik - Wirtschaft -*

Politik. Schriftenreihe des FhG-ISI, Bd 18, Heidelberg: Fraunhofer Gemeinschaft – Institute for Systems and Innovations Research.

Dunning, J. (1992), *The Globalisation of Business*, London: Routledge.

ECOAnalyse (1995), *Tusen blomster: Løn, skatt og sysselsetting i ni industriland, Del 1, bilag 7 til Kommisionen om fremtidens ehrvervs- og beskæftigelsesmuligheder*, København: Ehrvervministeriet.

Economic Council of Canada (1991), *Employment in the Service Economy*, Ottawa: Economic Council of Canada.

Edquist, C. (1989), *Empirical Differences between OECD Countries in the Diffusion of New Product and Process Technologies*, paper presented at the International Conference on Diffusion of Technologies and Social Behaviour: Theories, Case Studies and Policy Applications, International Institute for Systems Analysis, Vienna.

Edquist, C. (1990), 'Audacious manufacturing but simple products', *Forskning och Framsteg* (December).

Edquist, C. (1992), *Technological and Organizational Innovations, Productivity and Employment*, Geneva: Technology and Employment Programme, International Labour Office.

Edquist, C. (1993a), *Systems of Innovation: A conceptual discussion and a research agenda*, paper presented at workshop 3: Globalization versus national or local systems of innovation, EUNETIC Network, Strasbourg, France: BETA.

Edquist, C. (1993b), *Innovationspolitik för förnyelse av svensk industri (Innovation Policy for Renewal of Swedish Industry)*, Linköping, Sweden: Department of Technology and Social Change, Linköping University.

Edquist, C. (1994a), *Technological Unemployment and Innovation Policy in a Small, Open Economy*, Linköping, Sweden: Department of Technology and Social Change, Linköping University.

Edquist, C. (1994b), 'Technology policy: The interaction between governments and markets', in G. Aichholzer and G. Schienstock (eds), *Technology Policy: Towards an integration of social and ecological concerns*, New York: Walter De Gruyter, pp. 67–91.

Edquist, C. (1997a), 'Systems of innovation approaches: Their emergence and characteristics', in C. Edquist (ed.), *Systems of Innovation: Technologies, organisations and institutions*, London: Pinter Publishers/Cassell Academic.

Edquist, C. (1997b), 'Product versus process innovation: A conceptual framework for assessing employment impacts', *Creativity, innovation and job creation*, Paris: OECD.

Edquist, C. (ed.) (1998), *The ISE Final Report: Scientific findings and policy conclusions of the 'Innovation systems and European integration' (ISE) research project*, Linköping, Sweden: Systems of Innovation Research

Programme, Department of Technology and Social Change, Linköping University.

Edquist, C. (2001), 'Innovation policy: A systemic approach', in D. Archibugi and B.-Å. Lundvall (eds), *The Globalising Learning Economy: Major socio-economic trends and European innovation policy*, Oxford: Oxford University Press.

Edquist, C. and Hommen, L. (1999), 'Systems of innovation: Theory and policy for the demand side', *Technology In Society*, **21**, 63–79.

Edquist, C. and Jacobsson, S. (1988), *Flexible Automation - The global diffusion of new technology in the engineering industry*, Oxford: Basil Blackwell.

Edquist, C. and Johnson, B. (1997), 'Institutions and organisations in systems of innovation', in C. Edquist (ed.), *Systems of Innovation: Technologies, organisations and institutions*, London: Pinter Publishers/Cassell Academic, pp. 41–63.

Edquist, C. and McKelvey, M. (1992), *The Diffusion of New Product Technologies and Productivity Growth in Swedish Industry*, Berkeley, CA: Center for Research in Management, University of California at Berkeley.

Edquist, C. and McKelvey, M. (1996), 'The Swedish paradox: High R&D intensity without high-tech products', in K. Nielsen and B. Johnson (eds), *Evolution of Institutions, Organizations and Technology*, Aldershot: Edward Elgar.

Edquist, C. and McKelvey, M. (eds) (2000), *Systems of Innovation: Growth, competitiveness and employment*, Cheltenham, UK and Northampton, US: Edward Elgar.

Edquist, C. and Riddell, W.C. (2000), 'The role of knowledge and innovation for economic growth and employment in the ICT era', in K. Rubenson and H.G. Schuetze (eds), *Transition to the Knowledge Society: Policies and strategies for individual participation and learning*, Vancouver, BC, Canada: Human Resources Development Canada/Institute for European Studies, University of British Columbia, pp. 3–32.

Edquist, C. and Texier, F. (1996), 'The perverted growth pattern of Swedish industry - Current situation and policy implications', in O. Kuusi (ed.), *Innovation Systems and Competitiveness*, Helsinki: Taloustieto Oy.

Edquist, C. and Texier, F. (eds) (1998), *ISE: Innovation systems and European integration*, Linköping, Sweden: Systems of Innovation Research Programme, Department of Technology and Social Change, Linköping University.

Edquist, C., Eriksson, M.-L. and Sjögren, H. (2000), 'Collaboration in product innovation in the East Gothia regional system of innovation', *Enterprise and Innovation Management Studies*, **1** (1), 37–56.

Edquist, C., Hommen, L. and Tsipouri, L. (eds) (2000), *Public Technology Procurement and Innovation*, Boston/Dordrecht/London: Kluwer Academic Publishers.

Edquist, C., Hommen, L., Johnson, B., Lemola, T., Malerba, F., Reiss, T. and Smith, K. (1998), *The ISE Policy Statement: The innovation policy implications of the 'Innovation Systems and European Integration' research project*, Linköping, Sweden: Unitryck (University of Linköping Press).

Elfring, T. (1988), *Service Employment in the Advanced Economies: A comparative analysis of its implications for economic growth*, Aldershot: Avebury.

Ellis, E.D. (1980), *Canadian Patent Data Base: Construction and application*, paper presented at the Science and Technology Indicators Conference, Paris.

Enos, J. and Park, W.-H. (1988), *The Adoption and Diffusion of Imported Technology: The case of Korea*, London: Croom Helm.

ENRS (1995), *The European Observatory for SMEs*, Zoetermeer: ENRS.

Ergas, H. (1987), 'The importance of technology policy', in S.P. and P. Dasgupta (eds), *Economic Policy and Technological Performance*, Cambridge: Cambridge University Press.

Ernst, D. and O'Connor, D. (1992), *Competing in the Electronics Industry: The experience of newly industrialising economies*, Paris: OECD Development Centre.

Escher, J.S. (1997), *Wireless Portable Communications Trends and Challenges*, paper presented at the IEEE Radio Frequency Integrated Circuits Forum.

European Commission (1993), *E.C. Harmonized Innovation Surveys, 1992/1993: Final questionnaire*, Brussels: European Commission.

Evangelista, R. (2000), 'Innovation and employment in services: Results from the Italian innovation survey', in M. Vivarelli and M. Pianta (eds), *The Employment Impact of Innovation: Evidence and policy*, London/NewYork: Routledge, pp. 121–48.

Evangelista, R. and Sirilli, G. (1995), 'Measuring innovation in services', *Research Evaluation*, **5** (3), 207–15.

Fagerberg, J. (1988a), 'Why growth rates differ', in G. Dosi, C. Freeman, R. Nelson, G. Silverberg and L. Soete (eds), *Technical Change and Economic Theory*, London: Pinter Publishers.

Fagerberg, J. (1988b), 'International competitiveness', *Economic Journal*, **98**, 355–74.

Fagerberg, J. (1999), 'The economic challenge for Europe: Adapting to innovation-based growth', in D. Archibugi and B.-Å. Lundvall (eds), *The Globalising Learning Economy: Major socio-economic trends and European innovation policy*, Oxford: Oxford University Press.

Fagerberg, J., Guerreri, P. and Verspagen, B. (eds) (1999), *The Economic Challenge for Europe: Adapting to innovation-based growth*, Cheltenham, UK: Edward Elgar.

Finansdepartementet (1987), *Metoder, modeller och beräkningnar: Bilaga 1 till LU 87*, Stockholm: Finansdepartementet.

Fincham, R., Fleck, J., Procter, R., Scarborough, H., Tierney, M. and Williams, R. (1994), *Expertise and Innovation: Information technology strategies in the financial services sector*, Oxford: Oxford University Press.

Fontaine, C. (1987), *L'Expansion des services: Un quart de siecle en France et dans le monde développé, I-III*, Paris: Rexervices.

Fransman, M. (1997), 'Is national technology policy obsolete in a globalised world? The Japanese response', in D. Archibugi and J. Michie (eds), *Technology, Globalisation and Economic Performance*, Cambridge: Cambridge University Press.

Freeman, C. (1974), *The Economics of Industrial Innovation* (2nd edn), London: Frances Pinter.

Freeman, C. (1987), *Technology Policy and Economic Performance: Lessons from Japan*, London: Pinter Publishers.

Freeman, C. (1988), 'Japan: A new national system of innovation?', in G. Dosi, C. Freeman, R. Nelson, G. Silverberg and L. Soete (eds), *Technical Change and Economic Theory*, London: Pinter Publishers.

Freeman, C. (1991), 'Networks of innovators: A synthesis of research issues', *Research Policy*, **20** (5), 499-514.

Freeman, C. (1995), 'The "national system of innovation" in historical perspective', *Cambridge Journal of Economics*, **19** (1), 5-24.

Freeman, C. and Perez, C. (1988), 'Structural crises of adjustment: Business cycles and investment behaviour', in G. Dosi, C. Freeman, R. Nelson, G. Silverberg and L. Soete (eds), *Technical Change and Economic Theory*, London: Pinter Publishers.

Freeman, C. and Soete, L. (1987), *Technical Change and Full Employment*, Oxford: Basil Blackwell.

Freeman, C. and Soete, L. (1994), *Work for All or Mass Unemployment: Computerised technical change into the 21st century*, London: Pinter Publishers.

Freeman, C., Clark, J. and Soete, L. (1982), *Unemployment and Technical Innovation: A study of long waves of technological development*, London: Frances Pinter.

Freeman, C., Soete, L. and Townsend, J. (1982), *Fluctuations in the Number of Product and Process Innovations, 1920-1980*, Paris: OECD.

Fridlund, M. (2000), 'Switching relations and trajectories: The development procurement of the AXE Swedish switching technology', in C. Edquist, L. Hommen and L. Tsipouri (eds), *Public Technology Procurement and*

Innovation, Boston/Dordrecht/London: Kluwer Academic Publishers, pp. 143–66.

Furåker, B. (1990), *Labour Markets and Labour Market Flexibility in Canada and Sweden*, Umeå, Sweden: Sociologiska Institutionen, Umeå Universitet.

Gadrey, J. (1986), *Société de services ou de self-services? Examen du cas Français*, Lille: Johns Hopkins European Centre for Regional Planning and Research.

Gadrey, J. (1988), 'Des facteurs de croissance des services aux rapports sociaux de service', *Revue d'Economie Industrielle*, **43**, 34–48.

Gadrey, J. (1992), *L'Economie des services*, Paris: La Découverte.

Gallouj, C. (1994), *L'outplacement: Evolutions du métier et interprétations dans le cadre des nouvelles théories du marché du travail*, paper presented at the Third Annual International Research Seminar in Service Management – 'Le management des services: Rapports multidisciplinaires', Aix-en-Provence.

Gershuny, J. and Miles, I. (1983), *The New Service Economy: The transformation of employment in industrial societies*, London: Frances Pinter.

Gjerding, A.N. (1992), 'Work organization and the innovation design dilemma', in B.-Å. Lundvall (ed.), *National Systems of Innovation: Towards a theory of innovation and interactive learning*, London: Pinter Publishers, pp. 95–115.

Green, M.J. (1985), 'The development of market services in the European Communities, the United States and Japan', *European Economy*, **25**, 69–96.

Greenan, N. (1995), *Technologie, changement organisationnel, qualifications et emploi: Une étude empirique sur l'industrie manufacturière - Document du travail*, no. G9504, Paris: INSEE.

Greenan, N. and Guellec, D. (1996), *Technological Innovation and Employment Reallocation*, Paris: INSEE.

Gregersen, B. and Johnson, B. (1998a), 'How do innovations affect growth and employment? Some different approaches in economic theory – Report for ISE project 3.1.2', in C. Edquist and F. Texier (eds), *ISE: Innovation systems and European integration* [CD ROM], Linköping, Sweden: Systems of Innovation Research Programme, Department of Technology and Social Change, Linköping University.

Gregersen, B. and Johnson, B. (1998b), 'How do innovations affect economic growth? Some different approaches in economic theory', in L. Herlitz (ed.), *Mellan økonomi og historie*, Aalborg, Denmark: Aalborg Universitetsforlag, pp. 83–111.

Griliches, Z. (1957), 'Hybrid corn: An exploration in the economics of technological change', *Econometrica*, **25** (October), 501–22.

Griliches, Z. (1992), *Output Measurement in the Service Sectors*, Chicago: University of Chicago Press.

Habbakuk, H. (1962), *American and British Technology in the Nineteenth Century*, Cambridge: Cambridge University Press.

Hammer, M. and Champy, J. (1993), *Re-engineering the Corporation: A manifesto for business revolution*, New York: HarperCollins.

Hannan, M.T. and Freeman, J. (1989), *Organizational Ecology*, Cambridge, MA: Harvard University Press.

Hansson, B. (1991), 'Measuring and modelling technical change', unpublished Doktorsavhandling, Uppsala Universitet, Uppsala, Sweden.

Hauknes, J. (1994), *Tjenesteyende næringer - Ökonomi og teknologi*, Oslo, Norway: Studies in Technology, Innovation and Economic Policy.

Hauknes, J. (1996), *Innovation in the Service Economy*, Oslo, Norway: Studies in Technology, Innovation and Economic Policy.

Hauknes, J. and Miles, I. (1996), *Services in European Innovation Systems: A review of issues - STEP report 6 (1996)* (Report 6), Oslo: STEP.

Henderson, R.M. and Clark, K.B. (1990), 'Architectural innovation: The reconfiguration of existing product technologies and the failure of established firms', *Administrative Science Quarterly*, **35** (March), 9–30.

Henderson, W.O. (1965), *Britain and Industrial Europe, 1750–1870: Studies in British influence on the industrial revolution in Western Europe*, Leicester: Leicester University Press.

Herzlinger, R. (1997), *Market Driven Health Care: Who wins and who loses in the transformation of America's largest service industry*, Reading, MA: Perseus Books.

Hicks, J.R. (1932), *The Theory of Wages*, London: Macmillan.

Hill, P. (1997), *Tangibles, Intangibles and Services: A new taxonomy for the classification of output*, paper presented at the CSLS Conference on Service Sector Productivity and the Productivity Paradox, Ottawa, Canada.

Hirschhorn, L. (1988), 'The post-industrial economy: Labour skills and the new mode of production', *The Service Industries Journal*, **8** (1), 19–38.

Hodgson, G. (1991), 'Evolution and intention in evolutionary theory', in P. Saviotti and S. Metcalfe (eds), *Evolutionary Theories of Economic and Technological Change: Present status and future prospects*, Reading, UK: Harwood.

Hodgson, G. (1993), *Economics and Evolution*, Aldershot: Edward Elgar.

Hollingsworth, J.R., Schmitter, P.C. and Streeck, W. (1994), 'Capitalism, sectors, institutions, and performance', in J.R. Hollingsworth, P.C. Schmitter and W. Streeck (eds), *Governing Capitalist Economies*, New York: Oxford University Press, pp. 3–16.

Howell, D. (1996), 'Information technology, skill mismatch and the wage collapse: A perspective on the U.S. experience', in D. Foray and B.-Å. Lundvall (eds), *Employment and Growth in the Knowledge-based Economy*, Paris: OECD, pp. 291–306.

Howells, J. and Wood, M. (1993), *The Globalisation of Production and Technology*, London: Bellhaven Press.

Hörte, S.-Å. and Lindberg, P. (1992), *Performance Effects of Human and Technological Development — Working paper*, Göteborg, Sweden: Arbetsvetenskapliga Kolliget.

Hunt, L. (1984), 'Robotics, technology and employment', in *Proceedings of the 1st International Conference on 'Human Factors in Manufacturing'*, London: IFS Publications Ltd/North-Holland.

Ichniowski, C., Shaw, K. and Prennushi, G. (1994), *The Effects of Human Resource Management Practices on Productivity: Working paper*, New York: Columbia University.

Illeris, S. (1996), *The Service Economy: A geographical approach*, Chichester: John Wiley & Sons.

Imai, K.-I. (1996), 'Information infrastructures and the creation of new markets: Japan's perspective', in D. Foray and B.-Å. Lundvall (eds), *Employment and Growth in the Knowledge-based Economy*, Paris: OECD, pp. 101–14.

Jeremy, D.J. (1981), *Transatlantic Industrial Revolution: The diffusion of textile technologies between Britain and America, 1790-1830s*, Oxford: Blackwell.

Johnson, B. (1992), 'Institutional learning', in B.-Å. Lundvall (ed.), *National Systems of Innovation: Towards a theory of innovation and interactive learning*, London: Pinter Publishers, pp. 23–67.

Johnson, K. (1995), 'Productivity and unemployment: Review of the evidence', *The OECD Jobs Study: Investment, productivity and employment*, Paris: OECD.

Juran, J.M. (1993), 'Made in U.S.A.: A renaissance in quality', *Harvard Business Review* (July–August), 42–50.

Kantrow, A.M. (1980), 'The strategy–technology connection', *Harvard Business Review* (July–August).

Katsoulacos, Y. (1984), 'Product innovation and employment', *European Economic Review*, **26**, 83–108.

Kelly, D. (1995), 'Service sector productivity growth and growth in living standards', *The Service Economy*, **9** (4), 9–15.

Kenney, M. and Florida, R. (1993), *Beyond Mass Production: The Japanese system and its transfer to the U.S.*, New York: Oxford University Press.

KISIN (1996), *The Strategic Role of Knowledge-intensive Services for Transmission and Application of Technical Management Innovation*, London: University of London, Department of Geography/Knowledge-Intensive Services and Innovation Network (KISIN).

Klevorick, A., Levin, R., Nelson, R. and Winter, S. (1995), 'On the sources

and significance of interindustry differences in technological opportunities',
Research Policy, **24**, 185-205.

Koike, K. and Inoki, T. (1990), *Skill Formation in Japan and South East Asia*,
Tokyo: University of Tokyo Press.

Koivusalo, M. (1995), *Kipinästä tuli syttyy: Suomolaisen radio-
puhelinteollisuuden kehitys ja tulvaisuuden haasteet*, Tyväskylä:
Gummerus Kirjapaino.

Kraft, K. (1990), 'Are product and process innovations independent of each
other?', *Applied Economics*, **22**, 1029-38.

Kuznets, S. (1972), 'Innovations and adjustments in economic growth',
Swedish Journal of Economics, **74**, 431-51.

Landes, D. (1969), *The Unbound Prometheus: Technological change and
industrial development in Western Europe from 1750 to the present*,
Cambridge: Cambridge University Press.

Lansbury, R.D. and Bamber, G.J. (1997), 'Australia: Restructuring for
survival', in T.A. Kochan, R.D. Lansbury and J.P. MacDuffie (eds), *After
Lean Production: Evolving employment practices in the world auto
industry*, Ithaca, NY: Cornell University Press.

Layard, R., Nickell, S. and Jackman, R. (1991), *Unemployment:
Macroeconomic performance and the labour market*, Oxford: Oxford
University Press.

Layton, E. (1974), 'Technology as knowledge', *Technology and Culture*, **15**,
31-41.

Lazonick, W. (1994), 'Learning and the dynamics of international compara-
tive advantage', in Y. Shinonoya and M. Perlman (eds), *Technology,
Industries and Institutions: Studies in Schumpeterian perspectives*, Ann
Arbor, MI: The University of Michigan Press, pp. 189-211.

Lazonick, W., O'Sullivan, M. and Smith, K. (1996), *Governance of
Innovation for Economic Development - Draft report*, paper presented at
the ISE Workshop, Milan, Italy, September.

Lee, F.C. and Has, H. (1995), *A Quantitative Assessment of High-knowledge
versus Low-knowledge Industries* (discussion paper, preliminary draft),
Ottawa: Industry Canada.

Levy, R., Bowes, M. and Jondrow, J. (1984), 'Technical advance and other
sources of employment change in basic industry', in E. Collings and
L. Tanner (eds), *American Jobs and the Changing Industrial Base*,
Cambridge, MA: Ballinger.

Lipsey, R.G. (2000), 'New growth theory and economic policy for the
knowledge society', in K. Rubenson and H.G. Schuetze (eds), *Transition to
the Knowledge Society: Policies and strategies for individual participation
and learning*, Vancouver, BC, Canada: Human Resources Canada/Institute
for European Studies, University of British Columbia, pp. 33-61.

Lipsey, R.G. and Carlaw, K. (1998), *A Structuralist Assessment of Technology Policies - Taking Schumpeter seriously in policy: Working paper*, no. 25, Ottawa: Industry Canada.

Loveman, G. and Sengenberger, W. (1990), 'Introduction - Economic and social reorganisation in the small and medium-sized enterprise sector', in G. Loveman, M.J. Piore and W. Sengenberger (eds), *The Re-emergence of Small Enterprises: Industrial restructuring in industrialised countries*, Geneva: International Institute for Labour Studies.

Lundvall, B.-Å. (1985), *Product Innovation and User-Producer Interaction*, Aalborg: Aalborg University Press.

Lundvall, B.-Å. (1988), 'Innovation as an interactive process: From user-producer interaction to the national system of innovation', in G. Dosi, C. Freeman, R. Nelson, G. Silverberg and L. Soete (eds), *Technical Change and Economic Theory*, London: Pinter Publishers, pp. 349-69.

Lundvall, B.-Å. (ed.) (1992), *National Systems of Innovation: Towards a theory of innovation and interactive learning*, London: Pinter Publishers.

Lunn, J. (1986), 'An empirical analysis of process and product patenting: A simultaneous equation framework', *Journal of Industrial Economics*, **34**, 319-29.

Lynch, L. and Black, S. (1995), *Beyond the Incidence of Training: Evidence from a national employers' survey*, Cambridge, MA: NBER.

Machlup, F. (1980), *Knowledge: Its creation, distribution and economic significance - Vol. 1: Knowledge and knowledge-production*, Princeton, NJ: Princeton University Press.

Maddison, A. (1991), *Dynamic Forces in Capitalist Development: A long-run comparative view*, New York: Oxford University Press.

Mäenpää, K. and Luukkainen, S. (1994), *Telekiniikasta monimuotoiseen viestintään*, Tampere: Tampere-Paino Oy.

Main, J. (1994), *Quality Wars: The triumphs and defeats of American business*, New York: Free Press.

Malerba, F. (1992), 'Learning by firms and incremental economic change', *Economic Journal*, **102**, 845-59.

Malerba, F. (1993), 'Italy', in R. Nelson (ed.), *National Systems of Innovation: A comparative study*, Oxford: Oxford University Press.

Malerba, F. (1998), 'Public policy and industrial dynamics: An evolutionary perspective', in C. Edquist and F. Texier (eds), *ISE: Innovation systems and European integration* [CD-ROM], Linköping, Sweden: Systems of Innovation Research Programme, Department of Technology and Social Change, Linköping University.

Mansfield, E. (1968), *Industrial Research and Technological Innovation: An econometric analysis*, New York: W.W. Norton.

Mansfield, E. (1988), 'Industrial innovation in Japan and the United States', *Science*, **241** (30), 1769–74.

Matthews, J. (1996), 'Organizational foundations of the knowledge-based economy', in D. Foray and B.-Å. Lundvall (eds), *Employment and Growth in the Knowledge-based Economy*, Paris: OECD, pp. 157–80.

McGuckin, R. (1994), *Evaluating the Role of Organizational Change in Firm Performance Using Longitudinal Firm Establishment Data*, paper presented at the OECD expert meeting on Job Creation and Job Destruction, Paris, November.

McKelvey, M. (1994), 'National systems of innovation', in G. Hodgson, W. Samuels and M. Tool (eds), *The Elgar Companion to Institutional and Evolutionary Economics*, Aldershot: Edward Elgar.

McKelvey, M. (1996), *Evolutionary Innovations: The business of biotechnology*, Oxford: Oxford University Press.

McKelvey, M. (1997), 'Delineating evolutionary systems of innovation', in C. Edquist (ed.), *Systems of Innovation: Technologies, organizations and institutions*, London: Pinter Publishers/Cassell Academic.

McKelvey, M. (2000, forthcoming), 'Network based dynamics: Does Linux represent a real alternative to Microsoft?', in R. Coombs, K. Green, V. Walsh and A. Richards (eds), *Demands, Markets, Users and Innovation*, Cheltenham, UK and Northampton, US: Edward Elgar.

McKelvey, M. and Edquist, C. (1997), *Swedish Specialisation in Research and Development: Strength or weakness? Working paper*, no. 178, Linköping, Sweden: Department of Technology and Social Change, University of Linköping.

McKelvey, M., Texier, F. and Alm, H. (1998), 'The dynamics of high-tech industry: Swedish firms developing mobile telecommunications systems', in C. Edquist and F. Texier (eds), *ISE: Innovation systems and European integration* [CD-ROM], Linköping, Sweden: Systems of Innovation Research Programme, Department of Technology and Social Change, Linköping University.

McKinsey Global Institute (1994), *Employment Performance*, Washington, DC: McKinsey Global Institute.

Mercer Management Consultants (1994), *Future Policy for Telecommunications Infrastructure and Cable TV Networks*, Boston, MA: Mercer Management Consultants.

Metcalfe, J.S. (1988), 'The diffusion of innovations: An interpretive survey', in G. Dosi, C. Freeman, R. Nelson, G. Silverberg and L. Soete (eds), *Technical Change and Economic Theory*, London: Pinter.

Metcalfe, J.S. (1997), 'Technology systems and technology policy in an evolutionary framework', in D. Archibugi and J. Michie (eds), *Technology,*

Globalisation and Economic Performance, Cambridge: Cambridge University Press, pp. 269–96.

Metcalfe, J.S. (1998), *Evolutionary Economics and Creative Destruction: The Graz Schumpeter lectures*, London/New York: Routledge.

Meyer-Krahmer, F. (ed.) (1989), *Sektorale und gesamtwirtschaftliche Auswirkungen moderner Technologien*, Berlin: DIW.

Meyer-Krahmer, F. (1992), 'The effects of new technology on employment', *Economics of Innovation and Technical Change*, **2**.

Meyer-Krahmer, F. (1996), 'Dynamics of R&D-intensive sectors and science and technology policy', in D. Foray and B.-Å. Lundvall (eds), *Employment and Growth in the Knowledge-based Economy*, Paris: OECD, pp. 213–36.

Michie, J. and Pitelis, C. (1998), 'Demand- and supply-side approaches to economic policy', in J. Michie and A. Reati (eds), *Employment, Technology and Economic Needs: Theory, evidence and policy*, Cheltenham, UK and Northampton, US: Edward Elgar, pp. 42–57.

Miles, I. (1987), 'Information technology and the services economy', in P. Zorkorsky (ed.), *Oxford Surveys in Information Technology*, Vol. 4, Oxford: Oxford University Press.

Miles, I. (1996), 'Infrastructure and the delivery of new services', in D. Foray and B.-Å. Lundvall (eds), *Employment and Growth in the Knowledge-based Economy*, Paris: OECD, pp. 115–31.

Miles, I., Kastrinos, N., Bilderbeek, R.H. and Hartog, P.D. (1995), *Knowledge Intensive Business Services: Users, carriers and sources of innovation* – EIMS publication no. 15, Brussels: EC/EIMS.

Miller, R. (1996), 'Towards the knowledge economy: New institutions for human capital accounting', in D. Foray and B.-Å. Lundvall (eds), *Employment and Growth in the Knowledge-based Economy*, Paris: OECD, pp. 69–80.

Ministry of Posts and Telecommunications, Japan (1994), *Reform Toward the Intellectual Creative Society of the 21st Century: Programme for establishment of high-performance info-communications structures*, Tokyo: Ministry of Posts and Telecommunications, Japan.

Mowery, D.C. (1995a), *US Postwar Technology Policy and the Creation of New Industries*, paper presented at the Conference on Creativity, Innovation and Job Creation, Oslo, Norway, 11–12 January.

Mowery, D.C. (1995b), 'The practice of technology policy', in P. Stoneman (ed.), *Handbook of the Economics of Innovation and Technical Change*, Oxford: Basil Blackwell.

National Research Council (1994), *Information Technology in the Service Society*, Washington, DC: National Academy Press.

Nelson, R. (1987), *Understanding Technical Change as an Evolutionary Process*, Amsterdam: Elsevier.

Nelson, R. (1990), 'US technological leadership: Where did it come from and where did it go?', *Research Policy*, **19**, 117–32.

Nelson, R. (1991), 'Why do firms differ and how does it matter?', *Strategic Management Journal*, **12**, 61–74.

Nelson, R. (ed.) (1993), *National Systems of Innovation: A comparative study*, Oxford: Oxford University Press.

Nelson, R. (1994), 'What has been the matter with neoclassical growth theory?', in G. Silverberg and L. Soete (eds), *The Economics of Growth and Technical Change - Technologies, nations, agents*, Aldershot: Edward Elgar.

Nelson, R. (1996), *The Sources of Economic Growth*, Cambridge, MA/ London: Harvard University Press.

Nelson, R. and Mowery, D. (eds) (1999), *Sources of Industrial Leadership: Studies of seven countries*, Cambridge: Cambridge University Press.

Nelson, R. and Rosenberg, N. (1993), 'Technical innovation and national systems - Introduction', in R. Nelson (ed.), *National Systems of Innovation: A comparative study*, Oxford: Oxford University Press.

Nelson, R. and Winter, S. (1977), 'In search of a useful theory of innovation', *Research Policy*, **6** (1), 36–76.

Nelson, R. and Winter, S. (1982), *An Evolutionary Theory of Economic Change*, Boston, MA: The Belknap Press of Harvard University Press.

Nielsen, K. (1991), 'Towards a flexible future - Theories and politics', in B. Jessop, H. Kastendiek, K. Nielsen and O.K. Pedersen (eds), *The Politics of Flexibility - Restructuring state and industry in Britain, Germany and Scandinavia*, Aldershot: Edward Elgar, pp. 3–30.

Niosi, J. (1995), *Flexible Innovation: Technological alliances in Canadian industry*, Montreal and Kingston: McGill – Queen's University Press.

Niosi, J. (1996), *The Diffusion of Organizational Innovations: Towards an evolutionary approach*, paper presented at the Annual Conference of the European Association for Evolutionary Political Economy, Antwerp, Belgium, 7–9 November.

North, D.C. (1990), *Institutions, Institutional Change and Economic Performance*, Cambridge: Cambridge University Press.

Nutek (1996), *Swedish Country Report*, Stockholm: Nutek.

Nyholm, J. (1995), *Information Technology, Organizational Changes and Productivity in Danish Manufacturing*, paper presented at the conference on Effects of Advanced Technologies and Innovation Practices on Firm Performance: Evidence from Establishment and Firm Data, Washington, DC, 1–2 May.

OECD (1986), *The Evolution of New Technology, Work and Skills in the Service Sector*, Paris: OECD.

OECD (1991), *Information Technology Standards: The economic dimension*, Paris: OECD.

OECD (1994a), *The OECD Jobs Study: Facts, analysis, strategies*, Paris: OECD.

OECD (1994b), *The OECD Jobs Study: Evidence and explanations - Part I: Labour market trends and the underlying forces of change*, Paris: OECD.

OECD (1994c), *The OECD Jobs Study: Evidence and explanations - Part II: The adjustment potential of the labour market*, Paris: OECD.

OECD (1995a), *Interim Report on Technology, Productivity and Job Creation*, Paris: OECD.

OECD (1995b), *The OECD Jobs Study: Investment, productivity and employment*, Paris: OECD.

OECD (1995c), *Industry and Technology: Scoreboard of indicators*, Paris: OECD.

OECD (1995d), *Canberra Manual - Manual on the measurement of human resources devoted to science and technology*, Paris: OECD.

OECD (1996a), *Technology, Productivity and Job Creation - Vol. 1: Highlights*, Paris: OECD.

OECD (1996b), *Technology, Productivity and Job Creation - Vol. 2: Analytical report*, Paris: OECD.

OECD (1996c), *Oslo Manual* (2nd edn), Paris: OECD.

OECD (1996d), *Science, Technology and Industry Outlook*, Paris: OECD.

OECD (1998a), *Science, Technology and Industry Outlook*, Paris: OECD.

OECD (1998b), *Technology, Productivity and Job Creation: Best policy practices*, Paris: OECD.

OECD (1999), *Communications Outlook - 1999*, Paris: OECD.

OECD/ICCP (1996), *Mobile Cellular Communications: Pricing strategies and competition*, Paris: OECD.

Osterman, P. (1990), 'New technology and work organization', in E. Deiaco, E. Hörnell and G. Vickery (eds), *Technology and Investment: Crucial issues for the 1990s*, London: Frances Pinter.

Palmberg, C. (1998), *Industrial Transformation through Public Technology Procurement - The case of Finnish telecommunications*, Åbo, Finland: Åbo Academy University Press.

Palmberg, C. (2000), 'Industrial transformation through public technology procurement? The case of Nokia and the Finnish telecommunications industry', in C. Edquist, L. Hommen and L. Tsipouri (eds), *Public Technology Procurement and Innovation*, Boston/Dordrecht/London: Kluwer Academic Publishers, pp. 167–96.

Palmer, L., Edquist, C. and Jacobsson, S. (1984), *Perspectives on Technical Change and Employment*, Lund, Sweden: Research Policy Institute, University of Lund.

Papaconstantinou, G., Sakurai, N. and Wyckoff, A. (1995), *Technology Diffusion, Productivity and Competitiveness: An empirical analysis for ten countries - Part 1: Technology diffusion patterns*, Luxembourg: European Innovation Monitoring System (EIMS).

Parker, P.M. (1992), 'Price elasticity dynamics over the adoption life cycle', *Journal of Marketing Research*, **XXIX** (August), 358–67.

Pasinetti, L. (1981), *Structural Change and Economic Growth*, Cambridge: Cambridge University Press.

Pearce, D.W. (ed.) (1986), *The MIT Dictionary of Modern Economics*, Cambridge, MA: MIT Press.

Perrow, C. (1993), 'Small firm networks', in S.-E. Sjöstrand (ed.), *Institutional Change: Theory and empirical findings*, London: M.E. Sharpe.

Petit, P. (1990), *Emploi, productivité et technologies de l'information: Le cas des services*, paper presented at the séminaire de l'IRIS sur Compétence et Compétitivité, Université de Paris.

Phillips, A. (1971), *Technology and Market Structure: A study of the aircraft industry*, Lexington, MA: Heath, Lexington.

Pianta, M. (1996), *S&T Specialization and Employment Patterns*, paper presented at the Conference on Creativity, Innovation and Job Creation organized by OECD and the Norwegian Ministry of Education, Research and Church Affairs, Oslo, 11–12 January.

Pianta, M. (2000), 'The employment impact of product and process innovation', in M. Vivarelli and M. Pianta (eds), *The Employment Impact of Innovation: Evidence and policy*, London/New York: Routledge, pp. 77–95.

Pianta, M. and Meliciana, V. (1994), *Technological Specialization and National Performances*, paper presented at the Conference on Technological Performances and Economic Performances, organized by GREGI, BETA and CERETIM, Le Mans, 14 October.

Pianta, M., Evangelista, R. and Perani, G. (1996), *The Dynamics of Innovation and Employment: An international comparison*, paper presented at the expert workshop on Technology, Productivity and Employment: Macro-economic and Sectoral Evidence, organized by OECD, Paris, 19–20 June.

Pollack, M. (1991), 'Research and development in the service sector', *The Service Economy* (July).

Posthuma, A. (1992), 'Japanese production techniques in Brazilian automobile firms', in T. Elger and C. Smith (eds), *Global Japanization?*, London: Routledge, pp. 348–77.

Powell, W.W. and Dimaggio, P.J. (eds) (1991), *The New Institutionalism in Organizational Analysis*, Chicago: University of Chicago Press.

Rapeli, J. (1995), 'UMTS: Targets, system concept and standardisation in a global framework', *IEEE Personal Communications*, **2** (1), 20–28.

Reati, A. (1996), *The Present Technological Change: Growth and employment perspectives*, paper presented at the Annual Conference of the European Association for Evolutionary Political Economy, Antwerp, Belgium, 7–9 November.

Rifkin, J. (1995), *The End of Work*, New York: G.P. Putnam's Sons.

Romer, P.M. (1986), 'Increasing returns and long run growth', *Journal of Political Economy*, **94**, 1002–37.

Romer, P.M. (1990), 'Endogenous technological change', *Journal of Political Economy*, **98**, 71–102.

Rosenberg, N. (1972), 'Factors affecting the diffusion of technology', *Explorations in Economic History*, **10**, 3–33.

Rosenberg, N. (1976), *Perspectives on Technology*, Cambridge: Cambridge University Press.

Rosenberg, N. (1982), *Inside the Black Box: Technology and economics*, New York: Cambridge University Press.

Rosenberg, N. (1986), 'The impact of technological innovation: A historical view', in R. Landau and N. Rosenberg (eds), *The Positive Sum Strategy: Harnessing technology for economic growth*, Washington, DC: National Academy Press, pp. 17–32.

Rosenberg, N. and Nelson, R. (1994), 'American universities and technical advance in industry', *Research Policy*, **23**, 323–48.

Rouvinen, P. (1996), *The Comparative Advantage of Finland*, Helsinki: Research Institute of the Finnish Economy (ETLA).

Sabel, C.F. (1989), 'Flexible specialisation and the re-emergence of regional economies', in P. Hirst and J. Zeitlin (eds), *Reversing Industrial Decline? Industrial structure and policy in Great Britain and her competitors*, Oxford: Berg.

Sakurai, N. (1995), 'Structural change and employment: Empirical evidence for eight OECD countries', *STI Review* (15), 133–76.

Sakurai, N., Ionnidis, E. and Papaconstantinou, G. (1996), *The Impact of R&D and of Technology Diffusion on Productivity Growth: Evidence from ten OECD countries in the 1970s and 1980s*, Paris: OECD.

Salter, W. (1966), *Productivity and Technical Change*, Cambridge: Cambridge University Press.

SCB (1991), *Forskningsstatistik - Tekniks och naturvtenskaplig forsknin och utveckling i företagssektors 1989*, Örebro, Sweden: Statistics Sweden (SCB).

Schmookler, J. (1966), *Invention and Economic Growth*, Cambridge, MA: Harvard University Press.

Schumpeter, J. (1911), *The Theory of Economic Development* (R. Opie, trans.) (1934 English edn), Cambridge, MA: Harvard University Press.

Schwartzman, D. (1975), *Innovation in the Pharmaceutical Industry*, Baltimore, MD: Johns Hopkins University Press.

Scott-Kemmis, D. and Bell, M. (1988), 'Technological dynamism and the technological content of collaboration: Are Indian firms missing opportunities?', in A. Desai (ed.), *Technology Absorption in Indian Industry*, New Delhi: Wiley Eastern.

Senker, J. (1992), *The Contribution of Tacit Knowledge to Innovation* (mimeo), Brighton: Science Policy Research Unit, University of Sussex.

Silver, H. (1987), 'So many hours a day: Time constraints, labour pools and demand for consumer services', *Service Industries Journal*, **7** (4), 26–45.

Silverberg, G. (1990a), 'Adoption and diffusion as a collective evolutionary process', in C. Freeman and L. Soete (eds), *New Explorations in the Economics of Technological Change*, London: Pinter Publishers, pp. 177–92.

Silverberg, G. (1990b), 'Dynamic vintage models with neo-Keynesian features', in OECD (ed.), *Technology and Productivity: The challenge for economic productivity*, Paris: OECD.

Simonetti, R. (1991), *The Definition of Product-innovation and Process-innovation*, Brighton: Science Policy Research Unit, University of Sussex.

Smith, K. (1997), 'Economic infrastructures and innovation systems', in C. Edquist (ed.), *Systems of Innovation: Technologies, organizations and institutions*, London: Pinter Publishers/Cassell Academic, pp. 86–106.

Smith, K. (1998), 'Systems approaches to innovation: Some policy issues', in C. Edquist and F. Texier (eds), *ISE: Innovation systems and European integration* [CD-ROM], Linköping, Sweden: Systems of Innovation Research Programme, Department of Technology and Social Change, Linköping University.

Soete, L. (1981), 'A general test of technological trade gap theory', *Weltwirtschaftliches Archiv*, **117**, 638–66.

Soete, L. and Verspagen, B. (1991), 'Recent comparative trends in technology indicators in the OECD area', *OECD Technology and Productivity*, Paris: OECD.

Solow, R. (1957), 'Technical change and the aggregate production function', *Review of Economics and Statistics* (August), 312–20.

Somit, A. and Peterson, S.A. (1992), *The Dynamics of Evolution: The punctuated equilibrium debate in the natural and the social sciences*, Ithaca/London: Cornell University Press.

Soskice, D. (1994), 'Reconciling markets and institutions: The German apprenticeship system', in L. Lynch (ed.), *Training and the Private Sector: International comparisons*, Chicago: University of Chicago Press.

Spitz, P.H. (1988), *Petrochemicals: The rise of an industry*, New York: Wiley.

Spriano, G. (1989), 'R&D networks: The emerging market for technological and scientific services', in A. Bressand and K. Nicolaidis (eds), *Strategic Trends in Services: An inquiry into the global service economy*, New York: Harper and Row, pp. 65–79.

Stern, D. (1996), 'Human resource development in the knowledge based economy: Roles of firms, schools and governments', in D. Foray and B.-Å. Lundvall (eds), *Employment and Growth in the Knowledge-based Economy*, Paris: OECD, pp. 189–203.

Stiglitz, J. (1987), 'Learning to learn, localized learning and technological progress', in P. Dasgupta and P. Stoneman (eds), *Technology Policy and Economic Performance*, Cambridge: Cambridge University Press.

Stiroh, K.J. (1999), 'Computers, productivity and input substitution', *Economic Inquiry*, forthcoming.

Streeck, W. (1989), 'Skills and the limits of neo-liberalism – The enterprise of the future as a place of learning', *Work, Employment and Society*, **3** (1), 89–104.

Tan, H. and Batra, G. (1995), *Enterprise Training in Developing Countries: Incidence, productivity effects and policy implications*, Washington, DC: Private Sector Development Department, World Bank.

Tassey, G. (1991), 'The functions of technology infrastructure in a competitive economy', *Research Policy*, **20** (4), 345–61.

Tinnilä, M. and Vepsäläinen, P.J. (1995), 'A model for strategic repositioning of service processes', *International Journal of Service Industry Management*, **6** (4), 57–80.

Tschetter, J. (1987), 'Producer services industries: Why are they growing so rapidly?', *Monthly Labor Review* (March), 10–32.

Tylecote, A. (1998), 'A micro-macro view of the causes and remedies for unemployment in an integrating Europe', in J. Michie and A. Reati (eds), *Employment, Technology and Economic Needs: Theory, evidence and policy*, Cheltenham, UK and Northampton, US: Edward Elgar, pp. 115–27.

Tyson, L. (1992), *Who's Bashing Whom? Trade conflict in high technology industries*, Washington, DC: Institute for International Economics.

Utterback, J. and Abernathy, W. (1975), 'A dynamic model of process and product innovation', *OMEGA*, **3** (6), 639–56.

Verspagen, B. (1992), 'Endogenous innovation in neoclassical growth models: A survey', *Journal of Macroeconomics*, **14** (Fall), 631–62.

Vivarelli, M. (1995), *The Economics of Technology and Employment – Theory and empirical evidence*, Aldershot: Edward Elgar.

Vivarelli, M. and Pianta, M. (eds) (2000), *The Employment Impact of Innovation: Evidence and policy*, London/New York: Routledge.

Vivarelli, M., Evangelista, R. and Pianta, M. (1995), *Innovation and Employment: Evidence from Italian manufacturing*, paper presented at the conference on Technology Adoption and Skill Levels, Wages and Employment, Washington, DC, 30 April–2 May.

Von Hippel, E. (1994), 'Sticky information and the locus of problem-solving: Implications for innovation', *Management Science*, **40** (April), 429–39.

Voss, C.A. (1988), 'Implementation – A key issue in manufacturing technology: The need for a field of study', *Research Policy* (17), 55–63.

Westphal, L., Kim, L. and Dahlman, C. (1985), 'Reflections on the Republic of Korea's acquisition of technological capability', in N. Rosenberg and C. Frischtak (eds), *International Technology Transfer*, New York: Praeger.

Wolf, M. (2000), 'Growing too fast for comfort', *Financial Times*.

Womack, J.P., Jones, D.T. and Roos, D. (1990), *The Machine that Changed the World*, New York: MacMillan.

Index